Love in RED CHINA'S GARDEN

Love in RED CHINA'S GARDEN

Adrian Webber

ROBERT HALE · LONDON

© Adrian Webber 2012
First published in Great Britain 2012

ISBN 978-0-7090-9388-6

Robert Hale Limited
Clerkenwell House
Clerkenwell Green
London EC1R 0HT

www.halebooks.com

A catalogue record for this book is available from the British Library

2 4 6 8 10 9 7 5 3 1

Typeset by e-type, Liverpool
Printed in Great Britain by the MPG Books Group,
Bodmin and King's Lynn

This book is dedicated to the people of northern China, who, despite all difficulties and disasters,
have maintained
a steely grip on what they hold dear,
family, friendship and compassion for others.
I believe that if their stories could only be
more widely told,
the whole world would salute them.

ACKNOWLEDGEMENTS

I would like to thank Barry Sharples for all his work and encouragement at the very start; Jenny Hawthorne, Lindsey Sanders and Peter Ellway for their suggestions; and John Pawsey for his help in reducing the script down to a manageable level.

Within Robert Hale I would first like to thank Gill Jackson for her immediate support, Linda Carroll for polishing the script and Nikki Edwards for putting everything into place.

To the many people in northern China who helped me I owe a debt of gratitude that I know I could never possibly repay.

CHAPTER 1

若不变方向，你会到达要去的地方

*'If we don't change our direction, we're likely
to end up where we're headed'*

The old rusting Chinese minibus skidded and slewed down the worn potholed road. The thickset Beijing driver, barely in control, made yet another sharp turn before quickly descending a steep hill with a busy road junction at the bottom of it. There, a Chinese traffic cop stood, busily waving his white-gloved hands, trying to get the vehicles on the intersecting roads to do his bidding. Our driver cursed and stood hard on the brake pedal.

I closed my eyes, unable to watch. Only an hour or so before, my scheduled BA flight from London had swooped low over the Great Wall of China and gently touched down at Beijing International Airport. All that worried me then was whether there would be anyone to meet me. It came as no surprise after frantically searching the arrivals hall that I found no one. I resigned myself there and then to a difficult-to-arrange taxi ride when I spotted two Chinese men asleep on a bench, each clutching a wooden pole with a large placard at the top. On both placards was printed one word: WEBBER.

Mr Chen, the younger of the two men, was asleep again now in the minibus which, considering the ride we were having, was a miracle in itself. The older man, Mr Huang, perhaps thirty years of age, difficult to tell, was unfortunately still very much awake. He had been droning on to me from across the other side of the bus for forty-five minutes. He kept talking not to me, but *at* me, in a low monotone about nothing in particular, until I had come to the conclusion that he wanted to practise his English; each phrase he spoke came out like a mantra, or someone repeating the same text, over and over again, by rote. What was he saying now?

'It takes approximately one and a half hours by bus from Beijing Botanical Garden to centre of Beijing, for example, but the Forbidden City may of course take longer, depending on speed of bus ...'

As he wouldn't stop talking, I studied his eyes. He wore steel-rimmed glasses that had thick lenses. From where I sat, his magnified eyes looked tired and sad; actually *sad* wasn't quite the right word. *Disappointed* was a more accurate description; yes, he seemed disappointed.

The burly cop jumped round, startled, as we skidded to a halt, blew his whistle hard, and slammed his hands down on to the dirty bonnet of the bus. A quick and furious exchange of words took place before the policeman abruptly broke away, turned on his heel, and stomped over to his motorcycle; he was still shaking his head as he rode off. Our driver, who seemed to have got the best of the argument, now turned and looked back at us with a baleful stare and shrugged his shoulders resignedly before revving the engine hard and dropping the clutch. We lurched off again, joining the streaming traffic for a few minutes, before turning right into a much quieter, tree-lined, road.

Here the pace was slow and gentle, with people of all ages quietly cycling to and fro. Teams of women, in dark-blue overalls and matching baggy slacks, swept the roads with long bamboo brushes, their heads protected by enormous woven coolie hats that they tied under the chin with beautifully coloured scarves. It was so elegant and co-ordinated that it didn't look like sweeping at all; rather, in the heat haze, they appeared to be gently rowing and sculling down the tarmac road, afloat on a calm black sea.

Wood smoke rose and curled into the air from cast iron braziers which, surrounded by small colourful tents, were dotted along the pavements; sitting on their haunches were women with wizened lined faces charcoal-grilling meat and vegetable kebabs, together with whole corn cobs and red-skinned sweet potatoes. Squinting through the smoke they carefully and patiently turned and basted the hot snacks. No sign of customers yet.

Also along the pavements were groups of chairs where middle-aged men sat nonchalantly receiving a haircut or, more commonly, a wet shave by young girls in the now familiar dark-blue overalls. As I watched these scenes my nostrils were assaulted by various smells: the acrid tang of wood smoke, the wonderful flowery scent of freshly brewed jasmine tea, overlaid by the all-pervasive heat which made everything you touched unusually soft or brittle hard.

As I looked at all the people we passed milling around in the streets or cycling along the road, it struck me that China was *not* multicultural. It did not seem to incorporate other nationalities at all. Come to think of it, that was made pretty clear back at the airport – when everyone entered the terminal, the Chinese quickly joined the queues forming in the multiple lanes beneath the sign 'Chinese Passport Holders', whereas I and the handful of other Westerners queued along a single immigration channel beneath the sign 'Foreigners'.

Mr Huang got up and shouted something at the driver who turned and nodded. 'Webber, we shall stop in a minute for your bed,' he said loudly to me over the noise of the engine.

'It's not far from here,' he shouted, turning to look forward through the dirty windscreen of the minibus.

Sure enough, a few hundred metres further on, the bus pulled over on to the concrete forecourt of what looked like a small factory or warehouse. A tiny old man wearing battered grey overalls was waiting patiently with a set of keys. As soon as he saw the minibus he strode over and unlocked a set of double doors, kicking one open before going inside to unbolt the other.

We screeched to an abrupt halt. Our driver switched off the engine and, in the sudden silence, heaved himself out of his seat and followed the old man into the building. They emerged together a couple of minutes later holding a battered wooden bed frame between them. This was hauled on to the roof of the minibus amid shouted curses, pleas and recriminations, followed by a straw mattress split along one side. Then came a huge wooden box painted white with louvred sides, rather like a weather station, with a sloping felt roof.

Mr Huang got out to help and a sharp knock on the window woke Mr Chen to press him into service. The four of them just managed to heave it up on top of the bed and everything was tied down with a ball of thin string.

Back on the road again, this time with the bed and everything bouncing up and down loudly on the roof, another heated argument broke out – with the driver clearly having very strong views on the subject. The younger of my two escorts, Mr Chen, noticed my confusion and smiled before saying: 'We were discussing where to go for lunch! Our driver was born around here and thinks our first choice has poor hygiene and would probably kill the foreigner, if not all of us as well, and so we have discussed other choices!'

I smiled nervously.

Soon we pulled up in a small shopping area shaded by plane trees. The glazed front door of the restaurant was opened for us and we were quickly ushered inside. The airy dining room was cool and relaxed, which provided a welcome contrast to the heat and dust of the road. We all sat down around a glass table and a waitress brought over a tray of drinks. There was a tall beer for each of us passengers and a fruit juice for our driver, which he immediately rejected and demanded *pijou* (beer). Another disagreement broke out, this time on the rights and wrongs of drinking and driving, but so vehement was the driver's invective that Mr Huang eventually gave in and the fruit juice was later substituted, discreetly, for a large glass of *pijou*. In that moment I was grateful that his way of dealing with me (the foreigner) was simply to pretend that I did not exist.

Mr Huang was busy taking a call on his mobile so I looked properly at Mr Chen for the first time, now that he was fully awake. He was very tall and handsome, with a shock of black hair that he tried to keep flat on his head, but little tufts kept springing up. Like his colleague Mr Huang, he wore steel-rimmed glasses and dressed very plainly, as I began to realize many Chinese men did – a smart open-necked white shirt, black trousers and black shoes.

What initially struck me most about Mr Chen, though, was his apparent gentleness. My Chinese classmate from the horticultural college, Zhu Renyuan, who was responsible for getting me to China in the first place, was a totally different type, a formidable force; a sort of modern-day incarnation of Bruce Lee, I remembered with a shudder.

I was still intrigued about the weather station, so I asked Mr Chen if they now intended to record meteorological conditions in the Botanical Garden.

'No, nothing like that,' he replied. 'It's your wash table!'

I couldn't think of any reply, so just looked at him, completely dumbfounded.

'You see, there is no wash table in the office where you will live,' he explained. 'And so we have had to get one for you.'

'Excuse me, but did you just say that I am going to live in an *office*?'

'Yes, of course,' he went on enthusiastically. 'It belongs to your classmate, Mr Zhu Renyuan. He is staying in your England for another year, yes?'

I nodded slowly.

'So, director of Botanical Garden just gave Mr Huang permission for you to use Mr Zhu's old office to live in; you will live there for the rest of your stay.'

I recalled Zhu Renyuan's words to me just before I left: 'Of course, Adrian, your accommodation will be *excellent*!'

So that was it. For the next three months or so, I was going to live and sleep in an office, upon a straw bed, and use a weather station as my only table. Well, I'm glad we've got all that out of the way, I thought.

The pretty waitress returned, this time carrying a huge tray of food which she carefully placed on the table before us. There were dishes of meat and fish, together with bowls of rice and wide glistening strands of what looked like transparent noodles. These in turn were accompanied by tiny bowls containing different-coloured dips. The driver immediately brought his dainty wooden bowl, piled high with food, up to his chin. He then expertly pushed the food into his mouth with a pair of chopsticks before he requested, or rather demanded, another glass of *pijou*; the first glass, I noticed, had already been drained.

My other companions were far more elegant in their eating habits, and picked carefully at the morsels of meat or fish, before placing them on the rice or noodles in their bowls. They all watched discreetly as I snapped open the wooden seal at the top of the chopsticks (this was to show they had not been in anyone else's mouth) and placed them in my right hand. I was very hungry, and so without further ado I nimbly picked up a piece of fish from a dish, dunked it in one of the dips, and carefully placed it on my tongue. Years of practice! This was met with a short burst of applause, but I nearly spat the fish back out again. It was stone cold! Everything on the table was at ambient temperature or less. But once I forgot the coldness of the dishes, I realized that my mouth was able to appreciate the various tastes and textures of the different foods. This, of course, was no accident, as I was later to learn.

All too soon it was time to go and we reluctantly filed out of the comfortable and cool dining room on to the burning pavement outside before pulling ourselves up into the airless minibus. It still smelt of petrol and hot engine oil. All eyes now were on the driver as we set off along the empty street. To our relief he took the first two bends well enough, but then braked hard, nearly over-shooting an entrance into the Garden; he spat out an oath as we slid down the long plastic-covered seats, but he still managed to swing the old bus into what looked like a private tree-lined road.

As I looked to my left I made out a grey brick two-storey building in the distance, its tiled roof glinting in the strong sun. It was set beneath a very pretty mountain and was surrounded by numerous glasshouses and coloured poly tunnels, rather like a medieval camp.

Mr Chen pointed at the building and shouted, above the din of the bus, 'Your new home, Webber Adrian!'

It was very dark inside after the brilliant sun and I struggled to get my bearings. I saw some light cast from an open doorway halfway down the windowless empty corridor. Inside, the room – my room – was completely bare except for a small writing desk and a sink with one tap. The floor was tiled and wet – it must just have been mopped – and the bare walls were painted white, or simply whitewashed. The only window was quite large and had a close mesh grill covering the outside, presumably to repel insects. The window had a pair of blue curtains that were made of plastic. And that was pretty much it.

The sound of scuffling and scraping came from the corridor and soon my bed emerged through the door. The driver and the other man refused my help with a quick shake of the head. The bed was soon assembled and the mattress, trailing straw, was dragged in and lifted on to the bed frame. Next came the weather station, which was carefully placed next to the sink.

'Your wash table,' Mr Chen said, smiling, clearly pleased with it.

I watched him pat the weather station's felt roof affectionately before walking out. I was more dubious as my table's roof, was at an angle of 30 degrees. And then at once I was alone. There was no sound at all apart from the cicadas chattering outside. The sun was still burning hot, so I pulled at the flimsy curtains and eventually managed to draw them across as I was desperate now for sleep. I climbed into bed, and the sheets beneath me just about protected my body from the scratchiness of the straw. Well here I was, after everything, in bed, in the People's Republic of China.

In that moment I realized how my life had been utterly changed. It seemed that my destiny was to follow a hospital career, but I had walked away from it, and sold up to pursue my dream of becoming a garden designer. I was now halfway through the course and had just exchanged my college room for an office here in China. And all because of a chance remark when my Chinese classmate, Zhu Renyuan, asked me where I was going to spend my summer placement. He suggested I go to his Botanical Garden in Beijing. Now, six weeks later, I was here and trying to get to sleep in his office ...

But as I lay there I couldn't help but reflect that as my material status declined, my life seemed to be going in the other direction – it was becoming richer, more varied. And I was now embarking on another adventure, which was already shaping up to be the greatest challenge of my life.

I woke with a start. Someone was banging on my door. I knew what it was, but somehow couldn't think what to do about it. I just lay there. The banging continued. All my limbs felt as though they were strapped tightly to the bed. I managed to raise my head a little; it was light outside. The banging stopped and then I heard my name being called, 'Webber! Webber, Adrian?'

This was followed by conversations in Chinese and then 'Webber!' was shouted again. I finally pulled myself out of bed and shuffled along the cool, tiled floor to the door, unlocked it, and tugged it open. My eyes were still half closed, so I smiled an apology to whoever stood there.

There was nobody there. Odd, I thought, and so decided to walk out into the corridor to check – but as I did so I knocked over a huge metal flask, scratching my shin. It was very heavy, full of recently boiled water. I dragged it back inside with me. Slowly, I remembered being told that a flask of hot water would be left outside my door each day. Yes, they said it was for making hot drinks or cooking noodles and it could also be used for washing, hence the size of it. In the West we boiled a kettle each time we wanted a hot drink; here they boiled it at the start of the day and stored it to be used as and when needed.

I looked at my watch, it was 6.30 in the morning. I had been asleep for over sixteen hours. Good, I thought. But after a while I realized that it *wasn't* 6.30 in the morning, it was 6.30 in the *evening*. I had been asleep for only five hours. Long after night-fall, I was still wide awake. I read through the night and eventually fell asleep just before dawn.

Slowly, I awoke to loud banging on my door, accompanied by a lot of excited shouts, two or three conversations going on at once, and bustling movement in the echoing corridor.

'Please wait one second!' I shouted, as loudly as I could.

There was immediate silence outside and then a low whispering in Chinese again. Couldn't find my flip-flops, damn, so I shambled over to the door with bare feet and flung it open. I was immediately confronted by a small muscular middle-aged man wearing gold-rimmed glasses hunched down in front of the door, who after a few seconds stopped talking to the people gathered around him and turned his attention to me. He stood up, and I noticed that he was extremely relaxed and confident. He was also clearly bursting with energy and not a little curiosity.

Without a word, he walked, good-naturedly, straight past me and looked carefully around the room, while the clamouring broke out again among the people strung out all along the corridor. He took his time and then at last nodded to himself and spat out an instruction to a man who immediately turned and left the room. Now I knew who my visitor must be – it could only be one person, the director himself, head of the Beijing Botanical Garden. He oozed authority and took his time over everything before he finally turned his attention to me. He looked into my eyes intently; the beginnings of a smile played on his round face as he carefully scrutinized me, then he grinned, and a shiny gold tooth inside his mouth gleamed as he did so.

He quickly cast a look at Mr Huang, who had met me at the airport yesterday and now stood next to him. No response. He nodded at me again, widened his smile further, and then flicked another look at Huang. I understood. He didn't speak English so he wanted Mr Huang, who spoke English, to introduce him. I looked at Huang more closely now. He seemed transfixed; he mouthed words but nothing came out. There was sweat on his upper lip, and his whole expression was strange. It was as though he had never seen me before, as if yesterday counted for nothing. Just ... *silence*.

As we stood there, a younger man standing behind them jumped between Huang and the director and said in perfect English, 'Mr Webber ... Adrian ... may I present Director Zhang, who is in charge of the Beijing Botanical Garden? He is here to welcome you and to make sure you have everything that you need.'

If the director was as surprised as I was at the sudden change of interpreters, he certainly didn't show it. Instead he continued to smile broadly even after I thanked him in Chinese and firmly shook his soft meaty hand. He nodded to himself and again took his time before casually saying something to the young man, while maintaining his gaze on me. The translator said, 'Our director would like to apologize for not being here to greet you personally yesterday, but he had an important meeting in central Beijing.'

'No problem,' I said. 'And please thank the director for coming here to see me now, especially at the weekend.'

This was quickly translated for the director as he again walked around the room and then nodded before replying. 'Director says, think nothing of it, he always works weekends, anyway.'

I watched him circle my room again before he stopped and sniffed, the inspection finally over; he was clearly satisfied with my arrangements. Suddenly he stooped down and stood up again, gingerly holding the flip-flops I hadn't been able to find. He studied them closely with some puzzlement, before dropping them back on to the floor, declaring flip-flops to be of ancient Chinese origin – which was news to me.

The director prepared to leave, but first said something else to me in Chinese, closed his hands together as if in prayer, and then waved them in my direction, smiling again. The young interpreter translated: 'Our director invites you to lunch today, at noon. I am to take you there, personally. He says goodbye for now.'

I smiled and stood there as they filed out, alone again and trying to calm down. Somehow, this wasn't what I expected.

Then a sudden movement in the corridor again. The director's head popped back around my doorway, 'Bye bye,' he said – in perfect, if heavily accented, English.

No. Not what I expected at all.

CHAPTER 2

我梦勿唤我醒，我醒勿让我睡

'If I am dreaming let me never awake, if I am awake, never let me sleep'

The sky had been overcast all morning but was now beginning to clear as the young interpreter, whose name was Zhao Shi Wei but who liked to be called 'William', walked with me down the drive of the research building, the temperature already rapidly climbing to over 30 degrees. Soon I felt the sweat starting to run down my back, although William seemed perfectly cool. At the end of the drive we stopped at the gatehouse and William introduced me to the four or five security staff who were expressionless, with none of them glancing at him or me as he explained that I was a friend of the Botanical Garden and they should let me through at any time and generally make sure I was OK. He also gave them a phone number for them to call if there was a problem.

The sun was beating down hard when he emerged from the shade of the gatehouse into the open sky of the road. For some reason we both turned and squinted back at the research building in the distance, whose roof tiles and windows were now gleaming in the sunlight. Frankly, it looked deserted.

'This is really an old area of the Botanical Garden,' William said, 'and is not open to the public any more. A lot of research still goes on, though – that and plant propagation. More of which you will find out about next week. Mr Huang is drawing up a work schedule for you which will include working here for two weeks, maybe more. We shall just have to see.'

I followed William down a narrow track which turned out to be a staff short-cut to the Botanical Garden proper. I looked dubiously at the undergrowth each side of the tiny path and said, 'I'm glad you're in front, William, for the snakes I mean ...'

'Don't worry, Adrian,' he rejoined smoothly over his shoulder, 'the snake always bites the *second* man ...'

We came to a huge wire fence where a gap had been made to allow staff to squeeze through. From that high spot on the other side, we turned and looked at the Garden that now stretched in front of us as far as the eye could see. It was a series of rich vistas which eventually stretched to the mountains in the far distance. The contrast in colours of the different foliages, together with the sheer scale of the view, made me gasp. I was quite overcome; it was simply beyond anything that I had ever imagined. I breathed out deeply and looked at William who, as if reading my mind, said calmly, 'It's about 2,500 of your acres, I think, perhaps a little more.'

I didn't know whether to laugh or cry. The Botanical Garden extended 2,500 acres – over a thousand hectares! I wanted to dance! All my adult life I had dreamed of such a place and now I was about to enter it. It was simply too wonderful. Too beautiful to imagine. Years ago at college I had come out of the university library and stopped to look at a newly planted sapling. I was marvelling at the young beech tree, especially its distinctively pointed, tightly coiled buds, when behind me another student had stopped and said: 'Webber, it's a tree ...'

I had chuckled to myself and ignored him. He obviously didn't share the fascination, but surely even he, standing here, would be similarly awed. By now the sunlight had become prickly and uncomfortable so we moved on into a shady walk ahead of us. We then descended a small hill path and finally stepped on to a huge wide concrete road which went as straight as a die in both directions.

It was the weekend and the whole place was full of Chinese families strolling about, enjoying the tranquil gardens. Young people and old mingled together, as they relaxed among the luxuriant plantings, some eating ice creams from the little vending huts or enjoying a picnic they had brought with them. Others merely paused to look at particular specimen plants and check both their botanical and common names, out of simple curiosity. It was all too much for me to take in. But on we went, further into this magical land.

We stood on the edge of a gigantic landscaped 'bowl' bursting with roses, which must have been 250 metres in diameter at least. Different varieties of rose were planted in terraces all the way down to the bottom, which had a perfect flat round in the middle. Suddenly, right on cue, a huge single jet of water flew straight up into the air which after 40 metres or so began to cascade back down to earth, showering those nearby, who scattered immediately before turning back and laughing to one another.

'Five of your acres, approximately, if you include everything, yes, this rose garden is 5 acres in size. Definitely,' William said flatly.

We skirted a peony rise and climbed some stone steps to a viewing platform shaped like a temple. Looking back, I could see the Xiang Shan mountain clearly, but the research building had completely disappeared.

'In autumn, all of the foliage on the mountain turns bright crimson. It becomes a *red mountain*. Many Chinese people visit then, although for some it is a spiritual journey, like your "Pilgrims", I think,' he continued.

'William, can I just say that your English and your knowledge of the West is a marvel. I mean it. Have you visited many Western countries?'

'Director has sent me to some countries, but mainly here in the East.'

Eventually we arrived at a very traditional Chinese building with a sweeping green-tiled roof and eaves that swept upwards like wings; small figures of animals were displayed in cameo along the roof line. I supposed they were used in a similar way to gargoyles on an English church. Stepping inside, it was impossible to see anything. It was pitch black. We stood there, trying to adjust to the darkness after the harsh sunlight, when I heard a very distinctive laugh. It had to belong to Director Zhang. He emerged from out of the gloom and grasped my shoulder tightly while looking back and shouting at some people seated around a large table behind him.

Whatever he said made them laugh uproariously. They were still applauding him when he turned round and impishly looked at me. He was chewing something and continued chewing as he looked at me intently. He was weighing me up, I could see that. He pulled me round so I was facing the table full of people, and clutched my shoulder. Nodding again – he was always nodding – he put a matchstick in his mouth and started to pick at his teeth with it. Clearly, he had already started on the feast and so had everyone else as they were sitting back in their chairs and raising their glasses of beer and toasting one another from time to time. They were all men as far as I could see, and most of them seemed to be smoking. His arm was now round my neck, and he looked at me and said: 'Webber ... eh ... *Webber ... hmm ... yes* ... !'

His face was so close to mine I could smell the alcohol on his breath.

William was standing in front of me holding two glasses of what looked like pale lager. 'My director asks if you like *pijou*, Adrian?'

Before I could reply, the director took a glass out of William's hand, passed it to me, clinked it with his own, and said 'Cheers!' in English.

'Cheers,' I responded, and repeated it to William, saluting both of them.

Somehow, though, my responses didn't seem enough – perhaps they were too polite, too formal? No matter, just get on with it,

I told myself. Everyone else in the huge room was now clinking glasses and shouting to each other rowdily. Then someone stood up and started singing a sentimental Chinese love song and was immediately joined by a man opposite and then another ... and another. Before long *everyone* was joining in. A tall old man then started to conduct and lead the singing with languid practised movements.

'Let's get something to eat, Adrian, there's plenty left,' William shouted in my ear.

And so we walked away from the noisy happy scene and to a corner of the room where it was suddenly much quieter.

'Are they *always* this happy?' I asked softly.

'Well, it is the weekend, and the men who are here have been selected because they helped to organize a festival in the Garden which went very well. In fact, our director was officially congratulated by the Beijing Parks Bureau, so he wanted to reward them.'

'Oh, I see,' I replied. 'In my country the director would probably have said it was all down to him and thank you very much!'

'That would be dishonest,' said William earnestly as he looked me directly in the eye.

It was quite clear that food here was to be not only enjoyed, but celebrated, relished. Each diner tucked into every dish with gusto. They showed not a bit of embarrassment as they smelt, sucked and savoured every delicious morsel. It was clear that they believed that this was what food was for, and no one was going to give it a second thought. Each man cheered the others on, 'Eat, eat, enjoy!' Huge strands of cold noodles were noisily sucked into the mouth of one middle-aged man who was congratulated loudly by his companion diners.

I turned round to find Director Zhang grinning down at me and then smiling at the other men on the table. He turned to face me, holding up an official-looking card with a lot of Chinese writing on it and an official stamp.

William took it from him and read it quickly. He turned to me and shouted above the din: 'Adrian, our director has given you an official entrance card to show at any of the entrances to the Botanical Garden. The card says: "Let foreigner through. He is guest of Botanical Garden." All ticket staff and security personnel are to let you through, and if they have any sort of query they are to telephone our deputy director, day or night. He speaks English.'

'*Xie xie*,' (thank you), I shouted through the noise.

The director nodded and laughed, clearly pleased. He then said something else to William.

'Director says,' William began, 'that arrangements have been made for you to eat your evening meal here. The cost is not high, $3 US. He thinks this must be cheap for you – you know, as a Westerner, he means.'

This director moved quickly, I thought to myself. It was just over twenty-four hours since I got off the boat and already I'm a paying guest at *his* restaurant!

'He says could you also be early, Adrian, because the staff finish work at 6.30 in the evening?'

He smiled at me and I smiled back.

CHAPTER 3

酸甜苦辣，都要品尝

'Sour, sweet, bitter, pungent, all must be tasted'

The food I ate at lunchtime had barely been digested when I opened the door. Outside, it said in huge letters 'Public Restaurant'. Its only problem was, as far as I could make out as I entered for the second time that day, the lack of customers. I was alone in the huge room. It was silent as well as empty. Everything from lunchtime had been cleared away. It was as if it had never happened. A tall thin man emerged from a door to the rear of the place and walked towards me.

'We ... look ... after ... you!' he announced, and then disappeared out the back again.

Behind the black lacquered bar decorated with exquisite golden cranes, a door was barged open. A tiny waitress, smartly dressed in black with a tight bobbed haircut, marched out carrying a black tray. Without a word she placed a small plastic cup in front of me which I could tell, from the dark earthy smell, contained coffee. I watched as the little *xio jie* delicately scooped three heaped spoonfuls of black sugar into the tiny cup before carefully stirring it. She stood back, looked at it, and then, with a final deft flourish, popped a long thin straw into the cup, turned on her heel, and was gone.

She quickly returned with two dishes of food and a bowl of plain rice. Again she said nothing, didn't look in my direction once, and then scuttled back to the kitchen. I could see that one of the dishes was mixed vegetables in a shiny brown sauce. I think it was mainly *pak choi*, easily recognizable by the white stalk part, which resembled a Chinese porcelain spoon.

The manager walked over, smiling. Clearing his throat in a theatrical sort of way, he beamed down at the other dish that I hadn't touched.

'It is turtle, that is what you call it, I think. You will enjoy this dish I think, yes! But come, you haven't yet touched it, please ... before it cools.'

He picked up a spoon and carefully, reverently almost, placed two, then three 'chunks' upon the bed of rice in my bowl and looked up, expectantly. It tasted like chicken, but the texture was completely different to anything I had ever put in my mouth before. It had a succulence that was hard to describe, an oily smoothness that was strange but at the same time quite wonderful. It was meaty and, at the same time, ever so faintly fishy.

Some more was placed in the lacquered bowl but I didn't even notice as I was lost in some private reverie. 'Ambrosial,' I said to myself. 'The food of the gods.' I then started laughing – I didn't even know why. Looking up, I watched the manager carefully pouring a bottle of beer into a glass before placing it in front of me. I raised it to him and remembered the required toast – *gan bei*. He smiled, retrieved his cigarette, and smoked it by way of reply. Standing next to him were the chef and the kitchen staff in their ordinary clothes, ready to go home. They watched me eat with no expression on their faces. They simply stared. A quick command from the manager and they mutely filed out through the main door and carefully closed it behind them.

There was a huge steel gate over 2 metres high across the entrance to the research building's driveway. In the twilight I could just make out some shadowy faces through the windows of the gatehouse, which was in complete darkness. I stood there not knowing what to do. I walked over to the gate and shook it, hoping it would open. Five pairs of eyes watched me do this. Still nothing. I was feeling in my pocket for the official pass that the director had given me earlier when a boy of about ten ran out of the sombre building and noisily unlocked the padlock and then pushed at the gate. It was too heavy for him, so I helped push it open just far enough for me to squeeze through the gap.

Then as I approached the building, the little caretaker ran out to meet me and kept looking behind him as he led me up the steps and ushered me – almost pushing me – inside before locking the doors quickly behind him. In the light I could see he was wearing a pair of pyjamas under his jacket. He must have been waiting up for me, although it was before 10 o'clock. I said *xie xie* to him, but he didn't seem to understand.

'Tortoise!' I shouted. 'You mean *tortoise* is what I ate last night in the public restaurant? Please tell me that's not right, William. I mean ...'

William casually shrugged his shoulders and slowly walked back up the staircase, before he shouted over his shoulder, 'You mean you would prefer it to have been *turtle*, Adrian ... *really...?*'

'Well no! No, of *course* not, but it's ... well, you must know what I mean, *surely?*'

Upset, I hastily turned on my heel and bumped bodily into Mr Huang, who unfortunately dropped all the papers from under his arm just as the caretaker opened the main door, allowing a hot wind to gust through. The good news was, as he slowly came back up the corridor with his papers clasped to his chest, that he had recovered his ability to speak: 'The local Security Bureau was notified of your arrival and they will make an official visit to assess all security issues related to your stay here. They are expected any time within the next few days. Please make sure you return here before the gates are closed at 8 p.m. in the future, *Mr* Webber,' he said coldly. 'I am able now to show you your washing facility, if you wish it?' he asked, somewhat dubiously.

'Yes, thanks, er, sure, whatever ...' I replied.

I followed him down the empty corridor past the door to my room – or 'cell', as I'd come to think of it. He unlocked a padlock on the double doors at the end of the corridor and I followed him in. Inside was an enormous laboratory. This I knew was the micro-propagation department; all around were the huge fitted work areas, sinks and gas pipes for Bunsen burners that I remembered from school. There were also huge fridges, ceiling high, dotted around. Wall hooks with white coats hanging on them. Yes, it was definitely a laboratory, that's for sure, I thought, but wasn't he meant to be showing me my washing facilities?

'Come this way, please, now,' he said gruffly.

He opened a door around a corner of the lab. Inside was a bare tiled room with a small frosted window. On one wall was a showerhead that was connected to a tiny plastic pipe that went into the wall above.

'Here you have shower in evening, Webber, when all staff from micro-propagation have gone home.'

'It's so near to my room it might as well be en-suite,' I said, brightly.

He ignored me and slowly walked past the shower and gestured for me to look around the corner. There in all its glory was a small rectangular tiled hole in the floor. I remembered such an arrangement from a school trip to France. But I was sure there had been a couple of handles for you to hold on to even back then. Clearly, this would have to be approached ... er ... free style.

'Yes, well thanks, I think I know what that's for,' I grinned.

He looked into my face again doubtfully for a few seconds and then walked past me and out of the door.

'Well, thanks again for everything,' I said, calling after him.

By the time I got to the outside doors he was standing there waiting for me, with a key in his hand. He quietly locked the padlock and handed me the key with great solemnity.

'Do not, please, lose this,' he said as if I'd lost it already.

As soon as he had gone I rushed to my room and got my

washing things. Bending down, I found that if you fiddled with the two knobs on the pipe that ran low along the wall and were patient enough, you could get a reasonable temperature that was also stable. The pressure of the water was quite good and at last it flooded over my shoulders; I squirted shampoo all over my body and then rinsed it off with the cooling water. Finally I dipped my head under the stream and felt ten times better at once. All the stresses, strains and pressures that had accumulated inside me, even before I came to China, seemed to flow out with the water, cleansing my very soul.

Sunlight flooded the room through the plastic shower curtains at my window and filled the air with unexpected heat. It soon became too hot under the covers, so I reluctantly pulled myself up and got out of bed. I opened the windows to allow some air in. There was a lovely freshness to the air for the first time since my arrival. No trace of humidity at all.

I spent the day quietly as there was no one around apart from the caretaker and I think even he had gone out. I pinched a wooden chair from another room so I could sit at my little mahogany desk and try to get to grips with the Chinese language book that I had brought with me. The problem as far as I could see was that apart from the words, it was the tonal character of speech that made it so difficult. You might get a word completely right, but in not pronouncing it the correct way it became completely unintelligible.

Walking back from dinner in the public restaurant, I could hear a rhythmic drumming in the distance from the Xiang Shan area and because it was before my 8 o'clock deadline I decided to investigate. In a square, a group of elderly Chinese women were dancing in lines while throwing brightly coloured rippling scarves into the air in time to the music from a band sitting on the ground.

A large crowd of local people had gathered to watch, and standing there with them I became immediately conscious of being a foreigner. I was the only Westerner there. It had been my intention all along to just live among Chinese people, but somehow at that point I seemed to almost lose my nerve. Perhaps it was the *Chineseness* of everything, the inability to understand things they obviously took for granted. I had anticipated children looking at me and staring, but if anything the adults were worse. And they made no attempt to hide it; it wasn't meant, I knew, to intimidate, it was completely guileless. But they never seemed to blink either, which made it more unnerving. And they were immensely curious, with a very high embarrassment threshold it seemed. Perversely, if you tried to interrupt the stare with a quick *ni hao* (hello), or even just smiled, it seemed to galvanize their curiosity even further – with the added problem that it usually attracted the attention of other Chinese who, up until that point, hadn't noticed me.

Looking around I felt a stab of recognition. It was the café cum restaurant that I had been taken to on the first day, the one on the corner. Emboldened, I decided to go in. My request for *pijou*, a beer, at once brought *everyone* out of the kitchen. All the kitchen staff, together with the *xio jie*, stood around me – clearly debating what it was the foreigner wanted. Many theories, it seemed, were being expounded. This all took a very long time and started to include theories from already seated customers who began to peddle their own suggestions as to what the foreigner *obviously* and *clearly* wanted. What this particular foreigner wanted at that particular moment was *out*, and fast.

This was not getting anyone anywhere and so the chefs began to bring out raw dishes to see which of them was the one I was after. Doing my best mime of a man with a desperate thirst and in need of a drink, the whole thing subsided back into calm. A glass of beer was brought out from the back, which I accepted with much gratitude and sat down. I was exhausted. Thank God I had eaten, I thought, because to have tried to order a meal here would have left me a nervous frothing wreck. The good news was that the beer had cost me 3 yuan, which was about 25p at home, and so seemed extraordinarily good value. Later, with a quiet sense of contentment, the guards let me through the gates to the research building. Home at last.

'Why were you in Xiang Shan town last night, Webber Adrian?'

'Pardon?' I replied, startled.

'You were seen coming back from the town by the security staff on the gate last night on your *own*, do you deny it?'

'No, of course not,' I said, a bit bewildered. 'It wasn't late, lots of people around, I couldn't see the harm ...'

Mr Huang looked at me levelly.

'You simply do not understand, Webber Adrian. These local people, they are not *city* people and they are not *country* people either, do you understand what I mean?'

'Well, to be honest, no, they seemed friendly enough, they stare at me all the time ... but that's not a crime ...'

'These people are a *hybrid* and cannot be trusted. I am responsible for your safety and I was very worried when I heard you had left the Garden alone.'

'I'm very sorry, really I am,' I replied lamely.

It was all I could think of to say in the circumstances. William, who sat quietly behind him, looked friendly enough, but he didn't say anything and I could see that he agreed with Mr Huang's assessment.

'We just don't want anything to happen to you, Webber Adrian, you've only been here a few days ...'

'OK, OK,' I said, putting my hands up high, whatever you fellows say, please, *please*. I don't want to cause any trouble, obviously.'

William's quiet confirmation of the situation drove it home to me what a nuisance I'd been and the consequences for them if something had happened to me ... I felt terrible. And yet ... I hadn't felt in the least bit threatened, every Chinese person I met had been nothing but friendly and helpful to me. Not the right time to state that of course, that much was obvious; clearly my status had already moved into the category of 'too independent'. What I didn't want was for it to fall even lower to 'rogue elephant', or worse.

And so it was in that atmosphere that I said, 'Oh, by the way, the Summer Palace is only just along the road a few miles. Is it all right if I catch the bus up there? I mean, obviously during the hours of daylight.'

Too late I realized that this perhaps wasn't the best time to mention this sort of thing, but it would be in daylight after all ... and ... Mr Huang's eyes rolled into the back of his head and then quickly narrowed into a frown.

'You don't mean go there on your own, do you, not after all we have just said ... !'

'Well ... *yes*,' was all I could think of by way of reply.

He sighed deeply as he slowly got to his feet, patted the desk, and walked out and into the office next door. Through the wall I could hear him on the phone to someone. Eventually he returned and sat down heavily. He then turned and faced me steadily and, I could see, with not a little self-control. After quite a few seconds he cleared his throat and then said quietly, 'I have just made arrangements for you to visit the Summer Palace this coming Friday, but remember this is on the basis that you will be accompanied by one of our English-speaking academic staff. Do you understand, *Mr* Webber? You understand what I am saying to you, please? You do, don't you ...?'

'Yes, don't leave town. If I do, I must have someone with me?' I replied quietly and contritely.

He got up, nodding, 'Precisely. Precisely. *Good*. We are still working out your programme by the way, but you do promise to stay within the Garden tomorrow and not go *wandering off*, yes? Yes!'

'Yes, I do. Of course!'

'Good, this pleases me,' Mr Huang replied, finally.

*

Two days later, still no work had been arranged for me so I decided to steal into Xiang Shan anyway. I promised not to go there the previous day, but no one said anything about today, had they? Anyway, I didn't see any Garden staff – perhaps, fortunately, because it was lunchtime. The guards let me through, and just watched me impassively as usual. After a fifteen-minute brisk walk I entered the town by the same parade of little shops and eating houses as I was taken to on my first day. This raised parade was directly in front of me overlooking the car park, which as usual had very few cars in it. The sun was climbing high now, which seemed to bring everything to a standstill. Everyone had gone inside. Out of the blistering July heat.

Suddenly hungry, I walked across the hot tarmac of the road to the raised parade which I knew housed the little café where I had my fateful beer a couple of evenings ago. As I entered, it had the same coolness inside, which was a great relief. I made my way to a corner table. The owner rushed out before I even had a chance to sit down. He was holding a menu and, to my surprise, he spoke to me in fluent English.

'Welcome again to my modest place, would you like to eat here, *Yin guo ren?*'

'Yes please, I would!' *Yin guo* I knew meant English, *ren* meant person from that place, hence *Yin guo ren*.

He spoke English, so why hadn't he used it the other night? Perhaps he thought he might lose face if I hadn't understood him? Yes, loss of face, in front of all his staff, too.

'I will give you a whole meal for 20 yuan, not $20, ha ha ha! – so cheap,' he laughed, more to himself than me.

Well, it was certainly cheaper than the Garden's public restaurant, I thought immediately. The cold dishes he served on the first day were superb and had made a deep impression on me. Good wholesome food. Not too fine, or artificial. *That* was the problem with the Garden's restaurant food, I now realized – it wasn't earthy enough, no roughage. You could eat it once in a while, but not twice a day as I had been doing. And what would he bring out this time I wondered?

A platter of crispy pancakes filled with cubes of meat in a nutty sauce was placed in front of me, together with a bowl of black rice placed to one side. A *xio jie* of about thirty, and very pretty, brought over a small earthenware jug and poured out a very dark pungent liquid.

'Chinese coffee,' she said.

This was also in perfect English. She said it demurely and cheekily at the same time. It turned out to be black Chinese tea. I laughed. So this was a Chinese joke, eh? Chinese 'coffee'.

Later, I walked over to the post office across the quiet car park, which shimmered in the midday sun, and climbed the smooth marble steps once again before pushing open the heavy glass door. The air conditioning always came as a very welcome shock. The counters were practically deserted, each one was fully furnished with an American computer, but the young man who served me still preferred to use an abacus on his desk to work out the cost of my four international letters.

As I walked back along the long parade of shops, I saw one shop window full of bottles of Chinese alcohol. I looked furtively up and down the street but saw no one I recognized, so I slipped inside. I came back out with a half-bottle of clear Chinese spirit. It had a pretty picture of a young girl standing beneath a willow tree on it and cost only a few yuan. There had been no Western equivalent unfortunately. Anyway, if this didn't blast me out of this continual jet lag I reasoned, nothing would.

That evening I did not have to go to the public restaurant as it was closed for a staff rest day. Instead I carefully unscrewed the cap of the bottle of Chinese spirit I had bought and poured some into an ornate cup that had been left in my room. It was completely clear and transparent and smelt sweet and very alcoholic. As I rotated the cup I noted that it had the consistency of a particularly oily wallpaper paste.

I sipped it very gingerly and ... nothing! That was until I

swallowed it, when I immediately gasped because it *tasted* like wallpaper paste. Somehow I forced it down. If it gave me a good night's sleep, it would be worth it because I had to start work first thing in the morning. It had been arranged for me to start in micro-propagation.

It was 8.30 a.m. when I reported for work just down the corridor at the micro-propagation laboratory. The wallpaper paste had got me to sleep, but the 60 per cent pure alcohol had woken me up less than two hours later with a raging thirst and a thumping headache.

I felt terrible as I knocked on the open laboratory door. A plain middle-aged woman in a white coat ushered me inside. Four other middle-aged women stood in the doorway and smiled shyly as I went in. One walked towards me with a white coat over her arm. She held it up and gestured for me to turn round. On tiptoe she tried to push it over my shoulders, but it was far too small.

She had to drag it back off me as another of the women ran out the back and returned with another coat which was simply enormous. I rolled up the sleeves so that my hands were free, and buttoned it, although it was so huge it just slumped down in front of me. They all laughed, embarrassed. Another younger woman entered, looked me up and down, and pointed back down the corridor where we could hear a noisy rumpus of some sort. The double doors were flung open to reveal Mr Huang. He looked flustered.

'You must come quickly, Webber Adrian, *now.*'

Everyone from the lab watched as I was marched down the corridor. Outside my door were a group of officials waiting impatiently. I unlocked the door as quickly as I could, with them all crowding round me. There were three men and a woman, and two of the men were in military uniform. The woman wore a smart dark-grey outfit and had thin-rimmed steel glasses. The other, younger, man in a baggy charcoal suit, who appeared to be in charge, glanced at me quickly and then said sharply, 'Your passport ... *please.*'

I walked over to my bed, felt inside the straw mattress, and handed it to him. He carefully checked it before passing it to his female colleague. Opening a small attaché case, he pulled out a long blue form.

'In this you fill in, please, *now*,' was all he said.

I sat down at my desk, but not before I had tucked the voluminous white coat under my stomach, which must have looked ridiculous, and filled in the green boxes on the blue form. It was quite straightforward – they wanted length of stay, purpose of visit, that type of thing. Fortunately, they didn't pick up on the fact that I had travelled out on a normal tourist visa, although I was technically required to have a work visa.

While I filled out the form, watched by the woman, the two uniformed men checked the window locks and the strength of my room door and its lock. The male civilian was asking Mr Huang a lot of searching questions and the caretaker was brought in and asked more questions. His ID card was carefully checked too. All the answers were carefully noted down.

This was all carried out, it had to be said, in a brisk, formal manner. At one point I saw William outside my door with the woman. They were talking very fast; William nodded quickly, then shook his head. And then they were gone. The noise of the front door being slammed shut echoed down the dark corridor, followed at once by an uncomfortable silence.

I slowly turned and walked back to the micro-propagation laboratory, a slightly different man, it has to be said, from the one who left it only half an hour before. The staff were subdued and would not meet my gaze. Well, I hadn't done anything *wrong*, I wanted to say. The head of the department, Miss Zhang, smiled at me weakly. She was a tall handsome woman in her late twenties, perhaps early thirties, her hair pulled back tight in a bun. She had a clear open face. Zhu had mentioned her before I left England.

'When she was a girl, a difficult period in our history, her parents were so persecuted,' Zhu had said, 'that they had committed suicide, jumped off a high building, together, hand in hand.'

'Webber, Adrian ... *Adrian*!' I wheeled around, a little startled, to see William standing in the doorway.

'Please take off your coat and follow me,' was all he said.

Out in the corridor I said to William, 'Am I to be arrested, then?'

He didn't laugh, but merely said, 'Our director wants you to attend a special lunch, please follow me, *now*.'

A large black car with a silver-haired driver was waiting outside and we both got in. It was air-conditioned and I immediately started to shiver. I was still hot and unnerved by the morning's events, and I hadn't been able to get down to any work – which was maddening. After all, it was supposed to be my first work day ... I quickly glanced at my watch. It was 11.30 a.m.

We pulled up at the public restaurant. No, not *again*, I thought to myself. I trudged down the steep path, resignedly. We went straight in. William strode over to a table full of young men in their twenties who were already eating. They all shifted along to make room and we sat down. Looking closely, I could see it wasn't all men after all; there was an extremely pretty girl sitting to one side, saying nothing and eating less. She had a short bob haircut and narrow eyes set in a face with wide high cheekbones. On her brown face, Beijing's hot sun had brought out tiny freckles on her nose; her tanned arms, thin but exquisitely formed, lay across her lap. Her elegant hands wore no rings or other adornments apart from a tasteful silver watch which had a delicate matching bracelet. She appeared aloof, but watchful, careful, I noted. I must have been staring at her for a long time because William had to tap me on the shoulder to get my attention: 'Adrian, let me introduce you to everyone.'

But before he could, a heavy hand slammed down on my shoulder. I didn't have to turn round. I knew who it was. The whole table fell silent at once. The familiar big round face craned around in front of me.

'Hello,' he said, in English.

He then turned slowly, theatrically, to William and a quick exchange followed: 'Adrian, our director asks whether you would be so kind as to accompany him to meet a group of distinguished professors who are visiting our Botanical Garden today?'

I nodded, and not for the first time tried to smile even though I didn't mean it. This was a tough call, I thought, as I got up; here I was halfway through a *diploma* in horticulture from a tiny horticulture college in England and I was about to meet some of China's finest botanists! What if one of the professors asked me a technical question?

'Please, this way, Webber Adrian,' someone said, and I was led in.

A long table stretched away in front of us like that from a medieval banquet. There were about fifty, quite elderly, distinguished-looking men and women sitting at the table. The meal was obviously finished. Many of them were smoking, using cigarette holders or drinking alcohol from small exquisite cups in a sort of diffident, sophisticated way, and they all appeared supremely confident and relaxed, which was a lot more than I could say for myself. All the men present immediately stood up. At first I thought that someone important had just come in behind me, but to my complete mortification it dawned on me that they were standing up for me! If my classmates back at college could only see this, well ...

Director Zhang immediately propelled me down one side of the table and introduced me in Chinese. I don't know what he said, but each professor looked at me deeply impressed, and nodded courteously, before shaking my hand warmly. We eventually reached the VIPs at the top of the table and even the female professors now rose to greet me. 'Chin chin!' someone shouted behind me. They all began to relax and soon ripples of laughter spread through the room. Then as I shook a tall, venerable man's hand he tilted his glass, tapped the bottom, and declaimed, in perfect English, 'Bottoms up, old boy!' Someone else yelled 'Cheers!' above the din and I started to relax a little. It was going to work ...

Back down the other side of the table we went and soon I was laughing too; their sense of fun was all too infectious. 'Mud is in your eye!' I heard someone shout nearby. All the while Director Zhang was slapping my back, grinning broadly, and shouting *gan bei* (cheers) to anyone who came into sight. Someone else shouted, 'I want to talk to you!' Then suddenly I was being ushered on to the last professor and out of the room altogether.

Back at our table I was ceremoniously placed back down on my seat. The director curled his arms around me. I could feel his deep breaths on my neck as he addressed the younger academic staff sitting around us.

'Webber, *penyou* [friend]. Webber ... *wo'de hao penyou!*' [my good friend!], he said slowly.

Clearly, I had helped him. Helped him a lot.

'Good face,' William muttered afterwards.

So. It hadn't mattered what my academic status was. I was a foreigner, *his* foreigner; and a foreigner in this country, isolated for so long, meant only one thing – *kudos*.

CHAPTER 4

经验是严厉的老师，先测后教

'Experience is a hard teacher, because it gives the test first and the lesson afterwards'

The alarm clock went off next to my ear. It was 7.30 a.m. and I'd been woken up by the shrill bell instead of laying there wide awake waiting for the time to pass before getting up. This was definite progress. After yesterday's events I was told not to go back to work, but just to return the following morning. I certainly didn't want another day like yesterday. One good thing had come out of it though: the director seemed to have a favourable opinion of me. It was a shame that Mr Huang hadn't been there to see it, only William.

Still it was definite progress after my recent transgressions. What was it William quipped after giving me the rest of the day off? 'Providing, of course, you don't go wandering off again, Adrian.'

So, I was still on probation, that was clear. But I was happy with things overall, and so it was with a spring in my step that I made my way down the 10 metres of corridor to work.

I knew from yesterday that Miss Zhang, the department head, could speak English and, bearing in mind Zhu Renyuan's warning about her personal history, I was determined to make a good impression. And so when I pushed my way through the double doors and saw her standing at the far end of the lab I walked straight up to her, gave a little bow by way of apology for yesterday, and said, 'I am sorry to have rushed off yesterday, but I am ready now to do whatever you ask of me, Miss Zhang.'

Pretty speech, Adrian. I congratulated myself and looked up at her expectantly. Silence.

'I am *not* Miss Zhang,' she replied.

More silence. I looked around at the others who had stopped what they were doing and were now staring at me. Perhaps I had got her name wrong?

'Miss Zhang has been called to a meeting in the main building. My name is Sun Yi, I am Miss Zhang's deputy.'

And double, I thought. Goodness, what a mistake to make!

'You will come this way, Webber Adrian,' she said, a touch primly.

I followed her through a heavy green door, down a long corridor, and then through another heavy door before emerging into an air-conditioned room not unlike an operating theatre.

'Put this on now, please, at once,' she said briskly.

She handed me a white face mask, followed by a green rubber gown and thin surgical gloves. We were definitely going to operate, I thought. She lit two Bunsen burners with a lighter and walked over to a huge glass door which she wrenched open. It made a hissing sound as the two different atmospheres met. It was a sort of cold store which had numerous fridges against the walls and stacks of insulated boxes on the tiled floor. Miss Sun Yi emerged with a tray full of little plastic boxes.

Carefully, she placed them on the bench and indicated for me to sit down on the wooden swivel chair. She then carefully opened one of the boxes. Inside were four little bell tubes, each sealed with a small orange stopper. She pulled one out and removed the stopper. Taking a pair of long tweezers from a jar of disinfectant, she used them to pull a tiny fragment of vegetable matter out of the jar; with her other hand holding the larger bell jar, she first sterilized it in the flame of the Bunsen burner before slipping the specimen into it. She then poured a special liquid into the bell jar before sealing it with a much larger stopper.

She turned to face me. All I could see were her little eyes, above the mask.

'Now *you* try, Webber Adrian.'

So began my first day in propagation.

Mr Huang was still working on the rest of my work schedule when I walked into his office. I had already asked him if I could work with either one of the Garden's landscaping teams or, more preferably, with the garden design team which I had learned was based in the main building. He looked doubtful and merely said I would be too much of a burden, but he would make enquiries if I really wanted to work there. He wanted me to work mainly within the propagation department itself, which was under his control, for the first month or so at least, but I thought perhaps that the possibility of shifting responsibility for me on to someone else might eventually appeal.

Finally, after a lot of persuasion he gave permission for me to walk down to Xiang Shan town on my own to make a phone call from the post office to Zhu Renyuan back in England. I wanted to thank him for getting me out here in the first place, but also to tell him that I had been met at the airport and I had got somewhere to sleep – his office.

The call lasted four minutes and the woman in charge of the public telephones held up a bill for 160 yuan and then smiled toothily at me. I realized that four-minute call had cost me £14 as I walked back out in the first stages of shock. I won't do that again I thought.

Walking back past the liquor store I realized that the jet lag had definitely gone, but had been replaced by a deeply disturbed stomach which, if anything, was getting worse. I had to face the truth. Eating Chinese food twice, sometimes three times, a day was taking its toll on my digestive system. I had to all intents and purposes *stopped* eating, even if I went for meals. Most of the food I was served went back to the kitchen.

I decided to ask for advice. 'Sun Yi,' I shouted through the door, 'Do you know anywhere, anywhere at all, I can find some Western food? You know to eat?'

'It's best if you take off the face mask, when you speak, Webber Adrian,' she said politely.

'I forgot, sorry, I just want to try to find somewhere to have a Western meal, you know for a change.'

'You don't like *Chinese* food?'

'No, no, I love it, *adore* it, of course. It's not that, just for a *change* you see,' I said, looking her straight in the eye.

I could see that she was now thinking hard; it wasn't the sort of question she was normally asked, after all. Then her face broke out into a rare wide smile, displaying a row of perfect white teeth.

'Of course! The Xiang Shan hotel!' she exclaimed. 'It's an international type of hotel just the other side of the town. They have a Western coffee lounge *and* a Western restaurant, I think it's *Fa guo* – French in your language. Yes, they serve French dinners there. My father went, years ago. I think they change foreign currency, too.'

Could I sneak out this evening, I wondered? As for the Garden's public restaurant, I could just say that my stomach was too upset to go there again. I also urgently needed to change some money too. The small amount I'd cashed at the airport had nearly been swallowed up in the phone call to Zhu Renyuan.

And still there had been no mention of wages, despite Zhu's previous reassurances; in fact, as I had seen, quite the reverse – the director was trying to get money out of *me*. No, I would have to risk it.

WESTERN RESTAURANT – CLOSED, SORRY! I stood in front of the sign. I was soaked to the skin from the storm that had started when I was less than halfway up the hill to this place. I walked slowly back down the thick carpeted staircase to the main foyer. A tall man of about thirty, wearing a black tie – evidently some sort of manager – stood in front of me. He looked me up and down, slowly leant forward, and said, 'Would you like a room, Sir, have you booked?'

I shook my head, for once lost for words.

'Have you come here to dine then, Sir?'

I nodded slowly, warily.

'Excellent, our restaurant is open; it serves some of the finest Chinese cuisine in the capital! Have you booked a table, are you meeting someone?' he asked solicitously.

I shook my head. He might not have known it, but he was looking at a broken man.

'There are plenty of tables, please come this way ... but first, you may use our superbly equipped cloakroom facilities, to dry off I mean, they are just ... *here*,' he said, pointing at the heavy teak door.

'You want a Chinese meal that is as ... *Western* as possible,' the *xio jie* repeated slowly in case she was missing something.

I nodded for the second time.

'OK, I'll talk to the chef,' she said brightly and sauntered back to the kitchen. At least I was now dry and, to be fair, they had changed some money for me at the main desk after the tall manager intervened on my behalf. Around fifteen minutes later I spied a large metal trolley being solemnly pushed towards me. With great panache, the *xio jie* laid two immaculately presented oval dishes down in front of me, together with a black lacquered bowl.

Her face beamed down at me as she said, pointing first at the dish nearest me, 'This one is *flamed duck hearts in a sour sauce* and very tasty it is, too; and this one,' pointing to an enormous mound in a dish, 'is *ants climbing a tree*, which has a very plain sauce, just right for Western people. And in the bowl here is *stir-fried glutinous rice*. Enjoy, Sir, please!'

Stunned, I simply could not think of a response. None at all. So I picked at the rice for a few minutes and then, when the coast was clear, tucked the right money under the receipt and quickly left.

*

Back in propagation I was starting to get the hang of the glass sterilization operation, and the healing of the earlier burns on my left hand was testament to it. Sun Yi, bless her, proved to be a good teacher and an incredibly patient one. It was also pleasant and soothing somehow to have a firm routine after all the recent traumas. Apparently, it was a Chinese curse to say, 'May you live in interesting times.' Yes, I reflected, what I needed was several years of *uninteresting* times. Interesting equals stressful.

A knock on the door; it was William.

'Adrian, we must go now,' was all he said.

Out in the corridor I gave William a serious, meaningful look. Ever the diplomat, he quickly explained that I had been invited to meet 'a very important man'.

'He has asked to see you, Adrian, it's quite a compliment actually, really ...'

OK, calm down, I told myself, at least you are not in any more trouble.

Outside, in front of the research building, William disappeared into the basement and returned pushing two bicycles in front of him. Unexpectedly behind him was the pretty girl from lunch the other day. She was, if anything, even more beguiling than I remembered.

I bowed my head towards her in greeting, but she wordlessly got on to the bicycle she herself had wheeled out and immediately set off behind William. I clambered on to the other bicycle and pedalled off furiously to catch up.

When I caught them up by the gate William turned right in the direction of the town. It was downhill all the way to the stream at the bottom and the edge of Xiang Shan town. We free-wheeled through the shallow stream with our legs held high to keep dry.

The pretty girl – I still had no idea of her name – dropped back as we made our way slowly up the steep incline on the far side of the stream but soon caught up again as we entered the town proper. We rode on past the café cum restaurant I had visited more than once now, and then eased our way left into a much wider, busier road and were immediately forced to dodge the deep potholes outside the entrance to the town's sprawling bus station. Now that was a useful discovery I thought to myself, as we flashed past. I bet you could go anywhere from there. Anywhere at all.

William skidded a little as we almost missed the turn into what I thought was known as the South Garden; we sped past blocks of laboratories and lecture rooms and scattered gaggles of students who lingered too long crossing the road as we went. Goodness, he rides fast I thought, but, hang on – I looked around to see the pretty Chinese girl right behind me; her face a complete blank, a mask. We pedalled on, leaving the university area behind us as we crossed a bridge over a dry riverbed and eventually pulled up outside a block of faceless flats, where an old man was waiting outside.

He was the man from the lunch, I remembered. He had shouted 'I want to talk to you.' We rested the bikes against a wall, and he came over to me with his arms outstretched.

'You are Webber, from England,' he said, chuckling.

I shook his hand gently, but he refused to let it go and led me inside. My two companions followed in silence. We were shown into a sunny room which was obviously his study. There were more books than I had ever seen in one room. He disappeared and there followed a loud conversation in another room before he eventually returned with a wooden tray which he put down before us. He slumped down in his huge desk chair which had obviously been specially padded in various parts to keep the old man comfortable. He had a shock of silver hair on a still boyish, handsome face. He talked in a husky quiet whisper, which commanded attention.

'My name is Professor Yu, although I am retired now,' he said simply.

He shifted in his seat and leant forward, looking at me

intently. I could see from the expression on the faces of my two companions that they were in total awe of this man. Neither made any attempt at communication but just sat there, quietly. He chuckled again, mainly to himself, then began to laugh, louder and louder.

William and I looked at each other and also started to laugh. It was so infectious that even the pretty girl smiled a little in a very demure way. Eventually he shook his head and slowly drew a cotton handkerchief from his trouser pocket and blew his nose noisily. Satisfied at last, he sniffed and got up from the chair and looked straight into my eyes.

'I wanted to meet you ever since I saw you at that lunch,' he said, more to himself than to me.

Reaching down, he handed me a cup.

'I've made you some coffee, Webber, would you like a cup?'

His English was completely natural, unforced, impeccable. He poured the coffee into my cup. William and the girl both refused politely and just sat there. He then quietly poured a cup for himself, before unhurriedly stirring three heaped spoonfuls of sugar into it.

'I visited Denmark as a young man you know, before China's "liberation" of course. I studied Western botany there for a year. Tried to get to your country, England, but it was just after the war and travel was still difficult. I went out to Europe by boat, you see, from Saigon, Vietnam; we eventually landed in Marseilles in the South of France. It took a total of thirty-two days to sail, as I recall.'

Apparently he had then travelled up through France somehow, before catching a train from Paris to Denmark. The energy of the man was truly remarkable. Even at the age of eighty he was still writing books that were eagerly awaited and read by Chinese academics and the general public. His knowledge and memory was prodigious. I was a little overcome by his generosity, which was completely unexpected. I hoped William would come to my aid, somehow, but he just sat there quietly, smiling.

Suddenly, the great man stood up and led us outside. The meeting was over. We walked over and pulled our bicycles from the wall and, with a quick wave, cycled off into the intensifying heat and sapping humidity. I expected William to lead us back the way we had come, but he crossed the main road instead of making a left turn, and headed eastwards along the busy road away from Xiang Shan town. After a mile or so, with huge lorries trundling slowly past us, he pulled sharply into the huge central entrance of the Botanical Garden itself. The groups of ticket staff paid us no heed as we pedalled quickly past them.

We pulled up outside a large two-storey building with a huge 'People's Republic of China' sign on its roof. People were milling in and out, some wearing green military uniforms – not unlike those worn by the security people in my room a few days back. This must be the main building I concluded, although William said nothing as we pushed our bicycles along behind him. We rounded the main building along a long arching path and then walked in the hot sunlight over to another adjoining building in the rear, which had large windows and a welcoming main door.

As we ducked inside we were instantly assailed by the noise of a hundred or so Chinese having lunch. There was a lot of shouting and loud laughing, which in a way I had come to expect, but it was still a shock every time I came across it. Everyone was just so happy! It had to be the main dining room, although where the food came from was a mystery.

We moved slowly into the ruck of people queueing to one side by a long wall. William shook his head and gestured for me to sit down at the only free table left. I did this very willingly as I hadn't a clue what was going on.

William slid a deep enamel bowl in front of me. It was extremely hot and steam billowed from it when he lifted its lid, which also had two of the familiar round white breads balanced on top of it. My companions both had the same.

The pretty girl, aloof as ever, was studying the contents of her bowl as well as blowing the surface from time to time to cool everything; she was already munching on one of her bread rolls. I envied her hunger and appetite. The bread was as white as a snowball and had a similar shape in her tiny brown hands, but all other comparisons ended there; the bread texture was gluey and elastic and required quite a lot of chewing before you could eventually swallow it.

'Northern Chinese, like Miss Wu, prefer bread,' William gestured at the pretty girl.

'I'm from the south, we prefer rice of course.'

I nodded. So she did have a name. Miss Wu? A very *short* name, to be sure. But easy to remember. Miss Wu made no attempt to reply, but continued eating eagerly. I liked that name, Miss *Wu*.

The food was quite simple and wholesome, so I nibbled at it. 'Why haven't you brought me to this dining room before?' I asked William, 'It seems to be cheap and cheerful.'

'Well, for one thing our director really wants you to eat in the public one for some reason, and anyway this was a little too far to come from the research building – just for a meal I mean,' he shrugged. 'I think I know what your problem with the food is, Adrian, it's just *too* fine there, even for Chinese people. It is proper restaurant food, completely opposite to good proper Chinese home cooking. That's probably why there are no customers normally, that and the *price*, of course.'

This was a great relief to hear and I felt myself relax. It was an unexpected confirmation of the view I had been slowly coming to. I looked across at Miss Wu, to see if she agreed with this discussion, but she was lost in her own private reverie, expertly twisting the noodles from the bowl around the tips of her chop-sticks before pushing them delicately into her sweet little mouth. She had turned this simple act into an art form, I thought distractedly.

Despite her non-existent conversation, I felt my eyes returning to this girl more and more as the lunch wore on.

The dining hall started to clear at last; the visitors were

evidently on their way out to continue their explorations. I saw now they were all dressed the same in white polo neck shirts and mid-blue work trousers. They all carefully put on their matching blue baseball caps before marching out into the hot summer afternoon.

As we watched the last of them reluctantly file out, Mr Huang approached with a tray of food. He slammed his tray down and sighed wearily. 'Those hungry wolves, they nearly ate everything! I was lucky to get this,' he said, holding up a bowl of clear soup and a single bread roll. 'I have some good news for you, Adrian,' he said, before spooning some hot soup into his mouth.

My goodness, I thought – first he smiled at me and now he's just called me *Adrian*, not Webber!

'Your schedule has been completed; please take a look at it now if you wish?' he said primly.

William passed the folded piece of paper over to me which I read through quickly. Tomorrow, it said, I would be driven to the Summer Palace (as he had promised) and I would be accompanied by Wu Shu, the Master. I presumed this meant she had an MSc. I nodded, and smiled my thanks to him and Miss Wu sitting opposite. So she had two names. The first was her family name, hence Miss Wu, and 'Shu' was therefore her given name – Wu Shu – well, that will do for now, I thought.

For the rest of the month, the paper stated, I would remain in plant propagation. I would move to 'cuttings' ('please make sure your secateurs are sharp'!) the following week.

But the unexpected news was that I would spend the whole of August in the design office as I had specially requested. Beneath the table I clutched my hands together and prayed thanks to all the gods for allowing this. And I was to work with the design staff on drawings for new projects within the Botanical Garden *and* within Beijing city itself under the direction of the head of design, Miss Liu Hong Bin.

'Professor Yu, who you met this morning, although retired, is still a leading authority on Chinese public garden design principles and has offered to be your tutor on all these aspects for the rest of your stay here. You may also still contact him when you return to England. Are you happy with all this, Adrian?'

I felt a deep groundswell of emotion rise within me, mixed with profound gratitude. I was overcome. I sat there feeling over-awed and could say nothing. Nothing. Instead I grinned my thanks.

Cycling back from the public restaurant after such a day, the best day I had had really since I arrived, I decided it was best to get to bed early, relax, and soak up all the things that had been done for me that had come as such a pleasant surprise. Again, I noted, the Chinese last-minute way of doing things had fooled me into thinking that nothing would ever be done. They had, in fact, completely understood. The problem again wasn't the lack of action, it was the lack of communication. They simply could not see the point in keeping me informed. All the pressure was off now – I could see my way clearly; and it promised, as the Chinese say, a rich harvest. And to top it all, tomorrow was the day of the visit to the Summer Palace – accompanied by the very attractive Miss Wu Shu. Master.

My room began to darken as the sun went down behind the mountains. I lay there in the twilight, listening to a song being played in a family home the other side of the perimeter fence. It was Lesley Garrett singing 'Tonight' from *West Side Story*. I laughed – the 'Tonight' was right, except it should of course have been '*East* Side Story'!

I was still grinning when I glanced up at the darkened ceiling, but abruptly stopped smiling. On the top corner of the ceiling I could see a faint light. It was twinkling. I shook my head; it must have been my imagination, surely. But then I looked up again. It was still there. All thoughts of the day vanished. I've been *bugged*, I whispered to myself. The cunning devils. They came in here making out that all they were worried about was my security, but instead they planted some listening device in my room. Bloody cheek!

Slowly, the twinkling light moved, uncertainly at first, across the dusky white ceiling, then it suddenly stopped. I watched, transfixed as it moved off again, still keeping to the surface of the ceiling. Although it wasn't attached in any way, the light was clearly flying ... then it stopped once again and went out. Then the light was on the move once more, flickering uncertainly as it began a long languid descent from the high ceiling. As it came slowly down, I relaxed. It was a *firefly*!

CHAPTER 5

甘蔗不能两头甜

'You can't expect both ends of a sugar cane to be sweet'

Today was the day; there was no need to force myself out of bed. I pushed the button down on the alarm clock and jogged happily across the cool tiled floor to the door, opening it just far enough to be able to reach round for the fresh hot water flask. Soon my hand felt it and I quickly drew the flask back through the door opening, before lifting it up and placing it on the weather station – jamming it up against the wall to prevent it from sliding off. After getting my shaving things ready I lifted up the heavy flask and poured the boiling water into the sink, as the plug always worked quite well, and lathered first the shaving brush and then my face. Dipping the razor into the hot water, I reached for the tiny plastic-rimmed mirror I had bought for a few pennies in the town and carefully shaved above and below my beard to give a clean line. Looking into the mirror for almost the first time since I arrived, a thinner face than I remembered looked back at me.

Shave over, I put out the best white linen shirt I had, together with my favourite light-blue sleeveless summer waistcoat, also made of linen. I was determined to look as respectable as possible. Today was my *official* visit to the Summer Palace *and* I was also to be accompanied by the extremely pretty 'Master'. This again was *official*.

Flopping my white Panama hat next to my ancient Pentax

camera, I checked my wallet for money. I counted 300 yuan, about £25 – that should be enough for today, surely? As I walked up the corridor towards the main entrance, I passed the entrance to the Ladies just as Miss Wu emerged with dripping hands. I knew there were no towels or paper with which to dry her hands; it was the same everywhere – in China these things were simply ignored. But as she walked down the shallow steps to the corridor level I had the strangest feeling I couldn't explain. It told me quite plainly that the situation was simply not good enough for *this* young lady – for *this* young lady deserved better.

'The bus is here, Mr Webber,' Miss Wu said. 'Miss Sun Yi is coming too. She has to collect laboratory materials from Beijing and so will travel on to the city after we have been dropped off at the Palace.'

As we walked to the main door I could see Sun Yi laughing with the driver outside by the bus. It was the same driver who picked me up from the airport. They weren't just laughing, it looked more like flirting. And he a married man, Sun Yi – tut, tut, I thought.

Soon we had left the Garden behind and now entered a small urban area that I hadn't visited before. It housed a small community who seemed to spend most waking hours in the busy dusty streets. There were traditional single-storey houses, some with courtyards, either side of the road. They were intermingled with tiny shops and kiosks selling foodstuffs. Huge green watermelons were stacked outside everywhere in thick wicker baskets. Some vendors had set up tiny stalls using trestle tables to show off the fruit and vegetables. Already they were fanning themselves as they waited for customers in the early morning heat. It wasn't even 9 a.m. yet.

We went round a sharp bend and Miss Wu pointed down a narrow alleyway, saying, 'My dormitory is down there, it is where I live.'

She said it in a matter-of-fact manner. A simple enough statement, but somehow it unsettled me, provoked me in some way. I wanted to tease her, but I decided against it and looked out of the window nonchalantly. She might have been deeply offended, and that was the last thing I wanted.

The traffic congestion intensified as we neared the Summer Palace whose outer walls loomed up now in front of us. I could see a busy roundabout coming up, and all the traffic from our carriageway was streaming round it in a patient, comparatively fluent, anticlockwise direction. All the traffic, that is, but for the bus in front of us whose driver had evidently decided it would be quicker if he took the roundabout on the *left-hand* side. Somehow, he got away with it. Another driver saw him in the mirror and let him into the right lane of traffic before he found himself head-on with someone coming the other way. I tore my gaze away from the traffic; it was enough to give you a headache just watching it, although it was also quite addictive. I remembered a Chinese national on the plane coming out of London who confided that she hadn't realized Chinese drivers were completely mad until she visited the West, where, by contrast, traffic was so ordered.

Our driver pulled up sharply as he bumped on to the pavement and bellowed something to Miss Wu over his shoulder. I quickly followed her out and looked around. If the roads seemed crowded, they were more than matched by the number of people on the pavements; but here everyone was relaxed, brightly dressed, enjoying the atmosphere, and the prospect of a day at leisure.

Miss Wu pointed up at the enormous Chinese arch of the main entrance just along the street. Already stretching across it was a line of women in immaculate green military-style uniforms, each wearing a green peaked cap and a smart leather belt. They looked very serious as they took, and carefully examined, everyone's entrance ticket before letting them through. Visitors had to queue patiently at the main ticket office, but not us. Diminutive Miss Wu expertly barged past those waiting, flashed an official pass at the ticket officer standing in front of her and quickly strode past. The middle-aged woman immediately held up her finger and pointed her white gloved hand at me. The 'Master' shook her head confidently and deftly reached behind, grabbed my arm, and then propelled me through the little entrance gate. The woman shouted after us, but when I looked back she had already turned to deal with the next visitor.

'I'm getting used to being yelled at,' I said, nervously. 'It seems to be happening wherever I go now.'

'That woman wanted to earn extra money by charging you "special price" as a foreigner, but I told her that you were a guest of the Public Parks Bureau,' Miss Wu explained quickly.

'She didn't seem very happy about it though,' I added, needlessly.

'It doesn't matter, she was just being greedy.'

We walked on in the lovely dappled sunlight. It was a beautiful day for what promised to be a memorable visit.

'Heh, wait!' someone shouted from behind us.

We turned and saw a tall girl in a black summer dress, with a contrasting white formal collar and matching white shoes, running after us.

'It's *me*!' she shouted.

Eventually she caught up with us and said breathlessly, 'You *are* Wu Shu, aren't you?'

Miss Wu did not reply, but just looked at her steadily.

'I'm your guide today,' she continued. 'Sorry I missed you at the gate, was there a problem?'

'No problem,' replied Miss Wu.

'Good, OK, my name is Miss Xu Zhihong, I am a graduate and academic officer for this area,' she said confidently.

Miss Wu had tiny eyes even by Chinese standards, but I could see that she was studying this young woman very, very carefully and again said nothing.

'Shall we go?' Miss Xu said brightly at last.

She pointed down a wide path which sloped away towards a large imposing building. As we walked down the path I tried to tune out her endless stream of chatter. But was my apparent irritation with our guide really about her, or was it because I resented not being alone with the mysterious Miss Wu? Perhaps it was the latter. Eventually we were beside a huge expanse of water which stretched for nearly as far as the eye could see, miles in all directions. It was calm and almost milky in the now overcast sky, which seemed to bleach all colour from the landscape. I tuned back in to Miss Xu's seamless commentary.

'Of course, the emperors used to come to the Palace to escape the hot, humid summers in Beijing, hence its name: the Summer Palace. One emperor decided that he wanted a sea to remind him of pleasurable trips to the coast and so he had this lake constructed ...'

But in spite of the wonderful history I couldn't tear my eyes away from Miss Wu, who drifted through the heavenly landscape as if part of it. I could sometimes just make out her tiny eyes beneath her immaculate fringe, though what she was thinking I had absolutely no idea. I also felt (was I imagining it?) that somehow we were walking in unison, in the same unconscious rhythm.

She quietly kept herself apart from our guide, I noticed, until I requested a picture of them by the lakeside. They stood together, very poised, ladylike, but also strangely ill at ease with one another, and quickly parted once the photo had been taken.

Then Miss Xu, our indefatigable guide, instantly slipped back into role, explaining, in her sing-song voice, that towards the end of the rule of the emperors the Summer Palace had been a favourite haunt of the infamous Empress Dowager, who preferred it to the Forbidden City, in the centre of Beijing.

The most famous story of course was about her supposed abuse of power which had deprived the Chinese navy of funds it needed to modernize itself and protect China from foreign incursion. Instead, the Empress Dowager had commissioned an *ornamental* boat hewn from local rock and now perennially moored by the side of the great lake. As it was built purely for pleasure purposes, she named it 'The Boat of Purity and Ease'. As we looked down at the rather ridiculous construction, I thought it scarcely possible that the money that built this tiny boat out of stone could have provided the Chinese navy with a squadron of modern ships capable of saving the entire country. It would have barely covered the cost of an old leaky junk, surely?

What seemed more interesting was the way in which the imperial court made ordinary things its own, such as certain colours that were immediately off limits to ordinary Chinese citizens, or the case of the number nine. The number nine ran pretty much through everything and was highly visible and public. The ancient Chinese believed that because nine was the highest *single* number, it had the most positive strength. So, for example, the imperial pagoda building would have nine storeys. Looking out on to the lake there was a beautiful ornate bridge of white marble. It had seventeen arches, allowing the one in the middle – yes, the ninth – to be used by the emperor alone.

One emperor had even created an exquisite shopping mall made of stone. There was a continuous quay that you could walk on, with parades of shops and an ornamental lake in the middle. In this way the emperor could have the shopping experience without having to face ordinary Chinese citizens because the shops were staffed by members of his household. Retail therapy for emperors! It was given an edge by getting eunuchs to work as pickpockets, very common in those times. If caught, though, the eunuch still faced the usual legal punishment – which was hardly fair, surely? And, in her own way, Miss Xu carried on this tradition by persuading me to part with more than *half* the money I had in my pocket to buy an admittedly beautiful hand-crafted blue cloth.

We were the only shoppers that morning, and so from each shop came an exquisitely dressed young woman who tried, through flattery, to get a sale.

'Buy something for your beautiful wife, *pleeese* ...'

'I haven't got a wife,' was my only reply.

'Then your *beauutiful* children, Sir?'

'I haven't got any children,' I said, laughing.

Miss Xu took a phone call and suddenly became very serious. She seemed nervous too.

'Please, we must hurry,' she said after the call, 'We are to have lunch with deputy director Hua. Please hurry, other guests are waiting.'

She turned on her heel and we quickly trotted after her along the long dark pavilion. Soon we lost sight of her, but could hear her heavy sandals on the wooden boards of the pavilion so we followed the sound. Why was she so terrified, I wondered?

Out of breath, we saw her at the top of a long flight of stone steps and she beckoned for us to follow. At the top, we had no time to compose ourselves before immediately being ushered through a silk curtain and into what I expected to be a shrine of some sort.

Inside it was so dark it took a few seconds to adapt after the glare of the sunshine. At first I could just make out a high, solid, wooden, horseshoe-form table, then I noticed an elderly man in a crisp white shirt, sitting alone at this table. He was clean-shaven beneath a shock of silvery hair parted in the middle. His face was completely impassive and he gave no word of welcome. As my eyes adjusted I noticed to his left, sitting at another table, a middle-aged couple, together with a younger Western man who began to smile – but then abruptly stopped himself.

The couple didn't appear to be Chinese, and later I found out they were visiting antique dealers from the island of Taiwan. They also ignored us, and looked down at the table as we entered.

A *xio jie* in full imperial era costume ushered us formally to the table opposite the other guests. I went first, followed by Miss Wu and Miss Xu. Still the man at the top table said nothing. No form of greeting. The *xio jie* then stood in the space between the tables and, in perfect English, announced, 'Today we will experience an authentic imperial light lunch, courtesy of deputy director Hua.'

Another girl then came in and played some bells discordantly, followed by three *xio jies* who each carried a silver tray containing ornate silver dishes with tiny portions of food. As they were placed on the tables, the head *xio jie* explained what the dishes contained. Nothing special as far as I could make out. I looked at the two girls to my right. Their faces were masks. Blank. I hoped mine was too.

At one point our host had a polite desultory conversation with the Taiwanese couple, but steadfastly refused to acknowledge our table. As the meal wore on, the younger man opposite gave me a plaintive look and I nodded slightly as if to say I understood, but what could we do? The deputy director Hua then began another polite conversation with the Taiwanese couple, which I noticed made them uncomfortable. This official was clearly being rude, but why? Perhaps he didn't like foreigners? The two girls continued to eat the extremely bland food and said nothing.

I could feel anger rising within me. Why on earth was I eating this obviously expensive but tasteless food, which I had no wish to consume, in an atmosphere that made everyone feel intimidated by a ridiculous official who presumably had nothing better to do? Before I could stop myself, I had interrupted his conversation with the old couple and asked him – in English of course – what the matter was.

He ignored me and continued embarrasing the Taiwanese couple, so I interrupted him again. The atmosphere became electric. Everyone was still. After what felt like ages, he turned and looked at me with blank, lifeless eyes and pulled a paper napkin towards him. And then, with a pen from his shirt pocket, he quickly sketched a satirical portrait of me on the napkin and passed it to me without a word. I deliberately gave it a cursory look (it was actually very well done) and discarded it as if it was of no use.

The meal broke up soon after. Everyone stood up. We all filed out as if we had just attended a church service with a three-hour sermon. Miss Xu whispered to me that it would be appropriate to thank deputy director Hua for the lunch. I looked at her incredulously, turned my back on all of them, and walked back down the steep stone steps without a word. The two girls reluctantly followed.

And that was that.

I'd mentioned before lunch that I was desperate to go further into the city to see if it was possible to get some Western-style bread, butter and jam to soothe my long-suffering stomach. The meal we had just endured had not helped, of course. Miss Xu offered to come with me, but was politely overruled by Miss Wu, who said to me later when we were alone, 'That girl is a graduate, not Master, like me …'

Did that mean she had just pulled rank? Clearly, I had underestimated this quiet, demure, young Chinese woman, and the word 'formidable' kept popping into my head as we walked back down the hill, thanking Miss Xu for her time. We left the Summer Palace by a side gate, then strolled into an open-air bus station.

We, along with many others, hopped on to the only bus that had a driver at the wheel, hoping to move off shortly. Soon there were twice as many people on the bus as there were seats. We then lurched off in a cloud of smoke and dust as the girl came round to take the fares. I noticed that anyone who asked for a receipt became her instant enemy – because the tax would have to be paid on that fare – but she returned to the front smiling. It hadn't been so bad. Happiness, after all, was a full bus!

Miss Wu sat directly in front of me. The Chinese seemed to have no embarrassment about telling each other what we in the West considered highly personal details like marital status or salary – she had already told me her age (twenty-five), and asked me some personal questions. She wanted to know if I was a university graduate (yes), what I studied (politics and history), did I have a sibling (one sister), and finally my full name (Adrian Austin Webber). The questions, I noticed, were carefully thought through, and when I finished each answer she had an endearing way of tilting her head when she either understood or was a little surprised at the reply. This tilting of the head was accompanied by the question: '*really?*'

Sitting next to her was a grandmother with a little chubby-cheeked baby girl on her lap. She had beautiful brightly coloured clothes, and on the top of her head her grandmother had made her a tiny ponytail which made me smile. I tried to pull funny faces to make the little girl laugh and the grandmother nodded in recognition.

'Chinese people think it a great honour if you make a fuss of their child,' Miss Wu said loudly above the noise of the truck.

'Well, all I can say is that you would have to be very hard-hearted not to find Chinese babies adorable,' I shouted back. Her sun-bronzed forehead creased slightly as she considered this for a few seconds before replying, 'No, Mr Webber, we Chinese think Western children are the prettiest in all the world.'

The bus was vibrating more slowly now and soon it was time to get off, which came as something of a relief as the heat inside had been stifling. My guide, the Master, immediately pushed on ahead and made her way to the side of a wide busy road. She quickly looked left, grabbed my hand, and pulled me on to the road, briefly waiting for a gaggle of cyclists to swish past, and then led me further into the car lanes. Here, trucks, cars and all manner of taxis roared past just inches from your face, all the time spewing out smoke and acrid fumes; but Miss Wu was still watching, and carefully judging their speed, before timing our run.

'Now!' she shouted.

She tugged my hand hard and we ran for all we were worth. By the time we got to the other side, cars and lorries were tooting their horns loudly at us.

'Miss Wu,' I asked plaintively. 'Are there any, you know, *bridges* in Beijing?'

But as I asked the question I was very careful to let her still hang on to my hand. It just felt nice, that was all ...

Unfortunately, she then remembered to take her hand back, but surprised me by asking brightly, 'Well, we're here now, so what would you like to do first, Mr Webber?'

I crushed the request in my mind, to ask for her little hand back, and instead laughed and shouted above the noise of the traffic, 'Well, a cup of coffee would be very nice, if that's possible, Miss Wu?'

'Wait here, Mr Webber,' she replied primly. 'I'll ask in here ...'

She lightly tripped up some steps and I followed her into a deserted restaurant. While she disappeared out the back to find someone, I looked around the eating area, which had just finished lunch service by the look of things. Although it took a while to get used to the subdued light after the glare of the street, I soon noticed a number of huge glass tanks that each had a tube leading into them that produced frothing bubbles of air. Large fish swam around inside the murky water; they were carp, I thought, by the look of their silver sides.

Beneath the large tanks on the saturated floor were yet more tanks, this time with giant frogs bobbing up and down, desperately trying to find a way out. As I peered into the tanks they started up a huge mass croaking. The loud croaking didn't disturb the clearly exhausted *xio jie*, who I found asleep with her head on a bare table next to them. Beside her were some shelves with curious shallow wire cages on them that were the size of cartwheels. Moving closer I wondered what they could possibly hold. With a sudden start, I realized. The thin cages were packed with live snakes coiled around each other like an animated Cumberland sausage. There were a couple of hundred at least! It was truly horrible. I staggered back, shocked, and collided with Miss Wu.

'Coffee this way, Mr Webber,' was all she said and darted outside.

Later, I looked at the time and saw that it had been well over three hours since we came into the coffee lounge. It was part of an international hotel and, yes, the coffee had had a calming effect on my mind, if not my soul. We had been talking non-stop since we arrived. It didn't really matter how long we talked as it was never going to be enough. And she was clearly not a thirsty young woman as she had, all the while, contented herself with just a pot of yoghurt.

'I'm sorry, Adrian, but we had better start back as it's quite a way. We'll have to find your English food another time,' she said quietly. Mr Huang told me you must be back by 8 o'clock at the latest.'

'Do you know, I've never viewed Mr Huang as my fairy godmother, but it does have a certain resonance. Sometimes, I think he would like to turn me into a pumpkin ... poof! ... you know ... just like that!' I clicked my fingers as loudly as I could.

'I do think you are a little naughty – *poor* Mr Huang ...' she said, laughing.

We got up to leave and I paid the bill, at the same time realizing that I now had less than 100 yuan left.

It was late when our bus eventually pulled into Xiang Shan bus station, and all the little eating places had shut for the night. Here I stood with one of the most attractive women I had ever met, and who had looked after me *all* day. The least I could do was buy her dinner! But where? There was only one option – the expensive Xiang Shan Hotel. My heart sank, but with as much dignity as I could muster I said, 'You must be my guest, you must be famished, please follow me!'

The waiter brought the extensive *à la carte* menu to our table with no little ceremony. If he had placed it on the floor, it could have doubled as a room divider! Miss Wu accepted it calmly and I lost sight of her temporarily as she peered inside it. I snatched mine from his hand and quickly scanned it, guided by one thing and one thing only – *price*.

They didn't take credit cards and all my travellers' cheques were in my room ... and I had less than 100 yuan in my pocket. The waiter returned. I slammed my menu shut and looked him straight in the eye, 'Two bowls of the special fried rice, please, and two glasses of water, tap,' I said.

Miss Wu handed the waiter her menu, then turned to me and smiled, 'Excellent choice, Adrian – we had *such* a large lunch.'

I smiled back.

Later, as we strolled back through Xiang Shan in the warm darkness, she said casually, 'Tomorrow, Adrian, I have to travel back into Beijing for the weekend.'

'Why?' I asked.

'To attend my GRE English lessons. I do them every weekend. I stay in some girlfriends' dormitory on Saturday and Sunday night.'

'Why don't you come back here each night?' I asked.

'The buses don't run late enough, so I would have to take a taxi. Male taxi drivers cannot be trusted with young girl in dark night. Too dangerous.'

I nodded and smiled.

Yes, *very* sensible, I thought, as we walked on; this girl could certainly handle herself. Very independent. It crossed my mind that perhaps circumstances had forced her to be independent.

As we walked away from a dark and hushed Xiang Shan town I thanked her for everything and said I would of course accompany her to her dormitory, which I now knew was on the other side of the Garden.

'Oh no,' she said. 'I come with you to research building.'

'No, no, you cannot see *me* home,' I said, a little startled.

She giggled a little, then replied, 'You do not understand, Adrian, I have a bed there too. In my office, upstairs.'

CHAPTER 6

吃一堑，长一智

'A fall into a ditch makes you wiser'

There was a loud knocking on my door, then a voice: 'Adrian, quick, it's me, William!'

Blearily, I wrenched myself from the warm bed and traipsed over to the door. I opened it and yawned loudly. It was William, but a William I had never seen, so excited, so *animated*. And then he'd gone. But from the bottom of the staircase he'd shouted back up, 'It's the opening ceremony, the Olympic Games in America – it will start in two minutes, quick or you'll miss the opening ceremony!'

I threw on some clothes, then bounded up the stairs to the library, where the building's only television set was located. The caretaker heard me and came out of his office, laughing, making him choke on his breakfast roll. I stopped and grinned at him. We had struck up an easy relationship although we only had two words in common – well, four, if you included *yue liang* (moon), which he taught me a few evenings earlier when we were both looking at the full moon. Unfortunately, knowing the Chinese for 'moon' did not really help me a great deal in everyday conversation.

I heard the portentous Olympic music even before I had opened the door to the library. I sat down at the long table in the middle of the room and William, his face glued to the television screen, pushed a mug of green tea across the table for me.

'How did you get on yesterday, by the way?' he asked.

'Oh, excellent, William, the Summer Palace was beyond my expectation, you could *feel* Chinese history there.'

'Was it Miss Xu who showed you around?' he asked casually, still staring at the television screen.

'Er, yes,' I replied.

'I thought it would be her. She is the Palace's best English speaker – by far, you know.'

'She could certainly talk – English, I mean,' I said, looking across at him.

William gave me a puzzled look before returning his gaze to the ancient television. 'Good, it's starting,' he muttered.

There was a Chinese introduction before the music struck up and the ceremony began. It was on an enormous scale and strangely moving. I felt a bit choked. But it wasn't just the music and beautiful choreography as I sat watching it all. No, I had just begun to realize, or perhaps *appreciate*, what was being done for me here in China. Nothing had been too much trouble. Here I was, a big chap by any standards, and yet I was being treated as though I needed help simply to breathe. Yet everything was carried out with such a light touch I was often barely aware of the degree of help I was receiving.

Everyone had been so supportive, I thought, as I looked across at William, who himself had been such a stalwart. Even Mr Huang in his own way had been helpful. Yet no one would ever accept a word of thanks. They simply resisted any form of sentimentality and just got on with things.

Ceremony over, William turned to me and, yawning gently, said, 'Adrian, would you like to see a giant panda?'

The huge bus pulled up outside Beijing Zoo and we stepped down into the heat and humidity of central Beijing. William strode over to the impassive entrance officials and flashed the magic pass that yet again allowed us in free and with no need to queue. We saw three pandas with their distinctive black and white fur – which must have made them feel uncomfortably hot.

'We call them *Da Xiong Mao*, it means "large bear cat",' William explained. 'A nice name, don't you think, Adrian?'

'Yes, and I can certainly see why the World Wildlife Fund uses them as its symbol,' I replied.

As we strolled among the throngs of people, William slowly told me about his life. He had married a girl that spring, who he had met at Beijing Forestry University where he had been studying for his doctorate. 'She is now visiting her family in a province to the south of China. It is quite a long way, actually. So I'm pleased to have you here for the company.'

I nodded slowly. It must be hard on him, I thought, to have just got married and then almost immediately to be left alone, while the woman he loved dearly had vanished back to her home in a distant province. And, as I understood it, with no intimation of when she would ever return? I decided there and then never to mention anything about it unless, of course, he did. Perhaps he was also losing face by her absence so soon after their marriage? All in all, it was clearly a very difficult situation for him.

It was Sunday. The sun was streaming through my plastic curtain, making everything jump and sparkle within the room. It was a welcome change after the hot overcast conditions of late. Although it was still early, I decided there and then that it was time to climb the Xiang Shan mountain.

At the foot of the mountain you were confronted with a huge entrance gate and the usual ticketing arrangements. When you were through all that, you were free to stare and marvel at the sheer size and grandeur of the revered mountain – and, I quickly realized, its overwhelming steepness.

Discreetly, to one side, there was a group of men with donkeys who would normally offer to take you up the easy way – but they looked at my bulk doubtfully, and I couldn't say I blamed them.

There were many Chinese tourists here, and as I passed a

couple with a toddler they immediately stooped down and pointed me out to her. She looked at me for only a few seconds before running back to bury her little head in her mother's bosom.

The view from the top was worth all the sweat and aching legs. It was so timeless and peaceful and the air was pure. Wood smoke rose lazily from a hill in the distance. It was perhaps China at its most tranquil and gentle, away from the madding crowd. The Botanical Garden, spread out before me in all its rolling acres, was a marvel in itself.

I had been told that the local Chinese often tried to bury their relatives on this mountain, even though it was illegal. As they thought it was sacred, many were willing to run the risk. And, sure enough, there in the distance as I looked down I could just make out a line of people walking along a narrow winding track. Further along it, but slightly above, were two men wearing Coolie hats who looked to be digging furiously with hatchets or mattocks.

It was clearly a burial party. After a few minutes a white cloth was stretched over the hole, and the corpse was laid on top of it. Almost immediately it was lowered into the grave, while the mourners, now in a tight group, quietly witnessed the internment.

No vicar, no priest, no one at all to officiate. The mourners were all dressed in white, as if for a wedding. The women, I noticed, were all crying openly, but the men just bowed their heads in grief.

When I eventually returned home I was still turning over in my mind what I had seen. William could help me understand, I thought – he was the man to ask – so I bounded up the stairs and down the long corridor to his living quarters. I had to knock on his door for a long time before he unbolted it.

I was shocked by what I saw. William was barely recognizable as the same man who had taken me to the zoo the previous day. His hair looked greasy and uncombed. His eyes were hollow and dark, and I had the distinct impression that he had been weeping. I apologized for having disturbed him.

'Do not worry, I was just having a doze, Adrian,' he said, and sniffed softly.

But then he seemed to cheer up and, in his usual charming way, said, 'And what can I do for you? What have you been up to, *English gentleman?*'

We both laughed. The spell had been broken.

'What's the colour of death in China? It isn't black, is it?'

He looked bemused, then gave a wry smile. 'Adrian, that is a very *strange* question to ask. No, it is white, why?'

I told him what I had seen on the mountain.

He nodded, thoughtfully. 'Adrian, you have just witnessed a Chinese funeral, that was all. By the way, were the women crying?'

I nodded.

'Well, in that case the dead person was probably young – below the age of seventy, anyway. You see, we believe that a human being has the right to live to the age of seventy. It is the normal allotted span. If they hadn't been crying, the deceased would have been older than seventy, when they had, therefore, exceeded what they had a right to.'

'So the mourners wouldn't have cried, I see.'

'No, it's more than that – they would laugh! They would show their joy at their friend or relative beating the odds.'

Ah, so that was it, the Chinese way of death. As usual, there was a hard, dry, unsentimental take on what was a very emotional subject. And then I wondered: if white was the colour of death, then what was the colour of marriage? I asked him.

My friend looked down at the floor slowly, and took a very deep breath before replying, 'Red ... it is red, Adrian.'

Too late, I realized my mistake. Tactless. *Stupid*. I reproached myself, but all I could do was watch as he quietly closed the door. The bolt was pulled back across. He was alone again.

*

Today was the first proper day of my work in propagation. No more tweezers, sterile procedures or the devilish Bunsen burner. Today I was to join a team of good old-fashioned 'cuttings' staff who buried their cuttings in proper sandy compost and placed them not in some futuristic refrigerator, but in a proper cold frame as we would in England.

The sun was already high in the sky when I pushed open the glass double doors of the research building and drew the warm fresh air deep into my lungs. The team were already sitting down across the road and were busily chatting among themselves as I strode purposefully towards them in my short-sleeved boiler suit. It was a thin all-in-one outfit which I considered to be manly and workmanlike; and clearly showed that I meant business. It also helped with my confidence as I already knew that not one of the team spoke English, and I was going to be working with them for at least the next fortnight.

The manager nodded to me as I walked over. I knew that he had been called back from retirement as the Garden hadn't found anyone good enough to replace him. In fact, he had been one of the first staff to be recruited back in 1956 when the Garden was established. By coincidence it was also the year that I was born. He was a thickset man, as many native Beijing men were, and had a ruddy shiny skin. He looked about fifty, but I knew he was over seventy and his hands trembled a little as he worked with his secateurs. He had a cheerful personality, but he never smiled once in all the time I knew him.

The other staff within the team were a mixture of ages, but they were basically easy-going and good-natured. They could do the job blindfolded, and so passed the time in idle banter and story telling. They sat around in a loose circle, either squatting on their haunches or sitting on tiny stools barely a few inches above the ground.

William, as ever, was on hand and came over to introduce me.

They all nodded politely before looking at each other, which was a bit unnerving. What on earth were they thinking? It was a question that often slipped in and out of my mind these days. Later on, I *did* find out what they were thinking. They judged the big foreigner as a friendly type who was open and could be trusted. On a somewhat less positive note, they also questioned why so large a foreigner found it necessary to wear a baby outfit? They decided, therefore, that I must be a big baby.

Unaware of this, I smiled at everyone in turn and they smiled back. But what was about to happen was only to provide ample confirmation of their original assessment of me. A pile of cuttings was placed at my feet. I smiled again because there was no chair or stool for me to sit on. Although I was perhaps neither young nor old, for me to sit on my haunches all morning was completely out of the question. Even if I managed it, my legs would be paralysed by then from being in the squatting position.

Still smiling, I stood there, not knowing what to do. A hand fell on my shoulder and I looked round to see the old manager had fetched a stool. It was placed, with some ceremony, on to the dirt floor by some of the younger members of the team. The manager clearly didn't want to get any more involved – and later on I understood why.

With a quick nervous cough, I looked down at the stool and blinked the sweat from my eyes. It looked very small with no one sitting on it. Very small indeed. Then, as I paused, someone rushed off and returned with a copy of *The China Daily*, which was carefully draped over the low stool. They had apparently interpreted my reluctance to sit down as a wish not to dirty my 'baby outfit'.

What none of them seemed to understand was that my reluctance was purely one of aiming my backside at the tiny stool as I sat down. It was always going to be a dodgy manoeuvre, but it had now been made ten times worse by covering the damn thing up. There was nothing for it but to 'go for it', so I positioned myself in front of the newspaper, calculated the centre of it, and released my considerable weight downwards.

Surely, I thought afterwards, to anyone with an *ounce* of compassion, the sight of the big 'baby-clothed' foreigner hitting the dirt on his back with a sickening thud, having missed the stool completely, would have been heart-rending? But not a bit of it.

As I lay there flat on my back with my legs in the air covered in dust, ten Chinese faces looked down at me. The manager still managed to remain aloof and dignified as I was hauled back to my feet and the dust was quickly brushed off me. But, to my eternal shame, the male members of the team then bodily lowered me back down on to the stool (which had been quietly repositioned) like a precious exhibit on to its plinth. The secateurs that I dropped as I hit the ground were slapped into my hand and my straw hat was placed back on my head.

I was now ready to start work.

I snatched up one of the shrub cuttings from the heap in front of me and proceeded to butcher the thing out of sheer frustration and humiliation. With a gruff instruction from the boss, my secateurs were taken from my hand by someone who disappeared into a nearby shed. A long metallic grinding noise filled the still air. It was apparent that my extremely expensive Swiss-made secateurs were not considered sharp enough for the Beijing Botanical Garden. Duly sharpened, they were placed back into my hand with an apologetic smile. I wondered whether my colleague's smile of apology was better or worse than the barely concealed choking laughter that seemed to affect his comrades when they caught each other's eyes?

At lunchtime, the prospect of going to eat in the dreaded public restaurant was too much for me to contemplate, although I was extremely hungry. In truth I had been hungry for *days* now. When I went to sleep, all my dreams were of food. Bacon and eggs with plain toast and marmalade was a recurring dream, together with fish and chips served in an (English) newspaper.

The simple truth was that my stomach could no longer 'tolerate' Chinese food.

So instead of going to the public restaurant, I went back inside to write some letters home in the cool library upstairs. I was halfway through the first when I heard someone open the library door behind me. I knew who it was, even before I turned round ... Miss Wu.

She was wearing her workaday laboratory coat, pure white, which only accentuated her tiny dark eyes. Apparently she had been conducting photosynthetic experiments in her lab downstairs, next to the micro-propagation department and nearly opposite my room.

There was something about this girl that disturbed me; she made me feel uncomfortable. I seemed to be lurching from one mini crisis to another. I was feeling wretchedly hungry, about to burst with embarrassment after this morning's events, and now *her*. What I felt I really needed was a complete rest – and I had been in China barely three weeks for goodness' sake.

Now, as she walked towards me, her little face as eye-catching as ever, I felt mesmerized. I couldn't move. Not a muscle. She was holding a large porcelain bowl with a handle and there was a pair of chopsticks sticking out from it. I turned back to my writing as I didn't know what to say to her.

I then felt her right behind me, and it was some seconds before she said, 'Is this your diary, Mr Webber?'

It was said in a whispering confidential tone as she leant over my shoulder to look down at my writing pad.

I felt my throat tighten even before I could think of a reply, so I merely shook my head.

'*Not* your diary?' she said softly, silkily, in her perfect English.

'No,' I managed to reply, weakly.

She was bending right over me now, not moving at all. Completely still. I steeled myself and eventually managed to look up. Her tiny eyes looked steadily back and, I felt, straight through me and down into my soul. She moved her head from side to side as she gazed down at me – which was another form of torture; it was so feminine and yet guileless and beautiful and, *and* ...

'This is *not* your diary, then ...' she said.

I could stand it no longer. With all my courage I had to stop this! A man, *any* man, surely, could only take so much *torment*, beautiful as it was. Those darling cat eyes ... her full lips ... and so close ...

I cleared my throat. 'Miss Wu?' I said hoarsely, at last.

She looked at me beguilingly, so beguilingly that I wanted to cup her head in my hands and kiss her so very gently and lovingly with all the care in the world, and just hold her so close and tenderly that I would never tire, and then see if it hurt, if I kissed her again ... but ... but ... I knew that this was impossible. So, instead, I reluctantly hardened my heart before I said as gently as I could: 'Miss Wu, please would you mind ... just taking yourself and that pretty little nose of yours ... somewhere, *anywhere*, so a man can get on and finish his task?'

To my amazement, she didn't move an inch. She just continued to peruse, in a mock exaggerated way, the letter that I had half written. Then, when she was good and ready and not a second before, she looked me full in the face, smiled dreamily, and slipped out of the room.

I now realized that I would be an emotional as well as physical wreck if this sort of thing carried on much longer. I had just managed to finish my letters when Miss Wu returned.

'Would you like me to show you around my Botanical Garden this evening, when it is cooler, Mr Webber?' she asked casually.

'Yes, that would be interesting and helpful,' I heard myself reply. 'Perhaps we could meet for an early dinner at the public restaurant before we start the tour. It's where I am supposed to eat normally, I said, and looked down, a little nervous.

When I looked up, she had gone.

*

Washed and changed, I arrived at the restaurant just as Miss Wu pulled up on her bicycle. The place was shut. After my increasingly erratic patronage of the place, I could hardly say I blamed them. They had cleared off home. In one way it was a relief not to have to eat there, but I had no other options and really I, or rather my stomach, was beginning to wilt. The recent heat made everything worse. The Beijing summer was now at its zenith which prevented a good night's sleep. So the lack of food *and* sleep combined to produce an ethereal quality to my day-to-day existence, making me feel slightly detached from the world.

Naturally Miss Wu was oblivious to all this, or she was too polite to comment as we walked into the Garden. But I felt very weak now and didn't know how much longer I could continue to walk. And then it happened. I just stopped and suddenly felt both dizzy and disoriented. I looked around. All I could see was heat and the sun beating down. The cicadas seemed louder, more magnified, and my brain throbbed and throbbed until I thought I would pass out.

Someone was talking to me.

'Mr Webber, you have become very pale, what is wrong with you? What is wrong, please tell me ... *please.*'

I just leant against a nearby tree to support myself and took some deep breaths. I couldn't pretend I was OK, no matter how embarrassing it was to nearly collapse in front of Miss Wu. But when it came down to it, the Chinese were practical and full of common sense. So I told her what was wrong.

'You must come to my dormitory now, it isn't far, and I will get you something to eat.'

I leant on the handlebars of her bicycle for support as she led me out of the Garden and slowly down the busy, dusty road. It wasn't too far, just as she said, and soon we were entering a brick courtyard off a narrow and scruffy lane. The courtyard was the communal area for five or six single-sex dormitories. As soon as we entered, the all-pervasive smell of Chinese cooking, fried onion and garlic, simmering soy sauce with ginger, instantaneously filled the nostrils; young men and women were milling around, obviously preparing their evening meal. So this was where Miss Wu lived. Some of the staff here were married, and had a private section. I was also told later that this was where my old classmate Mr Zhu Renyuan lived before he travelled to England. ('Your accommodation of course will be excellent, Adrian.') So this was where he thought I might live?

Miss Wu deposited me at a concrete table in the centre of the courtyard, said something I didn't catch, and disappeared out of the gate we had just entered. Feeling a little conspicuous and self-conscious, I cautiously looked around. An enormous man, much bigger than me, came out of a living area, shouted something over his shoulder, and strode past with a friendly nod. He wore thick heavy-rimmed glasses and was sweating profusely. He then returned from the kitchen with a flask of hot water.

'Hello, Webber, what brings you here?' someone said behind me.

I swivelled round slowly to see the familiar smiling face of Mr Chen, the man who had met me at the airport. I told him about my problem. He nodded thoughtfully and disappeared for a few moments.

'Here, drink this,' he said.

He placed a can of Coca-Cola on the table in front of me. I expected it to be chilled, but no, it was actually *hot*. Mr Chen was joined by his wife, who quickly said something to him and then walked on into the kitchen.

'My wife said that what you really needed was a glass of water, Webber, she has gone to fetch you one,' he said.

I smiled my thanks. A cooling glass of water would be very welcome, as my throat was parched.

'Here it is,' Mr Chen said.

His wife placed the glass down in front of me next to the hot

Coca-Cola. I looked closely at the water inside. It was so hot it was actually steaming.

'Hot water?' I asked.

'Of course!' he replied. 'That will cool you down, you'll see ...'

Miss Wu returned, holding in both hands an enamel bowl, also steaming. Delicately placed in front of me were approximately forty soft-dough boiled dumplings (*jiao zi*), with a small side bowl containing undiluted soy sauce for dipping. I smiled weakly at the people gathered, who were now nodding and murmuring their approval at Miss Wu's choice.

I managed to force myself to eat four, but as soon as Miss Wu disappeared again I quickly offered them to anyone who passed by. Fortunately, the big man I saw earlier sauntered by again and couldn't believe his luck when he walked off with the last fifteen or so. Anyway, my bowl was clean, so when Miss Wu returned she was a little surprised to say the least.

'You *were* hungry, you poor man!' she said sympathetically.

We recommenced our walk. I had eaten just enough to see me through until the following day, but no more. As we walked she made a number of observations about me that were, well, less than flattering, 'Why do you always look at the ground in front of you when you walk instead of the sky and the world around you? You appear to be strong *physically*, despite your food problem, but what about your *moral* strength? That is the most pertinent question.'

She said these things more to herself than to me and continued to frown as I replied that I didn't know the answers to her questions. By way of reply I told her that despite her petite figure and ladylike manner, she struck me as a most *formidable* person.

She accepted this easily and with good grace, then said, 'I think that perhaps you are a very *bad* man?'

I looked round at her, shocked. She noticed and chuckled to herself before walking on ahead. I knew I wasn't strong on understanding the female mind, let alone a *Chinese* female mind, so I resolved not to try.

She eventually stopped walking, then turned and faced me before saying, 'You may use the refrigerator in my laboratory to store your food if you wish.'

I told her that my real problem was that I had no food to put in it – no Western food I meant. In other words, anything I could actually *eat*.

CHAPTER 7

知错不改，错上加错

*'A man who has committed a mistake and doesn't correct
it, is committing another mistake'*

M r Huang took me to one side as I was about to set off for
my second day in 'cuttings' and informed me in a very
serious, confidential tone, 'My director told me that it was wrong
to send the foreigner to the public restaurant for his meals. He
would like you to be told that the money you owe our Garden,
the $3 US, for each meal, has been written off.'

Huang Yi Gong then looked at me gravely before walking
slowly back into his office. It was clear, as he told me this, that
he personally disagreed with his director's (misplaced) sense of
generosity towards me and that really my sporadic attendance
had all been down to me and my unreliable appetite!

And so it was in a mood of reflection that I began work. I tried
to maintain a cheerful exterior, but deep down I was still fatigued
from hunger and felt tired, even after a full night's sleep. But not
so my new comrades. They were clearly in the rudest health and
were game for anything; they still periodically snatched my Felco
secateurs from my hands when I least expected it and ran off to
sharpen them. The way things were going, I would be lucky to
have any metal blade left.

It was impossible to equate the world-view of China with the
people who surrounded me now. They were fun-loving, liked to
enjoy life, eat good food when possible, and were firm in the
support of their families and the love of their country. I had

found it impossible to record in my diary the barrage of emotions that China evoked within me. I suspected that I was being slowly seduced by the country, that there was something in the landscape that drew me in, made me want to love it, even protect it.

Perhaps China had already begun a process of change within me – I didn't know – but I certainly felt different. In some ways I felt stronger, but in other ways weaker, or just less sure than before. It definitely wasn't physical, but it had something to do with the way I perceived the world outside me.

I felt less confident about what I might find, but was *more* confident that I could deal with it. Chinese thinking was definitely not based on logic, that much was clear. It was based on a totally different system or rhythm that so far had eluded me, but I hoped to understand it one day.

For example, the other day I had been walking in the Garden when I was struck by an elderly couple coming along the path towards me. The husband was walking forward purposefully in the usual way, but the woman, presumably his wife, whose arm he was holding, was walking backwards. The woman had a deadly serious expression on her face, a look of determination. This was evidently no childish game.

Sun Yi, from micro-propagation, told me later that the old woman was probably ill with a serious medical condition; by walking backwards, she wanted to unravel the problem and make herself better. Sun Yi told me this in such a matter-of-fact way that I didn't really take it in at first.

That afternoon, unexpectedly, I had two visitors to my new workplace. First was a smartly dressed policeman who had been sent from the local security bureau. He introduced himself to our unsmiling boss, who curtly nodded, before jabbing a thumb in the direction where I was working a little way off in a poly tunnel. He took out a notebook and began to jot things down. Eventually he put his notebook back in his top pocket, and buttoned it carefully before sidling over to me. My co-workers stopped their usual banter and tried to hide their curiosity.

'You are the English *foreigner*, yes?' he said smoothly, in English. 'You have any problems here you wish to discuss with me, Mr Webber?' he asked blandly and looked around at everyone.

'Er, no. Everyone has been very kind, thank you,' I replied.

He eyed me steadily for a few moments. 'Good. I shall return to see you as often as I can,' he said, standing up straight.

'Why?' I asked vaguely.

'Why, to practise my English of course!'

He strode off laughing. Everyone now was looking up and watching him go. When he had disappeared around the corner they all shook their heads and gave each other sour looks. They didn't seem to like this type of official.

A more welcome visitor was Miss Wu. She appeared wearing a sky-blue baseball cap (of all things), to protect her head from the fierce sun. It was worn, I couldn't help noticing, at just the right angle to look chic. *Impossibly* chic, I noted, with a lump in my throat. She came over and introduced a Miss Dong, her best friend, who gently shook my hand. She appeared embarrassed, and kept glancing at Miss Wu before looking down at the ground.

'Our Garden has a shuttle bus into Beijing city this afternoon at 4.30 p.m.,' Miss Wu told me. 'All the shops will be open, including food shops. As I mentioned to you the other evening, I will accompany you there to search for your food. Mr Webber, would you like to go *this* evening?'

It was said almost as a challenge.

The staff bus pulled off sharp at 4.30 p.m. It was full of those who had finished work and were now returning home to their families in Beijing. The Garden was a big employer, with more than 500 staff. Some lived on site, but the majority had a more normal existence, commuting each day from their family homes. None of the staff on the bus were familiar to me. Miss Wu was still wearing the same alluring baseball cap, but now held a shopping bag folded carefully under one arm.

No one seemed to take any notice of us, but I already knew

that could be misleading. Chinese people missed very little and would certainly have registered the big foreigner with the pretty 'Master', neither of whom were regulars on the shuttle.

Most of the staff had got off the bus by the time Miss Wu nudged me and pointed towards an anonymous-looking department store just along the street. In the store's basement was a supermarket, and the atmosphere was deathly cold from all the open-topped refrigerators which contained anonymous raw meats, whole fish and crustaceans. I grabbed hold of a rusty metal shopping basket and began to look round. Soon my basket began to fill. I had packets of pasta (product of Vietnam), margarine (Australia), chicken stock cubes (Hong Kong), frozen prawns and white fish fillets, jam, cheese and salty – as opposed to sweet – Chinese bread. And a jar of Maxwell House coffee (processed in England), which cost an absolute fortune (nearly four times the price it would be at home).

Later we were both hungry and so we went into a fast food outlet selling 'Fish & Chips'. The food was only one or two degrees above ambient and, yes, the fish had been fried much earlier in the day and the chips *were* soggy, but at least it was food I could recognize. I became so preoccupied with this unexpected feast that I completely forgot to see how my pretty dining companion was getting on.

'Is this how you eat this food in your England, Mr Webber?' she asked.

I looked up to see Miss Wu holding the entire foot-long battered fish fillet in her tiny wooden chopsticks while nibbling it at one end.

'Yes, Miss Wu ... but not *quite* like that ... !'

Work-wise, I had now fallen into a routine and, thankfully, I was no longer the centre of attention. I was working to the standard expected, so there was no longer any constant checking; they just let me get on with things. Later in the week I worked with a team of three others on a particular genus, or group, of shrubs. These again were put into the same inexhaustible supply of cold frames and poly tunnels that the garden used for its supply of new planting.

I had also brought out from England a number of cuttings of particular hybrids that Zhu Renyuan had advised were wanted urgently by the Botanical Garden. Many of the original plants had come from China but hybridization lagged far behind the West, so China was desperate for the new hybrids that were often more attractive, disease resistant and vigorous than the originals.

The following week, after a period of just three days, our team of four, working together, had cut, prepared and then potted up over 1,000 plants of which I, for one, was particularly proud. A great Sino-Anglo achievement was the way that I viewed it. Even our dour manager nodded and, I'm certain, almost smiled. Well, I liked to think so, anyway.

After this I was granted an official day off to visit some important historical sites within Beijing city itself, accompanied again by Miss Wu, all organized courtesy of Mr Huang.

I was therefore up at first light that morning, unlocked my door, and scurried down the deserted corridor for a shower. Micro-propagation's double doors were swiftly opened and I had a welcome cooling shower before any of the lab staff arrived for work. I carefully locked the doors behind me and then unlocked the adjacent door to Miss Wu's laboratory with the key she had recently loaned me so I could get to her refrigerator and my food.

I boiled a couple of eggs using her tiny electric hob, which sat on the tiled floor. I used an old packing case as a table and sat down to eat while the old kettle slowly boiled some water for my coffee. I had laid in a stock of two sliced loaves of bread, one in the freezer, the other in the fridge, next to all the dubious-looking plant cultures and experiments that usually filled it. After I washed down the soft boiled eggs and bread with two cups of scalding black coffee, care of Messrs Maxwell House, I felt ready for anything.

Since the evening of a few days ago, I had only eaten what I had prepared myself, and the effect on my body had been one of smooth, uninterrupted healing. I now felt reinvigorated, as comfortable as everyone around me for almost the first time since I arrived in China one month earlier.

We set off at 7.30 a.m. sharp. It was the same Beijing driver as before, who I now knew was called Wing Yin. He was grumpy, I could tell, as we got in, but then he was always a little grumpy. He slammed the door shut behind us and, with no word of greeting, pulled off sharply. We bumped down the now familiar road. I could see Wing Yin's face half covered in wraparound shades, reflected in the rear view mirror. His expression was one of grim obstinacy.

We first visited the Temple of Heaven on the southern side of Beijing. Completed in 1420, it had a tremendous atmosphere. The emperors would come here during the winter solstice to offer sacrifices to heaven, amid much pageantry and ceremony, and pray for a good harvest. During the time of the emperors the whole area would have been off-limits to ordinary Chinese, similar to the Forbidden City itself. Now as we strolled through the great park surrounding the temple, thousands of ordinary Chinese were using it for recreation in the shade of the enormous trees. There was also kite flying, and many played the Chinese violin, but there were also wind instruments of all types, and of course the by-now familiar early morning ballroom dancing; many of the male dancers wore black tie and looked extremely elegant as they led their partners around the tree-lined dance area.

There were signs occasionally in both Chinese and English that reminded visitors that some of the Temple's treasures could not be viewed because British troops had unlawfully destroyed them in the late nineteenth century.

It was not yet noon but we all felt hungry and so I, with hindsight naively, suggested a lunch of Peking duck – we were in Peking after all. Wing Yin readily agreed but Miss Wu was not so sure, though she eventually said yes. And so we looked for the exit, but before we had gone more than a few metres, a furious argument suddenly broke out between my two companions.

Miss Wu simply *tore* into the driver with a fusillade of invective which went on uninterrupted for some time. Now, I had watched this driver in an argument before and he had so far beaten all comers, even a traffic cop, for goodness' sake, but I watched horrified as he was completely taken apart. He was simply being outclassed here. At one point – and this was his undoing – he tried to interrupt her, but to his utter astonishment this young Chinese girl simply upped the ante and immediately doubled the speed of her verbal delivery!

What *had* he said? What could possibly have been so offensive? It didn't seem to matter because he clearly had not expected the force of the response. After Wing Yin received a *further* forty-five-second verbal assault, he hunched his shoulders and literally limped off. I almost felt sorry for him.

But it was a completely composed Miss Wu who now walked beside me as we headed towards the exit.

'Do you know what this driver said to me, Mr Webber?' she asked quietly.

'No, Miss Wu, I have no idea whatsoever. But I think I can safely tell you one thing for sure.'

'And what is that?' she asked sweetly.

'He will think very long and hard before he says it *again*.'

She seemed perfectly satisfied with that answer. I really didn't care what he had said for the moment; no, it was the response from Miss Wu that I was trying to come to terms with as we walked faster to catch up our, by now, penitent driver and guide. He was a Beijing *ren* (native), so surely would know the places to eat?

He did.

We entered a grand building, apparently one of the oldest and most illustrious restaurants in the capital and it was easy to see why. The height of its ceiling would not have been out of place in a cathedral, or even a palace. And it had windows to match.

Deng Xioping, the de facto leader of China, was a regular, apparently, and had entertained many heads of state here, including, quite recently, ex-President Bill Clinton. I had to say that it wasn't quite the sort of place I had in mind when I suggested a meal of Peking duck.

Even by Chinese standards the ratio of staff to diners was astonishingly high. There were about ten 'meeters and greeters' on duty, standing by the huge glazed double doors; while a similar number stood to attention in the reception area proper. And this excluded all the waiting staff.

We were ushered inside as though they had been expecting us, which was both charming and a little surprising. All this began to set off a warning bell inside me. Who was going to pay for this? It had to be very expensive, surely? I noticed out of the corner of my eye Miss Wu saying something sharp to our driver, but he merely shrugged before sitting down and accepting the proffered menu.

I had hardly opened the menu when Wing Yin finished ordering, so it was taken very gently from me while two enormous glasses of ice-cold beer were discreetly placed on the table by one *xio jie* while another poured tea into an exquisite ornamental cup placed in front of Miss Wu.

Moments later, a large elegant plate was placed in front of us, a platter of cold glistening meats: roast pork, which was welcome and, less appetizingly perhaps, ducks' feet. The last our driver wolfed down like his career depended on it. Miss Wu and I picked at the pork.

The table was then cleared completely and new plates and chopsticks were put on it, together with pancakes, salads and dips. The duck was now on its way to us on a silver trolley, with an enormous matching silver cloche on top of it, pushed by a chef wearing a tall white hat.

He gave a smart bow before whipping off the cloche, and expertly carved the duck into bite-size slivers which had a sweet savouriness that I didn't know even existed. The skin was crisp and shiny and the meat, by contrast, was succulent and earthy. The meat, together with the onions and cucumber, was placed inside the large flannel-like pancake which was lubricated by a very tart sauce and rolled up before being eaten.

Later, the same chef returned with a soothing soup he had made, while we had been eating, from the carcass of the duck. Which again begged the question: exactly how much was all this going to *cost*? As I worried about this, I caught sight of Miss Wu. She hadn't gone to the Ladies, but had slipped off to pay for the meal. I rushed over to her. Everything had come to 270 yuan which, in English money, was £22 or so, and would have been excellent value in England, but, as Miss Wu confided later, this exceeded an average Beijing weekly wage. Only after much insistence would she allow me to reimburse the whole amount later on. Our driver, for his part, clearly considered it all as no more than a perk of his job that day.

In the afternoon we drove on to the most famous (and many would say infamous) landmark in the whole of China after the Great Wall itself. Tiananmen. The Square. Largest in all the world and scene of the 1989 student uprising so brutally and bloodily put down by the People's Liberation Army (PLA).

Miss Wu told me that the demonstrations, only seven years previously, hadn't been confined to the capital, but broke out in cities all over China; she had become caught up in one, aged nineteen, at her university near Xi'an. Tellingly, the students were supported by thousands of ordinary people who also donated food and other provisions to help them continue their protest.

I had to admit that despite the recent bloodshed, the atmosphere when you entered the Square was electric. It was perhaps the most beautiful, evocative place I had ever set foot in. It felt like walking through an open air cathedral, with all the religious intensity that one would expect from such a holy place.

As we walked across the Square towards the Gate of Heavenly Peace, where Mao had proclaimed the People's Republic in 1949, I was struck by how his huge portrait still hung over the Gate. He had been dead for twenty years now, but he was still up there.

Turning around, I was surprised to see a small crowd following us. They stopped dead when we looked at them. Soon a few shy smiles spread across some faces, but I was baffled. Surely they would be used to Westerners in the centre of Beijing – all tourists came here, after all.

'These people are not Beijing *ren*, Adrian, they are from other provinces, far from here, where there are no Western tourists at all,' Wu Shu whispered to me.

The small crowd continued to stop and stare. Their clothes, I began to notice, were very old-fashioned by local Beijing standards. Some of the older men standing at the back even wore forms of the famous Mao military-style suit. They were doing exactly the same as we were, taking in the sights, but they were astonished when they saw a foreigner and a Chinese girl talking together in what was presumably his language.

'Chinese people are very curious, Adrian,' Miss Wu stated flatly, and not for the first time.

They continued to follow us to the edge of the Square where our bus was parked. I climbed in and put my camera beneath the rear seat cover to protect it from the sun ... just as Miss Wu climbed in and sat down on it. She immediately jumped up – with a very ladylike start – before I could warn her. She thought I had done it deliberately and said quietly: 'You are a very bad man, *Mister* Webber.'

She then crossed her legs and faced the front of the bus with great dignity.

CHAPTER 8

一线不能织衣

'A cloth is not woven from a single thread'

The first thing you were confronted with on entering Miss Wu's first-floor office was a huge wardrobe placed carefully in front of the door to protect her privacy. Once you rounded that, you found yourself in a spacious airy room with a window and a low glass door that led on to a narrow balcony. In the corner behind the wardrobe stood her tiny wrought iron bed. This was a functional space, yet it was also cosy and feminine. It made me want to sit down and relax.

'I saw you arrive from here,' she said, gesturing towards the balcony.

'You mean the first day, when I arrived from the airport? Really?'

She nodded and smiled.

'You looked very tired and a little worried, we thought.'

'We?' I asked.

Apparently, her best friend had overheard that the bus was due to arrive any minute and so had gone up to Miss Wu's office to view the arrival of the foreigner. Her friend had been told bits of what Mr Huang had already said on the phone, presumably during one of the constant calls that I noticed on the bus.

'It doesn't matter if the foreigner likes Chinese food or not,' he had apparently said, laughing. 'He is such a big elephant that he can live on his body fat for the whole of the summer, if need be. No problem.'

Yes, he had definitely got it in for me from the very first.

Miss Wu and I chatted all that afternoon. It was hard to believe that this Chinese girl was a product of such a different society from mine as she understood everything I said with ease and economy of effort. We talked and talked until I forgot that she was conducting her side of the conversation in a second language. And then suddenly she sat up and told me she was hungry. I glanced at my watch. It was gone 8 o'clock already.

We filed out of her room and walked down the wide staircase to the ground floor, past my room and down the corridor to her laboratory. The door unlocked, we stood in front of her enormous fridge, which still contained many plant specimens and experiments, together with my Western food ingredients. Neither of us said a word as she carefully pulled some packets of dried noodles out of the fridge before setting up the single electric cooking ring on the tiled floor by the main window. It slowly began to glow in the twilight as she filled up a big pot of water from a tap in one of the two heavy dark-wood work stations in the laboratory, pulled a large stick of dried noodles from each packet, and placed them into the now boiling water. Our 'table' was an old packing case that I had used before, but this time Miss Wu briskly covered it with a copy of the now familiar newspaper, *The China Daily*. She then took a large jar from the fridge; this immediately made me nervous as I couldn't make out what it contained. I had just got my stomach back on to an even keel, after all. But everything had already taken on a dreamlike quality – just being alone with this young woman – so I no longer really cared.

Listening to and gazing at this beautiful girl was an intoxicating experience. I bathed in her company. How she felt about me, if she felt anything, was a complete mystery. Maybe, for all I knew, she was just being polite. Chinese hospitality.

How could such a simple meal, eaten on an old packing case, in a *laboratory* of all places, taste and feel so special? I looked across at Miss Wu who was expertly folding the strands of noodle around her chopsticks before elegantly devouring them as only a Chinese lady could. Again, I wondered what she was thinking, although she seemed perfectly content now as we finished the improvised meal.

She met my gaze, the atmosphere heavy with anticipation. I could feel my heart beating in my chest. Embarrassed, I wanted to look down as she wiped her full lips with a tiny handkerchief from her sleeve and said quietly, almost whispering, 'I will remember this meal all ... my ... *life*, ... Adrian ...'

I could scarcely believe my ears because that was how I felt – *exactly* the same. It was the best meal of my entire life. I could have stayed there eating noodles with this girl all night. I never wanted it to end, to break the magic spell. Never.

Today was the first Monday in August, and my first day with the prestigious design office was to start under its technical head, Miss Liu Hong Bin, who was a designer in her own right and oversaw all the projects within Beijing city as well as the Garden itself. A curious thing about Chinese names was that if a woman was married, she still retained her maiden name together with the title of 'Miss'. This led, as Miss Liu told me herself, to the often embarrassing situation in which people would 'introduce' you to suitable young men, completely unaware that you were in fact married.

Miss Liu was a tall woman in her mid-thirties who spoke excellent English. She had long black hair and wore studious dark-rimmed glasses. Her most distinguishing characteristic, however, was not physical. It was her ferocious intelligence, coupled with the direct and unsentimental way she viewed people and what went on around her. She was clearly nobody's fool, but it went much further than that. Miss Liu Hong Bin enjoyed an almost forensic ability to dissect any situation and accept the consequences of it without complaint. I immediately respected her.

She gave me little pen portraits of everyone I was likely to meet. First, their good points and then the less flattering ones. This was unexpected, but immediately it made me feel included and part of the team. She put me into the care of her two most trusted aides who apparently both spoke excellent English. I was introduced to Miss Han, but Miss Shi was away on a week's leave. Both lived off site with their parents in Beijing.

Miss Han was also quite tall and likewise wore studious glasses, but she had a short bob hairstyle and a more 'girly' way than her boss – although I felt intimidated by both of them. Miss Liu mentioned that we were due to visit one of the big landscape projects for a Beijing university in the heart of the city the following day and the two women looked at one another meaningfully before they both looked at me.

'Would you like to go and see a movie afterwards, in the city, Adrian?'

They were both film buffs, and as China only allowed twenty foreign films into the country each year they were keen not to miss any.

'Of course,' I replied shyly.

We had only just been introduced after all, and it was a little unexpected. Apparently they had set their hearts on going to see an animated American film called *Toy Story*, which I had never heard of.

I reflected, not for the first time, that everything that happened to me right from the moment I had entered China had been somehow unexpected. Even the small things. It made me feel permanently off balance, but I made a mental note to just say 'yes' to everything in the future and simply go with the flow.

I strolled into Miss Wu's laboratory that evening and prepared my basic pasta meal using the by-now familiar Australian ingredients. But I couldn't cook as the only cooking ring already had an enormous kettle of water boiling away on it. I switched it off before nipping upstairs to Miss Wu's office to see if she had forgotten her boiling kettle.

Two and a half hours later I was a quiet chastened man and all thoughts of food had been banished from my head. Huang Yi Gong had seen her in the library that afternoon and had talked seriously to her about gossip within the Garden that speculated on why she was often seen with the foreigner. Foreigners, after all, could never be trusted with young girls, and could therefore destroy any lady's reputation forever.

He went on to say that he only had her interests at heart and was concerned for her reputation within his department and the Garden generally. For all that, it still felt like a formal warning.

Miss Wu was rattled, as anyone in her position would have been, especially in a society where 'face' – and, by implication, reputation – was everything.

'Should we still see each other, Adrian?' she asked.

The question couldn't be ducked or avoided as it held the crux to everything. I tried to *think*. Yes, it was unfortunate, but neither of us had meant anything to happen and, well, nothing *had* happened for that matter. The two visits to Beijing had been arranged officially, after all, by Huang Yi Gong himself, and neither of us had anything to do with it. And yet, and yet … it was what people saw with their own eyes, that was what really mattered – coupled with their subjective prejudices of course.

'You *are* a foreigner. Adrian … if only you were a Chinese …'

By that time of the evening I thought I could be forgiven for saying, 'If only you were English …' but it hadn't seemed appropriate.

Miss Wu, meanwhile, with tears in her eyes, had made up her own mind it seemed: 'Adrian, we must stop all this and just be friends for the rest of our lives.'

I nodded, walked to the door, and quietly closed it behind me. She was right.

Miss Han spoke in a quiet calm voice, but with a very distinctive American accent.

'Was your English teacher American, by any chance, Miss Han?' I asked gently.

'How did you ever guess that?' she replied in her southern drawl.

I just grinned a reply and looked out of the window. It was another sunny day and the events of last night seemed more muted than they had been when I flopped into bed, my head reeling. Ruefully, I reflected that things could happen quickly in this country, but they could also *un*-happen even quicker.

I studied Miss Han's attitude towards me and was pretty sure that she at least had not heard the rumours. She lived off-campus for one thing and worked here, the far side of the Garden from the propagation areas and the research building. It seemed a world away, so I allowed myself to relax. Anyway we were soon off by bus to visit the landscape project where we would be joined later by Miss Liu who was already in the city.

Miss Han explained that the project was at a very early stage and so there wasn't that much to be seen, but later on in the site office the design that was rolled out seemed very impressive. It was dominated by a series of elliptically shaped water features which, with the planting, would make it an attractive public space. Money for the project, I noted, was not a problem. The Chinese were very willing to invest money in this type of civic project. Impressive.

As it turned out, Miss Liu was unexpectedly recalled to the Garden for a meeting, so Miss Han and I travelled on to the cinema alone. The cinema itself was a shock. It was built apparently with Russian expertise in a severe, almost brutal, communist style. It would have looked more at home in Moscow than Beijing. The American film was dubbed into Chinese and so I didn't understand a word of it, but it was visually funny. Strange. Here I was sitting in a Russian-built cinema situated in the heart of communist China, watching a quintessential American film, next to a Chinese girl who spoke English with an American accent.

It was late when the film ended so we went for a meal. Miss Han proved to be very sensitive, and said she understood about my stomach and ordered what proved to be an excellent choice. Stir-fried pork with aubergines, chicken with peanuts, plain boiled rice and a cold bottle of beer.

Before the food came I needed to use the toilets. I stood outside the two doors for a very long time, not knowing which of the two Chinese idiograms stood for 'man'. No one of either sex came out. But my dilemma was deferred in a uniquely Chinese way because a local power cut immediately plunged everything into darkness, so I had to feel my way back to our dining table, now illuminated by the soft glow of candlelight.

It made a welcome change, as ordinarily the Chinese frowned upon low lighting, seeing it as a sign of decadence or seediness. Perhaps that was why the fluorescent light was the appliance of choice even in people's homes. Brightness was good and wholesome, worn like a badge of honour.

Sitting at my drawing board as usual, I suddenly felt that I was being observed. A Chinese girl that I had never seen before, wearing a plain cotton dress and black low-heeled shoes, was walking towards me with a very serious look on her face. She had big, almost round eyes and a wide mouth within a pale face and not a trace of make-up. She said nothing as she approached, but studied me very intently as she faced me. Without a word she stooped down a little to get a better view of me. I did not move. Her head was motionless, but her eyes moved first left then right. With her head fixed in that position, she moved around me slowly. Very slowly.

At first I tried to follow her gaze but became too embarrassed and so just sat there, resigned to this silent examination. Then, having completed her orbit, she nodded to herself and eased her round face towards mine. Her dark eyes and intent expression became almost hypnotic and so I stared back, unblinking, before she at last said something.

'Hello, you *are* the foreigner, yes? You are Webber Adrian, I believe?'

'I am Webber Adrian, yes. And who are *you* may I ask?'

'I am your older sister.'

Laying on my straw mattress the next morning I heard a delicate knock on my door. The hand had to belong to a woman, I thought.

'Please take an umbrella to work today as it may rain again later,' Miss Wu said in a very loud voice, from the other side of the door.

I sat up in bed and smiled to myself. Well, that was hardly 'low profile'! Not exactly a stage whisper, was it? Everyone in the building must have heard her voice echoing along the corridors.

As I got unsteadily to my feet, relieved by her lack of tact, I noticed a piece of paper had been slipped under my door. Reaching down, I could see that it had been folded expertly into the shape of an elegant dove. It was beautiful, and I felt touched even before I carefully unfolded it.

It read:

I loved the way you smiled so amiably at our Chinese tourists who were staring at you in the Tiananmen Square on Saturday.
    It had a deep effect upon me.
    Wu Shu

It did rain that day. In fact, it rained furiously, and later on, as I worked at my drawing board, it became so dark outside that my little drawing board lamp hardly lit my work. Instead it cast long shadows that were even darker and more impenetrable than the blackest night. Word came through as we worked that many Chinese people had already lost their lives that morning when a river had burst its banks. It did nothing for anyone's already gloomy mood, as the storm, slow and sullen, stalked its way across the city. The general darkness was only interrupted by occasional flashes of lightning, which were sinister and sudden. Not much work was done by anyone that day, and I was glad when it was time to finish and return to my room.

I ran up the steps to the research building and practically fell through the doorway such was my haste in getting out of the storm. I shook my head to get the rain out of my ears, and glanced down the empty dark corridor to my room. Everything felt cold and lifeless. I had got completely drenched as I cycled the length of the Garden to get back. To get home.

A hand fell on my shoulder and I spun round, startled. It was the little caretaker. How come I never saw or felt him approach? Everyone has their special skill – his seemed to be making me jump out of my wits every so often. He just grinned up at me and clamped my flask of hot water into my cold right hand.

He fired up the enormous gas burner outside his office, ready to cook his evening meal. It was a constant source of wonder to me how the ferociously hot gas jet didn't melt the old thin steel wok he used for cooking. I thought that he must be vegetarian because I never once saw him cook meat or fish; he only ever ate vegetables with different forms of noodles, and Chinese bread of course. But he always looked as though he was on the verge of a serious illness and he was going to bed earlier and earlier these days. Even before dusk. Frankly, I worried about him.

Miss Liu, my new boss, had a very logical mind. She was also completely unsentimental, so it was always a pleasure to talk with her. She told me that the Chinese government would from time to time flatter intellectuals in the country and pretend to appreciate them to the extent that they claimed the working arrangement would last indefinitely. But once they had got the information they wanted, they would drop the professionals they had so assiduously courted. A typical Liu remark – pithy, but accurate. She always said these types of things so lightly and without rancour that only when you properly digested what she had said were you shocked (or offended).

For example, as we had so many projects under construction there was much supervision and liaison work to be done, which meant requisitioning a car and travelling into the city almost daily. Miss Liu would often ask me to accompany her. As we walked to the car she always said, in her clear ladylike way, 'Adrian, you sit in front with the driver because you are fat.' A more diplomatic person might have said the seat was reserved for guests, but that would have been a lie to Miss Liu.

Today was different. We were to attend a lecture that afternoon by Professor Yu who had volunteered to be my academic tutor and would help in my dissertation on Chinese garden design for my college back in England. We would travel into Beijing where we would pick up my two 'older sisters', Miss Shi and Miss Han, and go on to the lecture.

As we left around 10 a.m. Miss Liu and I bumped into the director's bubbly female driver who I had met a couple of times. As usual she tried to touch my face and shoulder while cooing seductive Chinese asides. With her thick make-up and jewellery she resembled, somewhat disconcertingly, Imelda Marcos. She told me that she was thirty, and what did the foreigner think of *that*?

The foreigner didn't want to think anything at all about it, thank you very much. Miss Liu instead apparently told her that the foreigner thought she was still but a child at that age. (Thank you, Miss Liu!) At this she looked completely dumbfounded. Then she put her hands on her hips, laughed uproariously, and tried to grab my cheek again. It was another one of those social encounters that *always* seemed to spiral out of control.

As we drove out of the Garden we passed the many military areas that barracked soldiers of the People's Liberation Army. They seemed to have finished their military duties for the day, and some were now walking along the dusty broken paths by the road. It was of course from these local military bases that the soldiers had been sent to Tiananmen Square a few short years previously, although their tanks were kept well out of sight.

Instead they had put up rather amateurish painted signs which depicted members of the PLA in smiling poses, showing how they cared for ordinary Chinese families. A bit counter-productive I thought, as surely it only served to remind people what in fact they had done to them.

Many of these tough wiry soldiers were holding hands with one another. As if she read my mind, Liu Hong Bin touched me lightly on the shoulder, 'They are not gay, homosexual, I mean, Adrian,' she said confidentially. 'No. They are just friends, platonic friendship only. You do understand?'

Soon we were picking up Miss Shi and Miss Han on the outskirts of the city. They handed me an English language newspaper – a lovely gesture. But they were a couple of little rascals, though, and loved to laugh and tease.

'Say something in Chinese, Adrian, please ... please.'

'No way.'

'Oh, *please.*'

I spoke a short sentence, in what I considered perfectly executed Mandarin.

They both looked at me, open mouthed, then at each other, before bursting out laughing. I scowled back, pretending to be deeply offended.

'Adrian?' they said.

'What?' (in exaggerated irritable voice).

'Was that English or Chinese just then? Do please tell us!'

Miss Liu ignored them, but they were still laughing together as we pulled up outside the South Garden. This was attached to the Botanical Garden, but was completely academic and not open to the general public. Here Professor Yu was to give his lecture on Chinese garden design. All the English-speaking academic staff from the entire campus had been invited, but no one else at all because the eighty-year-old professor was to give the entire lecture in *English.*

We took our places among the hundred or so other staff who were already seated. There was a palpable sense of expectation.

Professor Yu was the author of many books printed in China; and now, in retirement, he was still turning them out. One story I had heard about him concerned a long-standing rivalry with another Beijing professor whose ideas he fundamentally disagreed with. After giving a lecture he had found to his surprise that he was to be followed on to the podium by his old rival.

As the rival professor took his place on the podium in front of the huge audience, Professor Yu decided to exit the hall instead of taking his place among the audience. But he seemed to have difficulty getting past the curtains strung across the way out. In fact, he got into so much difficulty that members of the audience felt duty-bound to go to his aid. All the while his rival was patiently waiting to begin his lecture. Yu had then walked to the front of the audience and publicly apologized for disrupting proceedings by disrupting proceedings even further ... Now *that* was chutzpah!

He then began a second lecture by complaining about the size of the apartment a Chinese professor such as he was expected to live in with all his books and papers. All this was done with much sly humour and of course in perfect English. It was coquettish, but I supposed that was the only way a man of his status could operate in a system that decided the number of square metres you were allowed for your accommodation.

I was very touched when he pointed me out before he began and told everyone that he particularly wanted me to understand what he had to say, and that for everyone else it was a good opportunity to practise their English! Everyone laughed.

We had the privilege of driving him home. He was clearly exhausted. How could a man of his years deliver a three-hour lecture, alone, flawlessly, in a second language? It was an awesome achievement for which I could not find the words to thank him enough.

CHAPTER 9

笼中只尖美丽的鸟

'A beautiful bird is the only kind we cage'

Since Miss Wu had sat on my camera believing (wrongly) that I had tried to startle her on purpose, the blasted thing had refused to work and seemed permanently jammed. Miss Han volunteered to accompany me into the city after work, so we could visit a large photo store she knew to see if they could help.

The *shifu* (assistant, expert) took the camera from my hands and disappeared out the back into some sort of laboratory. He returned ten minutes later all smiles and said in English 'All fixed, no charge, simple jam, OK', and waved us away to deal with the next customer.

Back out on the pavement I asked Miss Han as we were in the centre of the city if the embassy district was very far?

'You mean your British Embassy, Adie, don't you?' (My 'older sisters' had decided to call me Adie for some reason; the other English speakers called me Adrian. Even if my sisters had known, it would have made no difference – they did what they wanted to do and that was that.)

I suppose it was the tiniest form of homesickness. I really wanted to hear an English voice again. It was absurd really, and we both laughed about it as she hailed a taxi. Han Xu chose the cheapest type (roughly 10p per kilometre); they were yellow and were the nearest thing to a covered rickshaw, plus an engine. No air conditioning of course and a pretty rough ride, but the main disadvantage with all Beijing taxi drivers, was that they never seemed to know where you wanted to go. He managed to drop us the wrong side of the enormous compound from the main entrance. Not long after, this would be the site of mass demonstrations when a NATO bomber inadvertently dropped its payload on to a Chinese embassy in the Balkans, but all was calm that evening as we rounded the final corner and saw the impressive main entrance with its Union Jack flag fluttering brightly in the warm breeze. I felt a lump rise in my throat. I hadn't heard an English voice since I arrived, and thought naively that I was bound to hear one around this place.

Miss Han was trying to take a picture of me outside the enormous gates with my newly repaired Pentax when a short but very sturdy plain-clothed Chinese official busily – and not to say bossily – told me to go away. I think he actually said 'shoo!' We walked away from the embassy, and further down the wide road we witnessed the embassies' 'changing of the guard'.

Ten smartly dressed soldiers of the People's Liberation Army marched up the side of the road in single file towards us with a single officer following beside them, swagger stick clutched tightly beneath his arm. They were moving fast despite the incline, and we stood well back to let them pass. The soldiers were very tall and marched in high goose-step – which was a little threatening but we need not have worried. As each soldier drew abreast of us he shouted 'Hello' in perfect synchronization to his march rhythm. This 'Hello' was repeated ten times, once by each soldier – a beautiful and humbling experience. Their officer did not reprimand them but strode on past, eyes fixed ahead, ignoring us completely – which also felt right, somehow.

It was to be a whole evening of the Chinese military as we caught a bus to Tiananmen Square to watch the taking down of the national flag. There was already an expectant hush as an enormous crowd gathered to wait for dusk. A wide white line had been painted around the tall flag pole, and no member of the public was allowed to cross this.

I could feel the pride in everyone around me. Their eyes and faces were shiny with hope and trust in their great country. The middle kingdom locked away for so long was slowly emerging again, and here I was in its very heart watching its most important flag being slowly lowered with the utmost reverence. I caught the eye of some Chinese people standing there as the military band played the national anthem, its rhythms carrying across the huge traffic-free square. They were clearly watching my reaction; I maintained a sombre expression throughout the ceremony. What I could not tell them was that I felt touched and honoured to be there with them.

Then we entered the mercurial Forbidden City after dark. Its thick and impossibly high walls rose up around us, imprisoning us within their deep shadows. Suddenly from out of the gloom three extremely tall and handsome soldiers marched across our path in the now familiar goose-step march. The modern equivalent of the imperial guard. Each had a heavy machine gun strapped diagonally across his chest. They must have seen us flinch, dismayed by their sudden appearance, because they allayed our fear by parroting 'Do ... not ... be ... afraid!' as they crossed in front of us. They were gone as quickly as they had arrived and we were alone again. Yes, it had definitely been a military evening.

When I realized that I had left my wallet in the taxi home last night with $100 of travellers' cheques and 800 yuan (£60) inside, I should perhaps have felt sick or angry but I felt nothing of the kind. Why? Perhaps it gave me the chance to reflect once more on how lucky I had been since arriving in China. I had just expected to be treated as one of the workers and then largely forgotten about until it was time to leave. Instead I'd been treated like some sort of visiting dignitary, feted wherever I went, and I was overwhelmed by the friendliness and hospitality. The English-speaking staff in the Botanical Garden had told me I was famous: 'Adrian, you are the foreigner who is friendly to everyone.' Perhaps. But I was still a 'foreigner', I noted.

All these reflections cheered me up and gave me the courage to report my wallet's loss to my 'supervisor', the ever-strict Mr Huang. I came away afterwards with the distinct feeling that I had offended him somehow. Perhaps it was something to do with his prejudice against the English? I had since heard that he had spent a year working in the Windsor Great Park, just as Zhu Renyuan, my old classmate, was currently doing. Apparently Huang had taken against everybody there and locked himself in his room for the entire year, only coming out to work. It was also rumoured that his wife had an affair during his absence. We seemed destined not to get on, and the loss of my wallet was to make matters worse.

Later, as I casually pushed open the door to the design office, Miss Han walked straight over to me, her face flushed. Huang Yi Gong had just telephoned and remonstrated with her. He said, 'Webber Adrian was your responsibility last night and you completely failed in your duty. And now, look, even his wallet you allowed to be lost!' He then put the phone down.

He was as usual taking things a little too seriously and I regretted even telling him now.

Miss Han and I went outside to talk things over. There was a small pool with a fountain in a nearby courtyard and we sat down together on its ledge. I told her that the loss of the wallet was all my fault and I was sorry that she had been dragged into the long-running wrangle I seemed to have with Huang Yi Gong. She calmed down when she understood it really was nothing to do with her. As we talked I felt in my pocket and found a couple of low-value coins. I tossed them over my shoulder into the fountain and rubbed my hands together theatrically. I liked the finality of this gesture. Miss Han didn't miss a beat, 'Adie, you must now drink the wind, as a poor man, north and south, because it is cooler,' she said quietly and smiled.

*

When I returned to my room there was another beautifully constructed note which had been slipped beneath my door by Miss Wu. Inside it seemed to be a clear invitation to visit her upstairs in her office. I immediately dashed to micro-propagation for a quick and cooling shower, with the familiar knot in my stomach – this always seemed to occur when I had dealings with Miss Wu.

I heard her singing before I reached the top of the stairs and I stopped and listened. She seemed to be singing a sad love song in a quiet, lilting way. Was this good news or bad, I wondered, as I knocked on her door? The door was half open and I could see her sitting cross-legged with her back to me at her desk facing the window, her white lab coat draped elegantly over the back of her wooden chair.

Slowly she swivelled round and faced me with a sweet smile playing around the edges of her mouth. And then it became very serious and she said sternly, 'Mr Webber, I left that note beneath your door *hours* ago. Why did you not come to see me earlier? Do you know you can be a little haughty!'

I smiled with relief. Clearly, there were no sinister revelations to be communicated, today at least. Again her face and demeanour resembled a little cat's or, as I was beginning to appreciate more, the Chinese man's view of a girl such as this: *tiger*. She talked about the gossip again but this time without fear or rancour, more of a quiet acceptance. She kept switching tenses when she referred to us, so I didn't know how she felt. Were we still to be 'friends for the rest of our lives' or was there a chance of starting again?

We were sitting on her bed holding hands. It was midnight. She moved quickly to one side and beckoned me to lay my back against the wall. I saw her tiny dark eyes looking at me steadily from beneath her fringe. Then I felt her head on my shoulder as her short thick hair tickled my face; I didn't move a muscle, did nothing to resist breaking the spell; already I felt transported to a different world: China, this beautiful girl, both had seeped into my blood. I felt lighter, less burdened. I knew I would never be the same again.

Another long day in the design office, but it was getting familiar now. The design staff had become a lot more relaxed about having me around. Soon after I started in design, a small neat wrapped package had been waiting for me on my drawing board. There was no note and nothing was said. But when I opened it, a lump had come to my throat. Inside was a hard-boiled egg, two or three thick slices of *cha-sui* (Cantonese roast pork) and a Chinese round bread. Looking up, I saw Miss Shi standing there. In her slow lyrical way of speaking English, she explained: 'My mother thought that the foreigner must miss his English home cooking, but particularly his breakfast.'

She had heard that English gentlemen preferred a breakfast of bacon and egg. She knew bacon was pork and so this was her Chinese equivalent breakfast for me. I was very touched and told her to thank her mother from the bottom of my (foreign devil's) heart. A similar packet of food was waiting for me every morning until I left the design office a whole month later.

Wu Shu was due to travel into Beijing for her regular weekend of GRE English lessons, but she had agreed to have a meal with me that evening in a local Xiang Shan restaurant. We would go there separately of course to avoid being seen together. I hated this subterfuge. OK, I could understand Wu Shu's thinking, but it still rankled with me. Why couldn't two people have a meal out without someone leaping to the wrong conclusion?

And so it was in that mood that I strode down the familiar twisting road to Xiang Shan town: on past the small coal-fired power station, past the stall holders who edged the town, selling all manner of fruit and vegetables and calling out for custom. I could see Wu Shu in the far distance. Her thin ladylike legs looked slightly incongruous in the thick strappy white sandals she often wore, and yet she was still elegant and utterly feminine. What was that line from Iris Murdoch's *The Sea, The Sea*? 'She could run faster in high heeled shoes than any girl I ever knew ...' There was also something captivating in her purposeful walk. A determined sort of walk, I thought idly, as I kept a distance from her.

We couldn't stop talking to each other as usual and then I remembered the incident in the Beijing park when she had become so furious with the driver, Wing Yin. She pretended not to remember, but I persisted until she did.

'Oh, it was nothing really. He just said [I liked the *just*] that academic staff like me who worked in clean laboratory all day didn't know the meaning of work. If we had to work as hard as peasant in the field we all would surely die ...'

'Oh, I see. Well, you certainly put him straight about that, Miss Wu,' I said, comfortingly.

She went on to say that this same driver had to take her into Beijing the other day to collect some equipment for her photosynthesis experiments. He had refused to carry the equipment to the minibus, she said, 'in case they were contaminated with viruses'. 'He is a scoundrel and a hooligan,' she continued, 'The equipment was brand new, he could see that!'

So he had got his own back. It was typical of him. I had to laugh.

The rain had returned and was now falling in sheets as we reluctantly walked down the steps of the restaurant. It had been a good evening, but my mood darkened as I realized that this was Thursday and I wouldn't see her again until Monday at the earliest.

But we were holding hands beneath her tiny umbrella, which was a great consolation. It felt right somehow, walking along with this tiny Chinese girl in the warm rain.

'Do you know I am never tired when I walk with you, Mr Webber,' I heard her say over the noise of the traffic. 'Look, there's a bus!' she cried, and we just managed to catch it.

Wu Shu didn't want to sleep in her office because we would be seen together by the security guards on the entrance gate, so we trudged along the middle of the road to her dormitory, dodging the water-filled potholes as we went. Frustration at not being able to see her at the weekend, and all the pretence, burned a hole inside me and eventually I exploded: 'Look,' I said, 'we might as well pack it all in right now – the situation is, well, intolerable and I'm too proud quite honestly to keep skulking around pretending there is nothing going on between us, and I haven't even done anything to be remotely ashamed of and neither have you. It's just *unfair*, OK?'

I felt this tiny girl freeze as she looked up at me coolly, the rain pattering and then streaming off her coat hood. She turned and walked on ahead very, very slowly, obviously carefully considering my outburst. I hadn't meant to say all I had said, and certainly not so emotionally; she was so tiny and fragile and gentle and I never wanted to do anything that would hurt her, so *please* help me, God ...

She abruptly turned around, walked back, and pushed me hard until I moved backwards, and then pushed me again and again with all her strength into the privacy of a deserted brick courtyard, overshadowed by large-leafed trees that cast huge shadows in the full moonlight.

I felt my hand release the umbrella which fell, as if in slow motion, on to the wet earth as I stood there, shocked at what had just happened between us. We were both wet and out of breath. Wu Shu began to talk in a low steely voice: 'I have been in a dream too, Adrian, don't you know that? It's the same for *me*. Is this ... is this ... what people call *love* ... or is it something else? You tell me, Mr Webber. I'm just a young Chinese girl, not understanding; all right, I *am* Master, but everything has happened so quickly and I don't know what is happening to me. I can think of nothing else but I still don't *understand* – I don't *understand* what is happening, and do you know I am frightened. I'm frightened of the future and it's all your *fault*. Well, no, it isn't, but why do you come to my China? Answer me that! Before you came, everything was so calm and correct. No pain in my deep heart ... and ... no haunting thoughts either.'

I didn't know what to say. My mouth was dry. No words. I was left with no choice but to pull this tiny, exotic, intelligent girl towards me and just hold her close with my arms around her, wanting to comfort her, as the rain and tears streamed slowly down her beautiful face. I held her close to me. Squeezed her tight. Hold her. Hold her. Never let her go. Do *anything*, you must do anything ... everything to keep this girl.

The rain fell harder, and she pushed me gently away and said in a restrained and polite way, 'Goodnight.'

I just watched as she opened the gate and walked into her dormitory yard, closing the door quietly behind her.

I didn't try to make sense of what had just happened. I knew that it had been the most intense moment of my life. I remembered dropping the umbrella as I kissed and kissed her wet face. The rain mixed with the saltiness of her tears. And I told her how sorry I was to upset her and that I would never ever hurt her again and that my pride was all too stupid and ridiculous.

I had said many other things, but could no longer remember them as I climbed the high security gate; the guards watched impassively as usual. I woke the caretaker to let me into the building, and soon I climbed on to my straw mattress and waited for sleep to overwhelm all the thoughts and feelings that burned in my mind.

CHAPTER 10

香气只依附在献玫瑰花的手上

'A piece of fragrance always clings to the hand that gives you roses'

The sun was hot as I walked down the hill before turning into the bus station which had already filled up with local people making the trip into Beijing city that morning. I was to meet up with Miss Han who had kindly offered to show me the body of Mao Zedong in Tiananmen Square, and tomorrow night I had a dinner date with Professor Yu who wanted to take me to a French restaurant near the Summer Palace. 'Good for your sensitive stomach, Webber!' was all he said when he dropped off some coffee he had been given on an international conference trip that he had recently made.

Wu Shu was probably at her English class now. I missed her and wanted to be with her, but our separation was something that just had to be endured. Instead I resolved to enjoy the weekend, as I queued for what I hoped was the direct bus into the city. Occasionally someone would shout 'Hello' and then look away, embarrassed. I smiled back and nodded, just enough to be polite but not so much that it might provoke a salvo of 'hellos'. In between the sporadic 'hellos', some of the younger men gestured to me, holding up three fingers as they pointed at the bus. This meant the fare was 3 yuan (about 30p), and they were telling me not to be duped into paying more, state run or not.

The bus lumbered along, and just before nine I made out the figure of Miss Han wearing a smart sea-blue city dress at the central bus station. She hobbled towards the bus when she saw me. The poor girl had fallen when getting up from her seat on the bus last night, and had bruised her back and legs quite badly.

It was still too early to view Mao, so we crossed the Square, which was already sparkling in the weekend sunlight, and entered the Forbidden City as we had the other evening. This time the atmosphere was totally different. At once you could grasp its sheer size and scale. The city had been set out between 1406 and 1420 under the Emperor Yongle, who utilized a workforce of up to a million labourers at any one time. It was famously said that the city comprised 9,999 rooms – that number nine again. We looked down the distinctive high-walled alleyways that the young emperor, Puyi, cycled down in the film *The Last Emperor*.

At the other side of the sprawling city stood another emperor-inspired structure. This time a huge hill had been built to allow the emperor to view it from above, and it was certainly a serene spot. That was until a fast and furious fight broke out beside us. Two beefy Beijing men, both middle-aged, shouted their heads off as they grappled with one another before falling down the steps we were standing on. I saw blood sluice down the larger man's face from a nasty gash in his forehead as he looked around, dazed. He could see little as his eyes were both now badly swollen. Then a third man came storming up the steps and clubbed the larger man with a large plastic bottle full of frozen water, which sent him back down the steps now flecked with blood. He tried to look around him, and finally his wincing stare fell on me as I stood just a few feet away, trying to shield Miss Han as best I could. I dropped my gaze, not wishing to antagonize him further. He bent down slowly to pick up something he'd dropped and was gone.

We continued our way up the hill. Han Xu slowly shook her head: 'To take part in such a spectacle was a massive loss of face to a Chinese. That was bad enough and they would be deeply upset and embarrassed to have done it so publicly in front of Chinese people. But when they saw you, a foreigner, it made it a hundred times worse. I think that's why they left so quickly in the end. I'm sure of that.'

Later on we returned to Tiananmen Square where we joined the long queue snaking around the huge stone mausoleum, and patiently waited to see the mortal remains of Chairman Mao.

'If Mao is supposed to be so unpopular, why do all these people come?' Han Xu asked plaintively.

She had a point. Apparently, even now, twenty years after his death, there was no shortage of people wanting to catch a glimpse of the man who ruled China with such an iron fist. I was tempted to repeat what was said at the well-attended funeral of a Hollywood producer, notorious for his wickedness – everyone had come to make sure he really was dead.

But one look at Miss Han's anxious face, together with the unsmiling faces of the female security staff, told me that this was not the time for facetious comments of any sort as we were ushered reverently through into Mao's presence. It was really only possible to have a quick glimpse because the queue was so long. His very large face was immediately recognizable, but to me at least he somehow didn't look particularly Chinese. For a start he seemed too big, physically. And his face was shiny, wax-like, and so were his hands. I didn't want to linger.

His crimes were all too recent and familiar. A twentieth-century monster that humanity could have done without was my assessment of the 'old helmsman' as he liked to call himself. Good riddance.

I leant my rusty bicycle against the wall beside Professor Yu's apartment entrance and looked up at the evening sky. It looked bruised and swollen and I heard thunder in the distant hills. I found it difficult to believe that the professor was going to take me to a French restaurant. The Chinese were, after all, maddeningly emphatic about foreigners trying all manner of Chinese foods, but when offered examples of Western cuisine they stubbornly refused and gave the impression you were mad to have even suggested it. Once William had very reluctantly accepted a spoonful – a *spoonful*, mind you – of my spaghetti bolognese, before he rushed from the room to be physically sick.

Oblivious to the weather, the distinguished old man introduced me to his son-in-law, a schoolteacher. A typical burly Beijing native in his early forties, he looked me up and down before challenging me to an arm wrestling contest. Now I knew at home that I had a pretty good track record in this (male ego) trial of strength, and he was a schoolteacher after all, so I accepted readily. His meaty hand, surprisingly strong, completely enveloped mine as I looked into his impassive eyes.

'OK. Now we start!' he said in perfect English just as the professor re-entered the room. He watched with little interest as we pushed and strained. My opponent's eyes were still infuriatingly impassive as he upped the pressure, and I found myself under more strain than I ever remembered in an arm wrestle. My arm, locked in position, began to hurt ...

'Coffee?' our host asked nonchalantly and we both immediately released our grip. It had been a close-run thing for me to hang on as long as I had and I delicately rubbed my arm muscles to loosen them. A draw was declared. The old man's youngest son appeared in the doorway. He was our driver tonight. We followed him outside where the rain was now bucketing down, and climbed into a small van with rear side windows that had been converted into a sort of minibus.

We careered along the black road, dodging the boxes and other debris blown about by the fierce wind, now up to gale force. The rain hit the windscreen with such violence that the wipers were completely overwhelmed and just juddered to a halt. But this did not prevent our driver's solution to the problem – which was to drive even faster.

I wondered if Wu Shu had finished her classes and was now

out of this storm and in a safe place. I prayed she was somewhere warm and dry, perhaps with a bowl of her beloved noodles in front of her for comfort. Perhaps she was even thinking of me?

Suddenly everything went quiet; only the dull hammering of the rain on the roof could be heard. Slowly we came to a halt. Our driver was attempting to restart the engine, but with no success. It must have been overwhelmed by the rain, which was sheeting in horizontally on the gusting wind. The professor with his usual *sangfroid* turned to me and said, 'Not far to go now, Webber.'

He was still smiling as his son and son-in-law very reluctantly got out to bump-start the wretched thing. I moved to follow him, but the professor gripped my arm and pulled me back. 'You must not get out, you are my guest, please understand,' he said in a low whisper.

Reluctantly, I slid back into the rear seat. The old man turned round to look out of the rear window and gestured for me to do the same. Appalled, I watched as his son and son-in-law pushed the old van along the road, lashed by the rain. Again I asked to be allowed to help them, even by just getting out, but the professor sternly refused. Instead he turned round and watched them. By now their mouths were opening and closing like two enormous goldfish, magnified in a glass bowl. My host ducked down as the tears coursed down his face. He simply could not stop laughing.

MENU

Egg mayonnaise

Cream of mushroom soup

*Fried pork escalope in cream sauce,
served with French fries*

Dessert

A choice of beverages from the bar.

The meal of course was sublime – for me anyway. Whether my two dining companions shared my enthusiasm was difficult to tell as they were both natural gentlemen. They really just wanted me to enjoy it. Our driver refused all invitations to join us, and gave the distinct impression that he had suffered enough for one evening.

Another note had been slipped under my door. This time it had been folded in the shape of a Chinese dragon. Inside, in Wu Shu's unmistakable tiny handwriting, was a message:

> I was in my director's office today and saw Professor Yu who said you were very fond of the supper you had eaten with him last night. He thinks it was a great success.
>
> Bad news is that Security people have complained that you come back so late. Naughty person!
>
> Today I accompanied 20 foreigners who had special visit to our Buddha Temple. We also took them to Cherry Ditch area which is an important conservation area of our Garden.
>
> We saw limpid water of stream, cool in there because of Metasequoias.

This was followed by another note, this time in the shape of a swan:

> Thank you for washing my cup. You are so careful and kind. I am a naughty person. Always forget something. My mother often blames me on this point, but I cannot rectify myself. So I often make mistakes in my studying, working and other things. I want to ask you a question, that is: why you use such a word as 'cheeky' with me?! I know this word just now from my 'A New English – Chinese Dictionary'!
>
> I think I am not such a person with such a meaning. You also say that I have integrity, why use such a word on me!!!!!!!
>
> Wu Shu

Later we had our first argument. A misunderstanding really, but I left her office in a huff. On her way back from Beijing apparently Wu Shu discovered she could not get a connecting bus from the Summer Palace bus station as the traffic had ground to a halt. She stood there not knowing what to do when a young man got out of a truck and told her that the road was blocked by an accident or some such thing and if she liked he would take her to Xiang Shan by another route in his truck. She had looked in and saw that the truck contained an elderly man with a kind face and therefore thought it safe. When they dropped her off she gave the young man her *ming pian* (business card) and said that as they passed by regularly, she would give them a tour of the Garden at a later date.

I thought all this foolish in the extreme; to get into any vehicle when the occupants are not known to you, and to give your business card to a total stranger, could be misinterpreted. I was jealous, of course, but the latter point had been proved because he had left a dozen messages by phone.

Wu Shu, as a pretty, well-educated young lady of good family, had been pursued by countless young Chinese men ever since she had first left home. In the Chinese fashion, it had usually taken the polite form of a written letter expressing admiration for her educational achievements and other skills. They were all coy, but none the less the object was clear and well known. Each had received a very firm refusal, and that was the end of the matter. Wu Shu could on the face of it be sweet and trusting, but once she spotted trouble she could be ruthless in stamping on things. One man, who had been very firmly rebuffed, had said to everyone in her university class that Wu Shu walked with her (metaphorical) fist in front of her – and so it proved. At one point, even her own mother told her that she might be being a little harsh.

'I am a respectable girl and I have never encouraged their attention, so why should I be soft with them?' was her only reply.

One man, who had also been her classmate at university near

Xi'an, had not accepted the customary written rebuff, but had continued to pursue her, even after university when she had moved to Shanghai to undertake her MSc. At one point, fed up with his attention, she had dramatically confronted him and told him that he had not got a chance and so had better give it all up there and then.

'But why?' he asked incredulously.

'Because I do not like your personality. It does not attract me in the slightest.'

'I will *change* my personality, to suit you, do not worry,' he had replied, winningly.

She couldn't deter him and, even now, though he was married and his wife was expecting his child, he still found excuses to ring Wu Shu and try the same old nonsense. I knew all this, but calls continued to come in.

Also, an old classmate from school now lived in Beijing and had been very helpful when Wu Shu first moved to the city. Since then he had been quietly paying her his court until she told him to stop visiting her as she was too busy with her GRE English lessons.

All this did nothing for my morale. The real problem was that I simply didn't understand Chinese and so could not get a feel for anything.

Later there was a shy knock on my door. It was her. With a haunted smile, she gave me the things I had left in her office earlier. Tucked within was another letter, this time in the shape of an egg:

Adrian,

I hope you are fine. Although you left me in such bad mood you also hurted me so much that I promised never to meet with you again. You said I am playing game with you. How can you speak it out if you understand me? We can make joke at unusual time but we cannot make joke in our real life. Why we like each other in such a short time and then hurted each other so quickly? Why?

Why you could speak out that I philander boys' feelings? Maybe these words describe many young people in present society but you can't use it on me. You can't! Why you hurted me a lot and then hurted me in such a way? Use this 'game'? Why? Do you understand me, really?

I recalled you have ever asked me what I wanted in the future. I told you: A Warm Family. A Good Work. I select all along. I hope my husband must be such a man whom I like best and I'll use all my life to accompany him. Adrian, you have absolutely <u>disturbed</u> my life. Why can't you give me time to understand you more? I can't make a decision in a short time and nor can you with me. We should be serious with our choice. Do you agree?

I've missed these days when we visited the Summer Palace and Beijing park and when we went shopping. Both of us were so relaxing with each other; and that day we walked in the rain hand by hand.

Whatever will be, I hope we are good friends all along.

When would you want to visit Cherry Ditch [valley] with me? I'm look forward to it.

Wu Shu

The following morning before work I ran up the stairs as fast as I could and arrived at Wu Shu's door just as she opened it. She beckoned me in with a half smile and bowed her little head with her fluffy, shining bob haircut carefully brushed. I didn't know what to say, so I offered her my written response to the challenging letter she gave me the day before. Not knowing how to construct my letter in the form of an animal, real or mythical, I had just folded it as neatly as I could. She accepted it, put it carefully into her pocket, and gave a warm smile. It was what she wanted.

I went to leave and, as I passed her, she grabbed my arm and laid her perfect head on my chest. Only for a moment, but in that quick action, I knew all was truly well between us.

I tripped back down the stairs and grinned and grinned. Here was a man with a date, a date tonight with Wu Shu! To visit the Cherry Valley or, as she endearingly called it, the Cherry Ditch.

The cherry trees were indeed glorious as we strolled among them that evening. Wu Shu was a little more protective of me now, which I quite liked. No more pointed mentioning of Western 'openness'. Whenever I took a chance with her, it seemed some good came of it. Perhaps that was how relationships really developed? It wasn't all sweet nothings and innate under-standing, no matter how well matched you were.

Hungry, we wandered out of the Garden and found a tiny restaurant that from the outside looked shabby and unwel-coming. But inside it was the exact opposite. The *xio jie* buzzed around us, full of welcoming smiles. There was not too much in the way of decoration, but it was clean and comfortable. Chinese restaurants in Britain were perhaps too well furnished and upholstered. You really wanted your money to go on the food, surely? The food here was good. It was, as far as I could make out, simple home cooking. The rice was plain boiled and the meat and vegetable dishes didn't have that expensive gloss on them, which usually meant there was a myriad ingredients that you didn't really need.

Wu Shu began to relax and talked a little about her life. I noticed that she could be a little anxious, but this could be put down to having lived far from home since she was eighteen. Only one trip a year to the family home in Xining on the high Tibetan Plateau, a distant wild place even now. There was a long-haul train there out of Beijing three times each week. The journey took thirty-six hours.

She had been a bright student and modelled herself academi-cally on her father, who taught mathematics at the university in Xining. Her father's career, like so many in China, had been blighted by political considerations. He had been the eldest son of a wealthy landowning family growing up close to the coastal city of Shanghai. This meant that he was branded with the most dreaded word in the Mao political lexicon – 'landlord' – despite the fact that Mao Zedong came from a very similar background. The 'landlord' label did not just apply to his parents, but was applied equally to him, his three brothers and two sisters, and they would all share a similar fate under the political campaigns that Mao waged in China – loss of job, forced political confessions (her father as an academic was forced to wear a 'dunce's cap' in public) and, in the case of his younger brother, imprisonment. Their circumstances only improved after Mao's death in 1976.

'My mother was very naughty when we were growing up. She would always tell the same story during our evening meal about my Ba Ba [father] and how he lived before China's liberation in 1949.'

'Why? Was it privileged?'

'Oh, yes, *very*. Ba Ba was sent to an expensive private school each day and had a servant who walked behind him carrying a sack containing everything he needed for the day: books, papers, parcels of delicious food but, most important of all, his calligraphy set to practise his Chinese character writing.'

Her father's status had risen dramatically after Mao's death, not just for his academic work, but for his dark good looks and exquisite manners. It was clear that was where her beauty came from.

Her mother was totally different from her father. Short and chubby, she was known as 'little sweet' as a child. This had been modified, after giving birth to Wu Shu and three elder brothers, to 'little plum' as her torso now resembled one. It was an affectionate nickname though. More worryingly, she enjoyed another nickname which, when roughly translated, was 'knife mouth, tofu heart'. It was the 'knife' part that held my attention as she continued her story:

'My parents had four children because Mao led a public

campaign for Chinese couples to have as many children as possible. We know now why. He wanted a big population to do the work necessary to become powerful and to be able to withstand high casualties in time of war.'

I insisted on accompanying Wu Shu home to her dormitory despite her saying, 'I'll be fine, Adrian, you do not need worry.'

Then there was a final resigned acceptance in the usual cheeky Wu form, 'Oh, Mister Webber, you are so *manly* ...'

CHAPTER 11

犹如天气，一个人的运气可随夜而变

'Like weather, one's fortunes may change by the evening'

I found myself once again at the Summer Palace accompanying my friend William to judge the Annual English-speaking Guides Competition. Thankfully, he didn't need my help so I was free to wander around that enchanted place alone. Being a weekday it was largely empty, so it allowed me to go wherever I wanted; it also gave me the opportunity to reflect on the changes that had taken place since I was last there. I tried to pinpoint exactly how and when something happened between Wu Shu and me. Something definitely *had* happened here, but it was so subtle that perhaps we did not even feel it at the time, but instead it slowly grew inside us and, once there, it was impossible to ignore. I was already its prisoner and I had no choice but to act upon it. Neither of us were responsible; it was only possible between the two of us. Symbiotic?

Someone had said that when this happened you had really met your twin, that we all send out signals, unwittingly perhaps, trying to attract that person who is the same as ourselves. What you saw in the other person was really a reflection of your true self. I thought and thought about this girl as I wandered through the perfumed gardens and lingered for a while by the lake where Wu Shu had looked down at the darting fish. I had instinctively joined her here at this very spot and looked down too. It was a magical moment that made me shiver suddenly, despite the heat.

Whatever had passed between us happened here; it had already grown very fast and showed itself capable of shocking power.

As Wu Shu had asked that fateful evening, 'Is this what they call love ...?'

I knew that I loved her; she was already a very large part of me. Why had I thought that she deserved better when she came out of the Ladies with wet, dripping hands? I had seen girls from the design office, for example, do the same thing and merely ignored it. In fact, I thought it suited them. They were Chinese. End of story. But not Wu Shu. Oh no, not her ...

And she could make me laugh – laugh so much I wanted to cry. What did she call me the other day when I was brushing myself down and adjusting my hat, ready to go out? *Chou mei.* William later told me that it meant 'vain' ('who on earth said that, Adrian?'). Then, once, when I explained that I had been cooking Peking duck for many years at home, she dismissed this with one word: 'Braggadocio!'

Only the other day we had been having lunch with the ever-gloomy Mr Huang in the main dining room when, with her slim delicate fingers, Wu Shu had made a dagger of her two wooden chopsticks and speared one of the puffy round breads in the centre of the table as if it were a fish. A second later she was happily munching it and dipping it into her soup. I hooted with laughter, much to Huang's irritation. Wu Shu, intent on her food, raised her pretty head and looked quizzically at me from across the table.

I had been working hard on a difficult drawing for what only seemed like an hour after consuming my regular 'English breakfast', carefully prepared as usual by Miss Shi's mother, God bless her.

'Lunch, Adie!'

It was Miss Han and Miss Shi standing beside me with their US army-style canteen and metal spoon. It was 11.30 a.m.

'Come along, "little brother",' they said, 'your "big sisters" are waiting here patiently to take you to lunch and all you do is *pretend* to draw!'

Once I'd finished, I found them in our office's tiny kitchen where they were fastidiously washing all three canteens – mine and theirs – under the cold leaking tap.

'Tell me, why does rinsing a bowl you are going to eat from, with water you are forbidden to drink, actually make it cleaner rather than dirtier?' I casually asked.

They both clucked, shook their heads, and slowly looked up.

'Adie?' said Miss Han.

'Yes?' I replied.

'You are a man,' said Miss Shi.

'Yes,' I replied.

'*And* a foreigner,' said Miss Han.

'Uh huh ...'

'So how do you think you could possibly understand something so *simple* ...?' they both said as one.

I don't know, these *tigers* ...

We strolled back to the office from the works canteen, nibbling the piping hot food from our chopsticks as we went. I had come to love this daily ritual. We were so relaxed in each other's company and I began to realize that with these girls, as with Wu Shu, cultural differences were superficial. The real difference was that they were female. It was gender, not nationality, that made them so interesting. And I enjoyed their confidence in their own femininity. The Chinese girl was feminine, but she was also strong when she had to be, a point made a few minutes later by Director Zhang.

William appeared in our little rest room and announced that we would be joined by the director within a few minutes. He appeared with an enormous bowl of still steaming noodle soup, laughing as he did so. He sat down and said, in heavily accented English, 'Today we *eat* in English. No Mandarin.'

In spite of this he soon began to tell a story in Chinese which William smoothly translated for me. It was all about a Chinese tiger and how she beguiled a young man who met her deep in a tropical forest. Instead of attacking him, the tiger put on a spectacular display of her physical prowess – dazzled him with her lithe movements and long leaping skills. The tiger whirled and whirled around the man in a blur of speed and agility until his head spun. He lost touch with his need to escape as he watched spellbound as the tiger flashed her beautiful sharp teeth and stroked her soft fur against his limbs until he was hers and hers alone. By then he was sitting mutely on the soft earth as the tiger slowed her besotting whirls and leaps and padded slowly towards the by-now exhausted young man. He looked up to see her face so close that he could feel her warm breath on his face. The tigress roared her triumph.

All the while he recited this story, and indeed for the whole 'English lunch', the director had rested his left hand on my bare knee in a fatherly way. When he finished the story which, needless to say, I had grown more and more uncomfortable with, he shouted something, loudly even by Chinese standards, and everyone laughed uproariously, so much so that other people came to the door to join in the fun. I did not have to look up to know that they were all looking at me as they laughed. William, my friend as always, whispered in my ear what I already knew, 'Director says that maybe the foreigner will get himself a tiger, a Chinese tiger? I think you need to respond to director, Adrian.'

I sat up straight and said, 'Perhaps foreigners need to learn more Chinese and more about Chinese tigers before they come to China?'

It was just enough to end things there without any more tiger allusions, and thankfully everyone, still laughing, started to disperse and return to their work. The director, as ever, had been in good form and was happy with the way the lunch had gone. I could see now that he lived his life through people. A genuine extrovert who was also a natural-born entertainer. Perhaps that's why he frightened the life out of me? He was never embarrassed by *anything*. What I didn't know was that this very quality was to help me beyond anything I could have reasonably expected and would soon transform everything at a single stroke.

'Adrian, director says that he will take you soon to see the Great Wall, it isn't too far.'

I asked him to thank Director Zhang for all his hospitality and to say I would be delighted to see the Great Wall of China. We followed the director into the big meeting room and William began to pull down the blinds while Director Zhang fiddled with some video cassettes. As we sat down around him, the director barked something to William, before he embarked on his post-meal wrestling with a toothpick.

'Director says, tell Webber not to worry, these films are not *yellow*.'

'I beg your pardon?' I replied.

'Oh, I'm sorry, Adrian,' he said shyly. 'In your country pornographic films are *blue*, aren't they? Well, here in China they are *yellow* ...'

With that out of the way, we watched a series of films on the founding of the Botanical Garden forty years before and the important scientific work that had been undertaken since. The films included some good footage of a very dashing and youthful-looking Professor Yu, my host at the French restaurant the other evening, of whom I still had fond memories.

I skipped down the corridor to micro-propagation for a quick shower before work. As I opened the doors, I heard Wu Shu's name being called out from the office upstairs, but there was no answer. Another telephone call for her. Who was it this time I wondered to myself ruefully? Not another admirer, surely?

When I left work later that evening I took the outside staircase route for a change and bumped straight into her. She had only just returned from Beijing, looking desperately tired, but still as pretty as ever. She seemed nervous of me for some reason, but we walked on together the long way round to the research building to bypass most of the staff departments and blend in with the public. She

told me that the old schoolmate from her home city had telephoned her on Friday. He wanted to resume his regular visits and
hoped her English lessons had come to an end. He had already
lent Wu Shu a pretty silver watch when hers had broken and she
was wearing it now. Did I have a rival? He apparently worked as
a researcher for a food processing company in the centre of
Beijing. She was being matter of fact about it, or perhaps just
tactful? Perhaps they were even engaged? It was impossible to say.

A knot began to tighten in my stomach. I really didn't have a
clue what was going on. The whole Chinese cultural thing in
which I was hopelessly immersed had taken me out of my depth;
there were so many imponderables surrounding this girl. She was
extremely attractive, well educated, of good family and a
completely natural lady. Who was I to think that I had any hope?
I would return to England in less than three weeks. What was I
thinking? The situation was hopeless really.

And it was those uncomfortable thoughts that were stinging
through my mind as Wu Shu idly chatted about this man and
how her mother had always thought of him as a very gloomy
individual. On and on she went, laughing, until she stopped and
looked up at me, suddenly serious.

'Adrian, you don't mind me talking about this young man, do
you?'

I shrugged and feigned complete indifference before I heard
myself say, in a way that was both confused and angry, 'Well no,
because if you like him just give me the nod – I won't stand in
your way. I leave in a few weeks' time anyway.' My English
reserve seemed to have utterly dried up.

Wu Shu froze on the spot, turned to me, then said in a low
whisper, 'I was only talking honestly with you about my life. I am
a good girl, not bad.'

She turned and walked away down the long winding path by
the lake. I heard her little shoes ringing out in the warm still air.
I ran as fast as I could, caught up, and stood in front of her with
my hands on my knees, breathing heavily. She looked down with

her thick hair covering her face. I could hear her muffled sobs. Without looking up, I heard her say, 'I was only trying to tell you that I liked you best.'

She walked determinedly past me.

I had got it wrong again. How could I?

I set off after her again, but this time quickly caught up and gently put my arm around her shoulder. Wu Shu just stood there crying helplessly. I tucked her little head under my chin and held her tightly. I never wanted to let her go; I had got confused, missed the signals, or misinterpreted them. It was all my fault. I just hadn't been ready for this. It was so powerful. I had never believed in the idea of 'unrequited love'. It was either there between you both or it wasn't. You met your twin. You met your equal. You met your *match*. In every sense you met your *match*. I certainly had met mine. This girl might be crying, but it certainly wasn't out of weakness. No. She was crying because I had got it all wrong and that truly hurt.

Her arms were on my shoulders and she pulled me down before kissing my face. Her tiny dark eyes looked at me tenderly. 'I'm sorry,' we both said and then laughed. Together again, we walked over to a stone seat by the Garden's deserted main entrance. The full moon bathed us in the evening stillness. No people, no traffic, no birds. We were alone. Our foreheads gently touched as we shared hopes, confidences, all remaining barriers tumbling down. Nothing could be hidden now. It felt like a long slow leap into space, free of everything, accepting fate, pointless to resist, impossible ever to go back.

'Will you ... be my ... woman, Wu Shu?'

Her lovely head moved ever so slightly up and down, rubbing my forehead.

'I am yours,' she said simply.

I gently lifted her chin and looked into those mysterious eyes glittering like black pearls, smudged with half-dried tears. We rubbed noses. I told her that in some societies that meant love.

'Wu Shu, could you ever love me a little?' I asked her.

◁ A rare early family photo: Wu Shu aged six in the foreground beside her youngest brother Wu Shu Du. Behind them, Wu Shu Lu (left) and Wu Shu Bu (right) flank their father, with their mother on the far right. The friend who took the picture was the only person the family knew who owned a camera

Wu Shu's eldest brother Wu Shu Bu in full military dress with pistol – all borrowed from an army officer friend – Wu Shu Bu had never been in the People's Liberation Army (PLA) in his life! ▷

Wu Shu's father in 1957 about to embark on his career as a teacher within the People's Liberation Army Air Force (PLAAF), despite his 'landlord' status

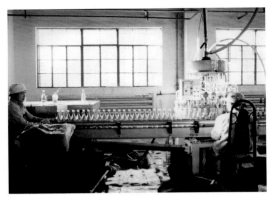

◁ The swelteringly hot Tibetan distillery whose raw '*jiu*' alcohol made me so ill

Wu Shu and her brother Wu Shu ▷ Du in his spartan accommodation near the printing company where he worked – high up on the Tibetan Plateau

◁ The research building where I lived in an office; the sacred Xiang Shan (Fragrant Mountain) towers above it

Our basic kitchen/dining facility ▷ located within Wu Shu's plant laboratory – the scene of our most memorable meal together

◁ A typically formidable cabin attendant in military-style uniform guarding the carriage entrance during a brief stop along the thirty-six-hour train journey from Beijing to Tibet

A view of the timeless Forbidden ▷ City, central Beijing, during a typically busy weekend

◁ Shot showing the destruction of the old Summer Palace – Yuan Ming Yuan – by Anglo-French troops in 1860, for which I later had to 'officially' apologize

My interpreter Wu Shu during ▷ the tour of the Summer Palace; she is standing in the specially built street lined with stores that enabled emperors to go shopping without encountering ordinary citizens

◁ Returning from Wu Shu's father's tomb high in the mountains above Xining city – we had just burned money for him to spend in the afterlife

The mighty Yangtze River rises ▷ close to Wu Shu's home in Xining on the Tibetan Plateau before travelling nearly 4,000 miles across China into the East China Sea, near Shanghai. The liquid equivalent, perhaps, of the Great Wall itself

◁ Typical Buddhist temples located high on the Tibetan Plateau. Tibetan flags would also be strung out across the mountains to send their peaceful messages to all beings – aided by the 'Wind Horse'

Wu Shu perfectly at home in ▷ a Xining city street, Tibetan Plateau, where she was born, although the oxygen in the air is only 50–60% of what you would expect at sea level

◁ Wu Shu's niece, Nan Nan, my little English-speaking friend, aged seven, Xining high street, Tibetan Plateau

People's Liberation Army soldiers ▷ 'changing the guard', similar to those who goose-stepped past me each chanting 'hello' in perfect English near the British Embassy, central Beijing

◁ Wu Shu, foreground, eating dinner with: from far left, seated, Mr Chen, his wife and Miss Zhang. The big man on the far right was to later save me from eating many *jiaozi* dumplings when my stomach and spirits were at their lowest ebb in China

Even in Tibet I was expected to ▷ repay the generous official hospitality by joining in with the entertainment afterwards. The restaurant's head chef had specially prepared a dish of roast beef with all the 'trimmings' (Chinese-style) in my honour

◁ Eldest brother Wu Shu Bu, as head of the family, carries his sister down three flights of steps from her family home to symbolically hand her to me before our marriage

Wu Shu and I arriving at ▷ the best hotel in Xining city for our formal wedding congratulation; a throng of local Chinese people, extremely curious, quickly gathered around us

Marriage certificate, Chinese style. We were both officially issued with a marriage passport in Beijing; this one is mine

◁ My closest colleagues within the design office, from left: my two 'elder sisters' Miss Shi and Miss Han and my manager Miss Liu

Some of my Propagation depart- ▷ ment co-workers; the man on the far right is the stoical manager in typical unsmiling pose

◁ A quick snap of Miss Xu Zhihong and Miss Wu taken during our tour of the Summer Palace – uncomfortable – they quickly parted once it was taken

Here I am flanked by my two ▷ 'elder sisters' Miss Shi and Miss Han, together with Miss Liu (far right) and other junior members of the design office

◁ Within a year of Wu Shu arriving to live in England our daughter Sophia was born – here she is wearing a Chinese hat I had not been able to resist when I saw it in a street market in Beijing

Wu Shu, despite previously rejecting any thought of being a mother, quickly adapted to motherhood; here she is a proud mother with our toddler daughter Sophia at home in the Cotswolds, England ▽

'Adrian, I have never loved you a little. I know now, in my deep heart, that I have always loved you *so very much*. I told you once that you disturb me, didn't you realize what I meant?'

She raised her head to mine and we kissed slowly and lovingly, all inhibitions now forgotten. Worries and concerns melted away in those moments as we kissed and kissed. I knew that I wanted to spend my whole life with her. She was so beautiful – as a person, as a young girl, and as my friend.

We stopped kissing and Wu Shu looked up at me and said, 'I belong to you.'

We held each other tight, her shiny hair touching my nose and tickling it. She brushed it back and I felt her warm breath on my face as a cool breeze shimmered between us. No one knew and we intended to keep it that way for now. Our secret.

Wu Shu became a little chilled and accepted my linen waistcoat as I pulled it around her shoulders. I had found my soulmate at last. I escorted Wu Shu back to her dormitory. She padded along beside me, and even in the moonlight I could see the enormous waistcoat draped over her petite body.

We parted at the entrance to her courtyard and I heard her friends call out to her through the darkness, so I knew she was safe. I loved her.

Some of her words ran through my mind: 'Sometimes I think you were meant to come to my China.'

'It does seem fateful, somehow.'

'If you leave your country to spend time in another, you must be looking for something you cannot find there.'

'Why am I never tired when I walk with you, Adrian?'

On a more practical level, I had quickly assured her that I would return to China as soon as possible. Unfortunately that meant Christmas because the autumn term of my course would not finish until the middle of December. Wu Shu had nodded her acceptance before saying, 'This girl has to wait for the return of her rotten English oak tree ... all along.'

CHAPTER 12

鞠躬，要鞠低躬

'When you bow, bow low'

I was awoken the next morning by Wu Shu. She seemed flushed and serious. She would not look up as I quizzed her on what was the matter. She looked so downcast and vulnerable I could not bear it and pulled her towards me, her head once again on my chest as she sobbed quietly in my arms.

She pulled away from me, wiped her eyes, and said, 'No time to talk, Adrian. Tonight I will tell you everything. I have done a brave thing just now I think.'

I had been given pride of place in the director's chauffeur-driven black limo for the trip to the Great Wall. Behind me, wreathed in smiles, sat the director with Madame Zhang on one side and William on the other. It was a Friday, a normal working day, the sun was shining and they were going to show the foreigner one of the wonders of the world; on the way they would have an agreeable lunch with many old colleagues and friends at the Ming Tombs, the traditional burial ground of the long-dead emperors of China.

The director's new amiable driver nosed the car carefully through the early morning commuter traffic before he opened up the huge car northwards on the dual carriageway. As we sped along Madame Zhang invited me, before I left China, to a family dinner. What I didn't know was that this was a great honour (she had a formidable reputation as a cook), and could be partly attributed to a dramatic meeting which had taken place that morning before we left. The invitation was sealed by her husband who slapped me on the shoulder with the words, 'OK, Adie. Good!'

The car slowed and turned through a series of sharp bends before emerging into a long wide boulevard lined with enormous stone animals. The *shan*, or mountain, above us, was known as the Mountain of Heavenly Longevity. We parked in a shaded area and walked down the Shen Dao (Street of Spirits) to the central Changling Tomb.

The road again was studded with statues of large animals, and Confucian officials, all beautifully carved in a light-coloured stone. In ancient times the whole complex was surrounded by high walls and was heavily guarded. The Ming dynasty emperors themselves were laid out in red-walled burial chambers, now mostly empty.

Inevitably there was a gift shop on route. It had a section of heavy dressing table items in the imperial tradition, some made of woven metal, others inlaid with semi-precious stones. One, in particular, caught my eye and I desperately wanted to buy it for Wu Shu, no matter what our future held. It was a heavy metal jewellery box in beautiful soft feminine colours. Inside was a mirror. It felt so right.

William, with his usual tact, came over and pretended it was for an important relative in England, 'Old English ladies like this sort of thing, I believe ...'

I nodded and smiled. It was priced at 385 yuan, but he eventually beat them down to 280 yuan (around £22) which was as much as I could afford. The reduction must have hurt because they refused to gift wrap it, which was usually free. It immediately felt like a talisman, an expensive good luck charm which gave me hope for the future. William immediately knocked me out of my reverie and upbraided me for not praising his negotiating skills. Quite right. Where were my manners?

Two pretty young *xio jie* escorted us formally into the private luncheon room. In front of us was a huge circular revolving table with the usual formal exquisite porcelain. Cups, bowls, little pouring pots and expensive, but very slippery, chopsticks on tiny mounts. Lots and lots of crisp white linen. There were about twenty other guests. All male and middle-aged, apart from Madame Zhang, who looked across at me and smiled. What a nice woman I thought. At least all the others looked as hot and uncomfortable as I felt, as I stood by my chair, and waited for something to happen. Eventually our host, the director of the Ming Tombs, arrived with a harassed-looking aide, also male and middle-aged.

He was now chatting with a whole group of men – presumably his administration team – and they were glancing over at me, which was a little disconcerting. William was trying to catch what they were saying, but he shook his head before straining some more. Something was building, that much was clear. I flicked a glance at our Director Zhang but he was, unusually, picking his teeth *before* the meal and smiling at everyone. Not a care in the world. No help there then.

There was that familiar sense of expectation as our host, at last, gestured formally for everyone to be seated. He remained standing and everyone fell silent as he made a little speech. The guests started to relax and soon they were nodding and even saying *dui* ('yes, right'), a little too portentously for my comfort. Some started to knock the table with their fists to signify their agreement. Ominously, I distinctly heard the name Yuan Ming Yuan crop up a couple of times in his speech – a huge historical site on the edge of Beijing, which I had already visited. I knew it was the official Summer Palace until it was largely destroyed by Anglo-French forces in 1860.

William's voice eventually penetrated, 'Adrian, our host, the esteemed director, has been discussing the terrible destruction of the Old Summer Palace – Yuan Ming Yuan – and the looting of its beautiful and priceless artefacts by your countrymen. They want you as an *Englishman* to make a formal apology, on behalf of your country, England.'

Everything went quiet and all eyes turned towards me although no one, I noticed, could hold my gaze and looked down into their laps instead. Even William now pulled himself formally upright.

Nothing for it, I had to get up. But just as I pushed back my chair, William whispered, 'They want you to apologize in *Chinese*, Adrian. No one here speaks English.'

'But so far I've only learnt thirteen Chinese words,' I hissed.

He gave me a look that said: you are on your own on this one – sorry and all that.

I stood up and began, '*Wo de penyou* [my friends] *Yuan Ming Yuan, zhe shi bu hao* [this was bad] *wo de Yin guo ren* [my Englishmen] *ta shi bu hao* [they were very bad] *qing* [please] *Zhong guo* [China] *qing* [please] *dui bu qi* [very sorry] *wo dui bu qi* [I am very sorry].'

As I said these words, and then repeated them in different ways, I held up my upturned hands in the hope that even if they didn't understand my halting Mandarin, they would understand the gesture. Unnervingly, throughout my little speech a stocky balding man, who sat directly opposite, glared at me.

I concluded with a very contrite bow and prayed that it was enough. Unbelievably, as if on some secret signal, they all stood up and gave me a polite but very long round of applause. I was about to relax until I saw that the balding man had left his place and was walking round the huge table in my direction. He stood in front of me with a glass in his muscular hand and said something in a deep gruff voice. At first even William could not understand his dialect, but then he whispered, 'This gentleman has just said that what was past could not be undone. It was past. You must salute his words, Adrian, *quickly*.'

I shook his hand and bowed my head formally.

Everyone now relaxed and began to chat freely as the doors opened and the food was wheeled in on huge trolleys by smiling servers. Each dish was carefully placed on the 'Lazy Susan' circular glass in front of the director, who rotated it in front of me and bade me sample each of the dishes first. This was clearly intended as an honour, but I'd lost my appetite. I was congratulated on my prowess with chopsticks as the food ended up in my mouth, not my lap. All compliments now, I thought! Director Zhang, I noticed, was still exercising his skill in talking to at least three people simultaneously while managing to fill their bowls *and* eat his own food at the same time. He was incorrigible really. Had he known what they planned to do? I never found out.

Without telling me or giving me any warning, Wu Shu had come to a decision. Perhaps rightly it was a decision that could only be made by her alone. She was in a situation that no one had foreseen, and she had nobody to turn to with sufficient authority to help and guide her. But I was hurt nonetheless.

Neither of us had time that morning when she came to my room to discuss it, but she had thoughtfully left a long note for my return and so it wasn't until after midnight that I got the full story.

Wu Shu had decided that the only way we had a chance of a future was if she got some powerful help. Her family, who lived on the high Tibetan Plateau, were just too far away and had no knowledge about, let alone influence within, the Botanical Garden. The only person who could help her was the man I had been with all day, although discreetly he hadn't mentioned it as that would have meant going through William. Presumably he had mentioned the situation with Wu Shu to his wife, who had beamed at me all day for reasons I could not understand at the time. And then there had been that sudden invitation to dine with them *en famille*.

Wu Shu had seen Director Zhang in the entrance of the research building waiting to pick up William and me. She asked for a private chat and he followed her up to her office on the first floor.

She had told him about us and the problems she had with staff gossip.

'My director, please tell me, do you think my relationship with the foreigner has a future?'

The director had sat down in front of her and listened patiently. He had a soft spot for her and had the habit of putting his arm around her shoulder. He smiled. 'It all depends on whether he returns as he says he will. If he returns, he must visit your family. We have some experience of this when another female member of staff formed a relationship with a man from Korea. They married and have a lovely little girl now.'

Wu Shu nodded and took all this in. Her director was being supportive, although he had the disconcerting habit of listening and then turning his head slowly towards her little bed in the corner before turning his head back again and smiling at her.

'Wait. All you can do is wait. From now on try to be discreet to protect yourself in case the foreigner does not return,' he said finally.

Meeting over, he got to his feet, patted her shoulder, and gave her another encouraging smile before leaving.

It was now Friday, so of course I couldn't see her. She was already in Beijing, at her English lessons, but her note made me forgive everything.

I read it and re-read it until I fell asleep.

CHAPTER 13

竹子长的越高，会弯的越低

'The taller the bamboo grows, the lower it bends'

Little cat. She had been well named. Every time I gave her a reply to a question, which was always framed in the same way – 'Adrian, I have a question, please do not mind ...' – she would look at me for a moment before narrowing her eyes and cocking her head to one side before saying: 'Really?' Yes. Little cat, feline and feminine. A tiger.

I was happy and could no longer remember ever being lonely. It was as though this wonderful girl had not only filled the present, but the past as well.

Those happy carefree thoughts were not destined to last though as suddenly, without warning, I got excruciating toothache. It was to last all night and so I only slept fitfully. In the morning Wu Shu and I walked together to an emergency dental service on the far side of Xiang Shan town. A moon gate welcomed those with dental problems. We walked through it into a small bare office illuminated by a single fluorescent light. A podgy little man wearing a crumpled white coat stood behind a battered dark wooden desk. His waxy face could just be made out behind a large pair of dark-rimmed spectacles. Without any form of greeting, he rummaged through the drawers of the desk, eventually emerging with a long metal torch. With a flick of the head, he motioned me to sit down and then advanced towards me, stretching his mouth open as he wanted me to do.

He shone the torch into my mouth for a few seconds before waving at me to relax. Going through the drawers again he found a packet of painkillers and tossed them on to the desk. They were to be taken every three to four hours to stave off the pain. I should report to the local hospital at 9 a.m. tomorrow (Monday) morning for treatment. I should not take the painkillers for longer than seventy-two hours or they would fry my brain. We were then ushered out of the door.

Out on the street I started to calculate whether I could nurse the tooth problem until I returned to England. Wu Shu stomped on this because she calculated I would be brain dead from the painkillers long before I ever reached Heathrow.

The hospital was busy, full of people patiently waiting their turn along the myriad corridors and departmental waiting rooms. Eventually we found the dental clinic and had to stand to wait as the few chairs were already taken. But within a minute or so a smartly dressed nurse came out, smiled, and said they needed to take down some particulars. As we sat behind a huge desk, all the staff came over to witness the foreigner's details being meticulously written down in an enormous hard-backed register. That done, I was led through into the surgery where a young dentist was waiting patiently for me.

He quickly went to work, probing and pushing with his metal instruments, while keeping up a non-stop commentary to Wu Shu in Chinese, and it was by no means all medical. Apparently I was the first Westerner he had ever worked on and he was *fascinated*. I choked as she told me that he found my long Western eyelashes *very* becoming. Then he said that my teeth were made of a different material to a Chinese person's and that my tongue was the largest he had ever seen. He pronounced finally that my previous dentist's work had been of inferior quality, certainly compared with his own, and there was no alternative but to fill the cavity again. *Now.*

I rinsed my mouth out and looked around. On the metal

trolley beside him was an array of different kidney dishes containing hypodermic needles of varying sizes immersed in some form of disinfectant. When challenged on whether he would use them on me he replied, 'Of course!'

'Why don't you use *disposable* needles?' I asked.

'Adrian, the dentist insists that his needles are better and sharper than your Western ones. There is nothing to worry about. Shall we commence with the procedure now?'

The sting of the needle moved around my mouth several times until he was satisfied that the area was completely anaesthetized. The nurse meanwhile had prepared the filling mixture. He'd already told Wu Shu not to worry as he had given the foreigner twice the level of anaesthetic he would have given a Chinese. Westerners, he knew, were very tender.

The next day, when I told Miss Liu, she nodded her head knowingly, 'Oh *him* ...' she said. 'And how many follow-up appointments did he give you?'

I shook my head.

'Pretty girls get two at least,' she laughed.

'And plain girls, how many do they get?'

'Oh, the same as you,' she smiled. 'None.'

'He's a *spy*!'
'Your mother said *what*?'

Apparently Wu Shu had rung her mother to tell her all about us the night I had gone to bed early with toothache.

'Adrian, I told her that was surely not possible, you couldn't be a spy, we were in a *botanical garden* after all, not something sensitive in China.'

'Good answer. What did she say to that?'

'He's a *deceiver*.'

'Oh.'

I tried to laugh and told her that her mother sounded quite a character, but Wu Shu then became more serious and told me that there had been more gossip about us within the Garden.

'They say I'm just your "plaything during the evenings", otherwise you would be bored.'

'Oh, I see,' I said quietly. 'It never lets up, does it?'

So this was how it would be from now on. That was clear. And with my imminent departure, Wu Shu would have to face it alone. Her own mother was not being supportive and her director had recently calculated when she saw him in his office how many prostitutes a Western man could enjoy for the price of a return airline ticket between London and Beijing.

'Adrian, he even put an abacus on his knee to make the horrible calculations as I just sat there in front of him, not knowing what to say or where to look!' she told me sorrowfully.

It would all have to be endured as an act of faith that I would return. That everything I said was true and that no, I was not a *deceiver* (or spy either).

One evening I met Wu Shu at her dormitory and we strolled back to her office to discuss the arrangements for my return. As we walked, Wu Shu skipped in front of me and said brightly, 'Why do I never get tired when I walk with you, my *Mister* Webber? I always feel so light.'

I smiled; she'd said that many times now. It was good to see her so relaxed.

'Why does everything feel like a dream? Why do I look so *old* when I look in the mirror? It's love, isn't it? It is all ... love. And it's all your fault, Adrian, my rotten to the core oak tree ...'

Why does she say my name in that special way? No one said my name like Wu Shu said it. No one, ever.

Love. We were giddy with it. Nothing seemed real any more. Intoxicated by anything and everything, a cloud as lonely as the poet, a beautiful flower, the alluring aroma of plain boiled noodles on a warm evening and the look of tenderness on Wu Shu's face as she gently stirred them. Sometimes I *envied* those noodles.

Before we went up to her room Wu Shu asked me to change a plug in her laboratory, so I fiddled in my suitcase for a screwdriver. I felt a little worried at changing a Chinese two-pinned plug, so I delicately unscrewed the back.

'Why is your screwdriver so old, Mr Webber?'

Typical Wu cheek, which wasn't helping my nerves, followed by, 'Adrian, why are you so timorous?'

'What the hell does that mean? Oh, *timid*, well, yes! I don't want to be remembered as the foreigner who burned down the research building, now do I?'

I laughed nervously. What was it she called me after I drank two tins of almond milk in a row the other day?

'Adrian, you are like animal!'

'What *sort*, Miss Wu? Camel ... elephant ...?'

'No. *Cow*.'

Cheek, I thought, and yet she was so serious with everyone else – that is, if she spoke at all.

Anyway, plug changed, the machine whirred into life, so no harm had been done.

Later that evening we spent so long discussing the travel arrangements in Wu Shu's office that we were surprised when we looked out of the window to see it was pitch black. By now we were both starving, so I volunteered to go back down to the lab and fix a bowl of noodles for us. As I returned and nudged open the door with my knee, the extension phone on her desk jangled into life.

I saw her talking very fast into the phone and motioning me to be quiet. It was her 'food processing admirer' and he had heard my voice. He had called to ask Wu Shu out to visit a Beijing park. Wu Shu had been a little curt and told him no, but he had not been put off until he heard my voice, and immediately rang off. We thought perhaps he had taken the hint and that was the end of the matter. But a couple of minutes later he was back on the phone. Wu Shu handed the phone to me with the words, 'He wants to speak to you.' He was angry.

'Get out. Get out!' he shouted. 'What are you doing there so late? Get out. *Get out!*'

Shocked by the emotion and anguish in his voice, I was completely lost for words. His intentions towards Wu Shu were anything but casual. He was in deadly earnest, secretly pinning all his hopes on this alliance.

When he again asked me what I was doing there so late, I decided I must tell him the truth. I covered the mouthpiece with my hand and asked Wu Shu for permission to do just that. She just nodded resignedly.

'The reason I am up here so late – not that it's any of your business actually – is that we are discussing the arrangements for me to return to China so that I can ask Wu Shu's family if they will give permission for me to marry her.'

Silence.

'Hello, hello, are you still there? *Hello?*' I shouted down the phone.

After what felt like an age, his guttural voice returned, but this time slower, more thoughtful (it must have been a huge shock after all): 'I want to speak to Wu Shu ... you must leave now ... I ... *hate* you ... !'

Slowly, nervously, I handed the phone back to Wu Shu. She said nothing as he was definitely doing the talking. He talked and talked. I watched her hold the heavy black handset in her delicate little hand as she listened to this distraught young man from her home city of Xining, on the high Tibetan Plateau. Perhaps his family there even knew of his intentions?

'*Dui ... dui*' ('yes') she kept repeating to his questions, raw and abject as they were, until he at last rang off. I took the handset from an emotionally drained Wu Shu and placed it back in its cradle. We looked at each other miserably. All thoughts of food gone now. She told me that he had just kept asking her the same question, 'Was it true?'

When she told him each time that it was, he simply asked her the same question again.

Finally, plaintively, he asked her, 'How could you agree to marry a man who you have known for such a short time when you have known me so many years? What is so special about this man?'

He had then asked her, finally, if there was any hope for him? Could he still win her affection? When she told him that it was impossible, he started to cry.

It was heart-rending for her. She could not ease his pain except by giving him what he so sincerely wanted.

CHAPTER 14

针只有一头尖

'A needle is sharp only at one end'

This particular night I had the honour of dining with Mr Zhang, director of the Botanical Garden, together with his wife and family. William would accompany me as interpreter; he had been nervous about this ever since the weekend when we first learned about the invitation. We then had a quiet meal together in the library. There was still no word of William's wife's return and he was very down. He had not seen her for over three months now and he looked tired, drained.

I had bought half a Peking duck and a variety of Chinese beers and made sure they were well chilled in Wu Shu's fridge before plying my friend with as much liquid solace as he could take. William had bought a box of spare ribs slathered in a hot tangy sauce and, a little surprisingly, chips! What a good friend ...

We drank to our women, without once mentioning them of course. Men didn't do that sort of thing, did they? William, of course, drank to his wife, who was over 1,000 miles away, and me to the woman I loved – who would shortly be 5,000 miles distant.

We talked about our childhoods: William about cycling to school in the hot southeastern part of China, famous for its rice and river fish. It was considered that heaven was in the sky, but his Jiang Su province was paradise on earth. A bright student, he had to cycle to a school further away than the other children's, and to dodge the snakes that had been run over as they crossed the road at night; the ones that survived were wounded and angry and tried to bite him as he warily circled them.

After yet more Chinese *pijou* we started to tease each other about our countries and their histories. Inevitably the Opium Wars came up. I was by now used to defending this one, but I got nowhere with William. In a last-ditch attempt to win the moral argument, I said, 'Look, we're giving you Hong Kong, aren't we?'

William shook his head slowly. Despite all the *pijou*, his mind was still razor sharp.

'No, Adrian,' he said. 'You are *returning* it.'

The car tooted its horn as it climbed the short incline to the research building. William looked smart in his blindingly white shirt and charcoal trousers. I wore my favourite white linen shirt and cream linen trousers. I had never seen him look so nervous. Where was Mr Cool tonight, I wondered? He hadn't stopped twisting his fingers for the last ten minutes as we waited, pausing only to look at his watch every thirty seconds. True, it was a rare honour to dine with the director at home, notwithstanding his wife's legendary culinary skills. William's status within the Garden's informal hierarchy, according to Miss Liu's unflinching analysis, hovered around 'head boy', so I supposed he didn't want to muck up.

Sitting in the car, I cradled my gift for the director, a presentation box containing a bottle of Johnny Walker whisky and two heavy tumblers. It had cost a fortune, but when I first saw it in a large department store in central Beijing I knew that it was the gift for him. Miss Liu had already briefed me on the Chinese protocol involved. It wasn't so much the giving part – that was easy – it was more how a Chinese *received* a gift that might surprise a Westerner, or even leave him feeling insulted when the recipient made a play of indifference. William confirmed this,

'We Chinese believe that to make a show of gratitude gives you bad face. You shouldn't after all be seen to be too needy. Can you understand this?'

Well, frankly, *no*, I thought as we pulled up outside the director's apartment that was located, somewhat curiously, within a local army base. We were to be joined by his two sons, a daughter-in-law and a small lively dog. The apartment was on the ground floor, not overly large, and had a distinctly 'lived in' look. The director was not materialistically minded. He was an extrovert character who lived his life through other people and enjoyed the sensuous pleasures of life. A fully paid-up member of the human race, in other words, and I thanked him silently for this. He had supported Wu Shu, and so he had supported me.

The dining room was lit by the now familiar single fluorescent light which was located to one side of the ceiling above the carefully prepared dining table. This was the first time I had eaten in a proper Chinese family home and I was determined not to be nervous but merely to enjoy it. After all, the director and I got on well. We had done almost from the beginning, but after I had helped him with the distinguished visiting professors our relationship had always been easy. I trusted him, too.

MENU

Peking duck

Duck eggs crystallized in a green jelly

FOLLOWED BY:

Mongolian hot pot

FOLLOWED BY:

three types of jiao-zi [dumplings]

FOLLOWED BY:

jiao zi tang [dumpling soup]

DRINKS

Cold pijou [beer]

OR:

Green tea

The food was sensational. I even managed a few of the *jiao-zi* dumplings so beloved of the northern Chinese, and Wu Shu in particular. It was the same unleavened suety skin filled with different savoury fillings of ground pork and vegetables. Not a hint of anything as mildly exotic as chillies even. William picked at the food, but I was ravenous and ate everything that was put in front of me.

The atmosphere had that rare quality of being both relaxed and charged with a tingle of excitement. I also never tired of watching the Chinese at the table, particularly coming from such an inhibited country as England. Eating was the Chinese hobby and they always thoroughly enjoyed the experience, which was guilt free. Enjoy. Enjoy! The rituals of *gan bei* (cheers) and putting food into other people's bowls was done with such gusto that you were simply swept along. Our glasses were always immediately re-filled by one of the sons.

I liked Madame Zhang enormously. She was a formidable cook, that was clear, but she approached everything so modestly and in such a ladylike way that she was clearly the epitome of the high official's wife. She must have helped her husband's career in many unsung ways. Her husband was the direct opposite: he relished everything, burped and slurped his way through the delicious feast, pausing only to laugh uproariously at any quip, joke or funny anecdote. And then he would slowly pick his teeth once he could eat not a scrap more. He was at home and he wasn't going to stand on ceremony.

I sat there, flattered to have even been asked in the first place, and aware that to be treated to this sublime feast in such a relaxed way was indeed an honour. As things slowed down, I told William that I wanted to present Director Zhang with a gift and he duly made the announcement. I had, of course, been forewarned not to expect any sort of fuss, but I was still surprised when everyone but the director got up from the table – as if it had suddenly become radioactive – and promptly departed the room. It was as though I had made a terrible social gaffe, dropped the brick of all bricks. But apparently it was just their way of reducing the embarrassment of being the recipient of a gift.

Suddenly alone with him, I felt shy and uneasy but I need not have worried. I was dealing with a consummate professional who just grinned his way through it. I could see, though, that he was quietly impressed; it gave him good face in front of his close family, and it came from a foreign devil, to boot.

He then called everyone back in as if to reassure them that he had survived the gift-giving intact, no problem. Through William, he told me that he had booked a leaving meal in my honour at the Wofosi Hotel the following night, and everyone who had worked with me had been invited. He went on to say that I would probably want to buy some gifts for my family and so his driver would be at my disposal the following morning when he would pick me up at 9 a.m. and take me into Beijing. I would of course require an English speaker to accompany me in the city and Wu Shu had been selected for this task. His office had already told her to make herself available.

I had underestimated this man. He was clever *and* discreet. I could not have asked more of him, and it was with a light-hearted feeling of elation that I said my goodbyes to the Zhangs before plunging into the warm dark night.

I could not sleep. No matter how hard I tried, nothing happened. Reluctantly, I pulled myself upright, pricking myself – not for the first time – on the straw protruding from the mattress, and walked over to the tiny sink to wash my face.

Feeling a little refreshed, I quietly got dressed. Careful so as not to wake the caretaker, I unlocked the main outer doors and stepped outside. The cold autumn air hit me straight away. Beijing had gradually become cooler as the weeks passed, especially now, just before the breaking of the dawn. I sat at the top of the stone steps and looked out at the twinkling lights on the mountains that surrounded this magical place.

Everything was still. Quiet in that special time just before daybreak. The moon bathed the road in front of me where I had first arrived, not knowing what to expect, or what would happen to me. I knew that I had to leave this place soon, but I really did not want to go. Wu Shu was part of this land. She was a product of it. What sort of system could produce someone as inherently gentle and placid as her? I looked out as the sun kissed the tips of the east-facing mountains before gradually bathing their steep slopes. A distant cockerel cried out its welcome to the new day. This land produced Wu Shu. A shiver juddered through me. I too felt part of this land.

'Adrian, I can feel your blood flow through my vein ...'

Perhaps in some ways I had become calmer and gentler, but in other ways stronger, more stoical. Less *tender*, to use the dentist's happy phrase. Perhaps it was also the sense of the great history of this country that informed the present. *The largest and most fractured of all histories*, someone had once said. It made you realize just how small and insignificant you really were. Perhaps that was part of growing up. Reducing the size of your ego. It was painful, of course, but perhaps the pain was a necessary part of the change process.

The director's driver dropped us off at the Grand Plaza area in the central northern part of Beijing. But just before he did, he turned and looked Wu Shu full in the face before quietly saying, 'You have unusual fate, but it is fate, none the less.'

This area of the city had become our favourite now. We had gone here after our first visit to the Summer Palace, when we had realized that we were falling in love. Uncanny. It was not spoken about or in any other way acknowledged, but it had happened here or hereabouts, we both knew that.

I had known it when she held my hand as she helped me cross the busy street. I had known it as I waited for her in the empty restaurant. I had known it when we walked back from the embarrassingly frugal meal at the Xiang Shan Hotel. It was just that I couldn't properly register it in my brain. It had never happened to me before.

And I think I had truly known it when we had been discussing childhood pets and Wu Shu said there had been a family dog. I asked her what happened to it.

'We ate it,' she replied.

'*Why*, Wu Shu?' I blustered.

'Because it was getting old ...'

I knew then, at that moment, that I loved her. She had said it so simply, so guilelessly. A definite Wu Shu moment. She told me much later that she herself had not actually eaten the family dog, but her father and three elder brothers had loved the meat and smilingly wolfed it down.

We strolled down the wide boulevard hand in hand. This drew the familiar stares. We knew that one girl in a similar position had been shouted at and accused of being a prostitute. But one look at Wu Shu, who never wore make-up and always dressed conservatively, surely dispelled such thoughts; no one ever said a word to her in the street.

But something was troubling her, I could see, so we ducked into an international hotel so we could have a quiet chat. Wu Shu slowly and thoughtfully stirred the sour yoghurt she ordered, then dissolved into tears. It was her suitor, the young 'food processing man'. He apparently telephoned her while I was having dinner with the Zhang family and threatened suicide. Said he was going to throw himself into one of Beijing's ornamental lakes.

I knew Wu Shu well enough to know that she would want to do the honourable thing – go to see him and somehow make things all right. But a feeling of irritation quietly seeped into my stomach and I immediately hardened my heart towards him. For one thing, I knew the Chinese relished stories of unrequited love. Somehow they found it romantic. In my view it was not romantic; it was plain wrong. It took two to tango and if one potential partner said 'no', that was it. End of story. *No story.*

'Wu Shu,' I began quietly, 'if a man has to ask why you could fall in love with someone you had known only a short while, instead of one you had known many years, he could never possibly understand. It is simply beyond his experience.'

She nodded slowly and said she would write him a short sincere letter that left him in no doubt that was the end of the matter. I was sorry that it had upset her and she had cried, but in the end – well, that's showbusiness, as they say.

Suddenly she turned and looked at me in a haunted way and said, 'Adrian, even if something goes wrong and you cannot return at Christmas, I will understand, OK?'

I said nothing. Where had that come from I wondered?

She then changed the subject back to the young man and said, 'I told him last night that I had decided to spend the rest of my life with you and would follow you wherever you decided to go.'

At last she dried her tears and smiled, 'Adrian. I love you, but I will never say it often. I am the lady.'

Yes, there was no doubt about that simple fact. Wu Shu was a lady. Later we returned to her dormitory and I could feel here the everyday Wu. She quietly showed me her collection of rare stamps and I promised to send her more from England when I returned. She looked around the room she shared with another girl and told me how simple her life had been until I had 'disturbed' her. She was wistful about that simple life now and I could understand. She looked down at me as I sat on her bed; her mosquito net was draped over one shoulder and she gazed into my eyes, 'Adrian, your *eye* spirit ... I love it very much, you know?'

'I love you too, my little Chinese girl,' I said.

At the same time I pulled her deep into my arms and hugged and hugged this little angel until I thought I would surely crush her.

'I may be tiny, but I can be a very strong Chinese girl, too, my *Mister* Webber, do you understand?' she said teasingly.

That evening William, Wu Shu and I cycled up the hill to the Wofosi Hotel located in a sacred part of the Garden. It included a shrine to the sleeping Buddha and received regular pilgrims from all over China. It had many ancient trees and enjoyed a special atmosphere. It was also noticeably cooler than in the lower part of the Garden. We were joined in the banqueting room by many of the propagation staff I first worked with and – yes – they teased me with imitations of a large foreigner trying to sit down on a low stool. More discreet were the design office girls who all looked tremendously poised and elegant. Senior members of the Beijing Parks Bureau were there, including the director himself, who was very friendly, along with the Garden's political officer. Ex-People's Liberation Army and compulsive smoker, he was an official member of the communist government and had the same formal status as Director Zhang, although he clearly reported elsewhere. We had met a few times and he had always been very friendly. It was he who had dubbed me *Da hu zi* (Big Beard) and almost certainly would have been briefed about Wu Shu and me by now.

The director was soon on the karaoke machine singing tender love songs with no musical accompaniment. Everyone was quiet as his voice soared and dipped – one song was clearly designed to tell a story because I kept getting odd looks from the very sober design girls. Apparently it told how a Chinese tiger saved a foreign gentleman in the mountains of China and how despite its natural fierceness he fell in love with the tiger.... The design girls were talking among themselves now before waving at me.

Wu Shu had carefully positioned herself well away from me at the far end of the table which, in view of her director's choice of songs, was just as well. Clearly no one had any real idea of who the Chinese girl in the songs – she was given no name – was. William, the epitome of discretion, just smiled at everyone. Once, towards the end of the evening the director kindly showed Wu Shu and me into a private room for a rest – until everyone burst in and pulled us out again. My last night in China was a wonderful send-off and I was more than a little drunk.

Eventually, everyone spilled out into the still warm, perfumed night, trying to stay upright on their bicycles as they set off. Some of the girls hitched rides by plopping themselves, side saddle, on to the back of the bikes before floating off down the long, winding, black road. Miss Han tried to get on mine, but soon changed her mind as I rocked uncertainly from side to side. Soon, having found a more steady rider, she too quietly disappeared into the night. The calm balmy air was filled with shouts and songs as we meandered our way down that enchanted hill.

When I eventually arrived back in the research building I said my goodbyes to Mr Huang and gave him his gift. It was all very awkward. There seemed to be too much going through his mind every time we met, but for the life of me I couldn't fathom what it was. The only time I ever met his wife she had, if anything, been even more hostile. But why? He accepted his gift of a fountain pen with the usual Chinese modesty, or was it complete indifference? It was difficult to tell.

The little caretaker was more effusive in accepting his gift. I bought him a heavy lighter as he usually used matches. He grinned as he weighed it in his thin bony hand. Wu Shu said later that, apart from the silk scarf I bought him a few weeks earlier, it was probably the most expensive thing he had ever owned as he came from a poor peasant family in a remote province. I was inordinately pleased to hear this until she then added, 'In fact, it was the very least you could do after everything this poor man has done for *you*, Adrian.'

Later on I climbed the stairs, more steady now, up to Wu Shu's office. Alone at last we fell into each other's arms. I thought Wu

Shu was going to say something romantic, but instead she said, in her stern mock-serious way, 'You smell too much of *pijou*, you are English drunkard, *not* English gentleman!'

'English gentleman, English gentleman! It's all Chinese girls ever talk about!' I cried. 'Besides, I thought you said I was your English *Quercus robur* [oak tree]?'

'No. You are my *rotten* English oak. And bad man!' she said flatly.

I laughed and said, 'Oh I see, this is Chinese *xio jie* joke time again, eh?' But as I looked down at my tiger, she was already weeping. How could I do this to such a sweet person as Wu Shu? Her sobbing slowly abated and I laid down beside her and pulled her beautiful little head on to my chest. I could see her tiny dark eyes in the moonlight that now streamed through the open window.

As she lay quietly in my arms, she told me how the director's second song was chosen with great care. The song, quite famous in China, was about the intense love a man and woman felt for each other who were destined to face many difficulties that would test them both hard. No wonder the design girls had given me such quizzical looks, when the previous song referred to how love recognized no boundaries. And this had been in front of all the senior staff from the Parks Bureau too, including its director, no less.

'Adrian, you came here so fast and you leave so quickly. *Why?*'

I kissed her little face and hugged her to me.

'You are a *cruel* man. Cruel to this little Chinese girl ...' she whispered.

With those words stinging in my ears, I trudged back to my bare room to spend my last night in China. Tomorrow a car would take me to the airport. It had again been decided that Wu Shu would accompany me as interpreter.

First thing in the morning she was there leaning against my doorway. She quietly watched me finish my packing.

'Chinese girl is here to help bad man pack his luggage. Today he returns to his England,' she said with determined casualness. She placed my battered straw hat pertly on her pretty head and smiled. She was wearing the dress that she knew I loved the best. It was cotton, aquamarine with dainty white spots. I took a couple of quick photos of her.

'No gift for Miss Wu, you know that and you know why, of course.'

Wu Shu smiled and whispered sternly, 'I would not want one, completely inappropriate, even for English "braggadocio" like *Mister* Webber, rotten to the core of his English oak, as he undoubtedly is!'

'That was quite a speech, Miss Wu, and I hope you are going to keep it up and write to me often, *little* Chinese girl.'

'Listen, bad man, if you write once a week I write once a fortnight. If you send me eight letters I will send you four, do you understand, my *Mister* Webber?'

As we neared Beijing International Airport we both became calmer. I would return in three months at the end of the autumn term and could probably stay for as long as a month before I had to return for the college's spring term, in the New Year.

Check-in could only be accessed through a security gate so we had to say our farewells straight away. We shook hands formally. The Chinese never seemed to kiss in public and Wu Shu, for one, would have been affronted to say the least. I passed through security and saw the girl that I loved standing there alone, impassive but ravishingly beautiful. I handed my passport to the uniformed white-gloved official and looked back one last time.

She was gone.

CHAPTER 15

笑一笑，十年少

'A smile will gain you ten years more of life'

It was nine in the morning and my hands were still shaking too much to eat the breakfast in front of me. Again I tried but it was no use, and so I simply sat there with both hands now clamped tight to my hot chest while I stared into space. It wasn't like this the first time I went to China; then, I didn't have a care in the world, I just hoped for the best and went for it. My big Chinese adventure. Now I knew what it would be like, and my whole body, if not my mind, was scared stiff. I was wracked with worry.

I wanted desperately to see Wu Shu. I had missed her so much. I hadn't seen her for over three months now. In truth, we had now been apart longer than we had been together. The only way we had been able to communicate was via letters, which took nearly ten days to arrive, and the very occasional phone call – which cost a pound per minute, and I had a quarterly bill of £320 to prove it. But this was nothing compared to the autumn term which seemed paralysed in its slowness. Still, it wasn't Wu Shu that I feared now. It was China.

When I had first returned to England Zhu Renyuan telephoned and asked me what I thought of his China. I replied that the more I understood, the more I realized what I didn't know. He laughed and said, 'Adrian, your knowledge is like an egg, it has grown, but your ignorance is like the egg's shell, it has grown too.'

He was right of course, but did that properly explain why my whole body was shaking now? Possibly, because I knew what to expect. Zhu Renyuan, my old classmate, went on to say two other things that were uncannily accurate as well as being perceptive. First, he told me that I had changed.

'China has made you calmer, Adrian. I always hoped for this when you first went out.'

True. And second?

'I also feel in my heart that you have found love in my China, too. Am I right?'

Again, uncanny.

'Well, if I had found love, as you say, who is the object of my love, Mr Zhu Renyuan? Answer me that,' I said light-heartedly.

He made a few guesses – Miss Han Xu, Miss Sun Yi ... but then I remembered that he hadn't met Wu Shu because he left China for England just before she arrived to take up her new post at the Botanical Garden.

'You haven't met the new Master in your Garden, have you?' I teased.

'Ah, the new Master, no. I heard that she is very handsome. Congratulations, Adrian, you lucky dog!'

'Thanks, Zhu, and I'll take all that as a compliment!'

As I slowly picked at the food I re-read Wu Shu's first letter after I left China:

Adrian,

Were you smoothly on your travel by plane? If you are in English time now? If your family and friends have said you become smaller and younger?

I felt empty when I came back from airport. In such a short time I experienced such a life, so different with before that sometimes I can't believe it. You came here in a hurry and you left so fast. Adrian, are you a real man? Although you aren't in here now, my heart can't be quiet as before. Just like rolling seas.

Are those halcyon days real? What is life? What is fate?

Adrian. Adrian. Adrian, where are you from? My god!

I try my best to calm myself. I want to go back to my life as before, but I can't. I still hope there always has a note under my door – I pick it up and read it with pleasure ...

The silence of dusk.

I re-called this song again 'Wherever you go, whatever you do, I'll be right here, waiting for you.'

Best wishes!

Love,
Wu Shu

I still found it heartbreaking to read, but it helped calm my nerves. I finished the meal – I needed the energy from the food for the ten-hour flight. I would be in China for just over a month. After a couple of days in the Botanical Garden, Wu Shu and I would take the train from Beijing to the end of the line – her home city of Xining located on the high Tibetan Plateau. The journey would take thirty-six hours and we would travel in a sleeper compartment.

My anxiety was probably caused by a number of things. Once you were in China, there was no way back out until your return ticket said so. And that was the problem. Once you were in, you were in. There were no half measures for me. No return to the familiar comforts of a Western chain hotel. Another problem was never knowing what was going to happen to you in the next month or so. And the day-to-day experience of being constantly stared at, being surprised, put me on the spot. Without the benefit of a common language, it tested my social skills to the very limit. Also, Wu Shu and I would have very little time to get to know each other again before being pitched into the social round, this time as a couple; we would be constantly on view within the Garden and then with her family. It was clear that as a couple, we would have to hit the ground running.

As soon as I met everyone in the Botanical Garden again, word would then spread about the foreigner's return. Then I would be off to meet Wu Shu's family on the edge of Tibet to ask if they would formally consent to me marrying her. None of whom spoke a word of English. Would they agree to my proposal? Would they even like me? Wu Shu's constant assertion of her three brothers' kung fu powers, and that 'They will fierce you, undoubtedly, my tender foreigner', did nothing for my confidence.

I shivered with anticipation. Another cup of coffee. That was the answer. That would calm me down. I had spent most of the previous evening carefully packing all the gifts I had bought, especially for Wu Shu's formidable widowed mother. She had not changed her verdict on me, I knew. It still stood as 'deceiver'. I preferred the original 'spy' verdict somehow – it must be the romantic in me.

The sun came up over the wing tip and then disappeared as the pilot banked the huge aircraft around Beijing airport. I looked down at the dark terminal below knowing that she was there. Her last note to me from China was short and to the point:

Adrian,

I think I'll live in my office from 20th November to your coming. You can call me day or night during this period with urgent thing. In case of this I have no other way. I'll stand chilly [in her freezing office] for you, Mr Webber.

The jumbo glided in before dropping its huge weight on to the long runway. As we taxied towards the terminal I remembered how on my first flight the Chinese quickly got to their feet, anxious to get out and get home; it was the same that morning. Over half the passengers on the plane were Chinese and in their twenties. I had done my best to help the Chinese mother next to me with her baby son during the long flight. We shook hands as we got off. Chinese children were adorable. And it was true – they rarely seemed to cry. No one seemed to know why.

I managed to find a trolley. Rusty, it just about moved, although not exactly where I wanted it to go. Eventually I got it moving and after a while descended a steep ramp and cursed loudly when it got stuck up against a metal barrier. Something made me look up, straight into the face of Wu Shu. It took me a few seconds to recognize her. She was wearing new glasses, her hair was longer, and her usually round face was thinner – but she looked as radiant as ever. She was also very, very serious and pointed for me to go left, not right, and to generally stop mucking about. I tried to keep up with her as she walked briskly out of the terminal to the car.

The director's driver was waiting patiently at the airport's pick-up spot. Clearly, the director had swapped the excitable woman driver, who always managed to embarrass me, for this much calmer, phlegmatic man. We were soon off and joined the usual airport traffic. I quickly glanced at Wu Shu who was stiff and ladylike. It had been no small act of faith organizing, even requesting, this airport pick-up.

The car soon accelerated as the traffic thinned out. I couldn't help contrasting in my mind the heated car and the bare scenery with my first arrival on that summer's day, travelling in the airless minibus when Beijing was at its hottest and most raucous. Then the Chinese lived their daily lives out of doors, but now it was a different story – everything looked closed and shuttered.

Wu Shu, I noticed, was wearing a very lovely dark brown over-coat and a fetching cream silk scarf around her neck. She also wore a traditional brown plastic hairband in her hair, which I spent some time admiring before being told to face the front with the words, 'Mr Webber, you ogle me ...'

Soon the driver's mobile was ringing. It was his boss, the director. He confirmed the package had arrived and where did he want it delivered? He was quickly given instructions on where to take me and soon we were pulling into the car park of a very large glass-fronted restaurant which neither of us recognized. I hadn't slept on the plane and had now been on the go for twenty-four hours at least. But I was back in China and that meant hospitality of the highest order. It was no time to curl up in bed and sleep the sleep of the gods. No, it was all smiles for a serious multi-course Sunday lunch, Chinese style. More miserably, my reunion with Wu Shu would have to await the end of the formalities.

Director Zhang was already waiting at the top of the wide stone steps of the restaurant, beaming a huge smile of welcome. As we went in he clapped me on the back several times and kept his arm around me as he signalled to his wife that we had arrived. Wu Shu had already dubbed him our 'Red Mama', the traditional term for someone, usually a woman, who success-fully introduced a Chinese man to a Chinese woman. Now our relationship would be public at last. We would be said to have 'held hands', signalling that it was a serious relationship. A traditional Chinese girl would only 'hold hands' once. More than that would damage her reputation, usually permanently. Other names would then be applied to her. 'Worn shoes' was one I had been told.

I saw the familiar face of Madame Zhang who smiled broadly and welcomed us by waving her hand. She was surrounded by her family. They were dressed for the winter and noticeably quieter as well. Muted. The change of seasons had slowed everyone down. It was like being reintroduced to someone at a formal business meeting whom you had first met at a lively party.

Director Zhang discreetly showed us over to a separate banquette so we could be alone. Wu Shu was, if anything, even *more* stiff and formal than she had been at the airport which I didn't really understand. I thought, perhaps naively, that once I returned, all anxieties about gossip would be swept away. But she realized already that there would necessarily be an uncom-fortable period of adjustment as people came to understand our situation. In many ways, though, the time of year itself proved to be a great help to us. The Beijing winter was extremely cold and the ground completely frozen. This meant there were very few visitors to deal with and little physical work could be done by the Garden's manual workers. If the staff came in, it was only to sit around in isolated groups, with the men playing cards, and the women typically playing mah jong. The whole official communication system no longer functioned as it ordinarily did. And nor did the unofficial communication system – gossip – either. We saw very few staff and the ones we did were not ordinarily meeting and talking with staff much beyond their own department.

But inevitably word gradually crept out. This was confirmed to Wu Shu only the following day when a woman who worked in the Pay Office said, 'Why does the foreigner like you? Your eyes are so *small*. *Everyone* knows foreigners only like big eyes.'

Professor Yu, my old friend, had already instructed his daughter to help us when we arrived at the South Garden's only hotel. She carefully placed my luggage from the car on to her heavy black bicycle and wheeled it in front of us to my room, located in a separate part of the sprawling hotel. It was already dark and we felt the hot flame from the hotel's coal-fired boiler as we passed it in the cold blackness. But it was the silence, even more than the cold, that continued to surprise me as we walked behind the professor's daughter. Even the urban landscape was drained of all vitality. Life had ebbed out with the heat. It was replaced by the pervasive smell of burning charcoal and coal smoke.

The room was part of a long single-storey block and had an en-suite bathroom which was a pleasant surprise, together with a proper mattress in the room. Its most distinctive feature, though, was the enormous old-fashioned cast iron radiator which pulsed out all the heat you would ever need, even as the temperature dropped rapidly outside. Wu Shu would spend as much time here as possible, but would sleep in her dormitory on the other side of the main road. Anything less would, of course, attract an explosion of gossip.

The Garden would hold a formal welcome dinner for me tomorrow night, but until then our time was our own. With that comforting knowledge, we fell into each other's arms. It had been too long, far too long, and I couldn't kiss her enough. My little Chinese girl was mine to hold and I wished with all my heart that I would never have to let her go again. Wu Shu wept softly as we held each other close. All we were able to feel was relief.

Later the next day, after Wu Shu returned from work, we decided to split my luggage and take what wasn't immediately required up to her office in the research building. It was six in the evening and pitch black as we strapped it on to Wu Shu's bicycle and pushed it up the road towards Xiang Shan. The streets were familiar, but all the shops and restaurants were closed and shuttered as if for protection from the now biting Beijing cold. Occasionally we thought we saw a faint glow from a still open shop, just visible in the uncertain murky night. Our voices echoed in the deserted streets. And then it began to snow. Just flurries at first, and then becoming heavier and heavier. It was some time before we could make out the research building. Covered in snow, it had been transformed from hot house to ice house.

It was only 7 p.m., but the caretaker had already locked up for the night and so we banged on his office window to let us in. Bent nearly double, like many people who are accustomed to opening doors for a living, his face turned to one of shock when he saw me fall into the building behind Wu Shu. Clearly, the gossip hadn't extended to him. Not knowing what to say, I grabbed him around his bony shoulders and laughed. Soon he started to laugh, too, and pointed towards Wu Shu and then me. I nodded to him slowly and grinned.

From the corner of my eye I made out the form of Huang Yi Gong approaching. This I knew was going to test my nerve. After I left China, Wu Shu and I corresponded a great deal by post.

(Unfortunately, email was completely unheard of at the time.) But despite my spacing out the sending of letters every few days, mine to Wu Shu seemed to accumulate in the Beijing postal system before being delivered to the main building of the Garden. After that it was up to someone who was passing. If they were going to the research building, they would usually pick up the post and carry it over with them.

One day, unfortunately, it fell to Mr Huang to undertake this chore. He walked the mile or so to the research building, sorting the post out as he went. He soon discovered that the foreigner who had only recently left had sent no fewer than seven letters to Miss Wu. Later he knocked on Wu Shu's office door with a strange expression on his face.

'Why has the foreigner written so many letters to you, Wu Shu?' he asked quietly, but firmly.

'We are penfriends,' she replied brightly.

She snatched the letters from his hand and quickly closed the door. It was a long time before she heard his footsteps retreat down the long corridor and slowly descend the stairs.

Later that evening, she had just locked the door of her laboratory so that she could wash her hair in one of the large sinks when she heard a loud banging on the door. It was Huang Yi Gong.

'I invite you to have supper in Xiang Shan restaurant,' he shouted through the heavy door.

Wu Shu told him that she had already eaten noodles and was no longer hungry, but he persisted.

'I need to talk to you, it's very important! You must talk with me now!' he said sternly.

Once again, she told him that she had already eaten.

'You can just have a snack while we chat,' he insisted.

He continued to knock on the door for some minutes. Eventually, although a little frightened by then, she reluctantly opened it and pointed to her wet hair. She repeated that she had no interest in food and needed the time to write up an important experiment. He walked away, dejectedly, and then turned back and said, 'It's colder now, keep warm, care for yourself.'

Back in her office the phone rang. It was Huang Yi Gong again.

'I have bought some delicious spiced breads, they are still warm – would you like to try some?'

'No thank you, Mr Huang, I am just going to bed. Goodnight,' she said firmly, and put the phone down.

Knowing all this, I watched as Huang Yi Gong came up to me. He murmured something quickly that I didn't catch, but he didn't bother to repeat it as he shook my hand. It felt like shaking hands with a very dead, wet fish.

'Nice to see you again,' he managed eventually.

'Me, too,' I smiled.

I walked away and bounded up the cold stairs to see my old friend William. I heard his wife had eventually returned from the bosom of her family and was now living with him in his first-floor quarters. Man and wife. Because it was dinner time, I didn't stay long. I quickly shoved my gift of a bottle of whisky into his hand and waved goodbye. William, I could see, was a happy and contented man. And yes, his young wife, who I managed to catch a glimpse of, was indeed a beauty.

We carefully stored the unwanted luggage in one corner of Wu Shu's office and I saw, to my surprise, my steel-toe capped boots beneath her desk. I recalled one of Wu Shu's letters:

Adrian, you left your heavy boots behind in my room because of weight for aeroplane. I felt them like monster when I saw them in first glance; but it become so handsome when I polished it with my new brush. I was lost in thought when I looked at it. I want to know where you have walked through with it?

On our return to the South Garden we called on Professor Yu. Despite the cold, and his eighty-four years, he was as bright as a button and ushered us both in. His wife was playing mah jong in the next room with friends. She was apparently addicted to it.

Once satisfied with the hospitality he had carefully provided, the old man didn't beat about the bush.

'Webber [he always thought this was my Christian name], you have this girl ... yes ... now go! *Go!* Take her and fly her away to your England. Make her a comfortable little home but keep a room spare for old friend Professor Yu to come and visit you from time to time, eh?'

'Well, perhaps it's not as simple as ...' I tried to say.

'Leave now! Before the Chinese people and its government take another plunge into insanity and it's too late! Pay off Wu Shu's remaining salary. Get that done and you're off!'

In many ways, of course, he was right, Wu Shu was committed to paying off her remaining five-year salary contract if she left before the five years were up. I told him that he had a good point, but there were many rules and regulations with regard to the UK authorities as well as China's. We were to visit the British Embassy in Beijing after we returned from Tibet. The old man leant forward in his chair until he faced me squarely, 'By the way, Webber, you *must* call Wu Shu's mother "Ayi". It literally means "aunty" in your language, but it doesn't have the same meaning in Chinese. But don't forget, it's *important*. And you *must* get the family on your side if you are to fly away easily. Do you understand? Remember to call her "Ayi" as she is your potential mother-in-law. It's vital to do this. Do you understand, Webber...?'

I thanked him, although I was surprised by his almost desperate earnestness. Truly, he was a good friend. He understood the whole picture, whereas I simply didn't. Back in the hotel Wu Shu left me to have a quick jet-lag snooze before dinner and went to a local clothes shop to buy me some thermal long johns. These, she maintained, were an essential day-to-day clothing item even to walk around the city streets during the day; her home city, being some 7,000 feet above sea level, was an extremely cold and inhospitable place. Temperatures, even on sunny days, rarely rose above minus 5 degrees. I found it all difficult to imagine. Beijing at sea level, and constantly bathed in sunshine, was cold enough.

CHAPTER 16

老马识途

'The old horse will know the way'

Beijing's West Station was impressive, even at a distance. It rose behind the busy road and seemingly threatened to swallow everything and anyone who ventured near it. The driver eased through the bustling traffic before depositing us right outside the main entrance. I had only just set down our luggage on the pavement when two people tripped over it, such was their haste to get to the queue at the ticket office; in fact it was not really a *queue* – more like a seething crowd who had just heard the bank was in trouble and wanted to get their money out.

'Adrian, you should see this station at Spring Festival time. It has a million Chinese here at least.'

I shuddered inwardly.

Fortunately, we were able to skirt round the ticket queue as Wu Shu had got some friends in the city to buy ours when it was quieter. They had to use *guan xi* to be able to buy them in advance. I knew something of this ancient Chinese system which was based on an informal network of mutual back scratching. Someone did something for you; it wasn't forgotten – it was a form of debt that you were expected to repay by doing something in return. Each Chinese person had access to something that another wanted and so on. And it happened at every level of society.

There was an old cynical saying: 'there are only two types of

Chinese, those who take bribes and those who offer them'. Either way, it was with relief that we were able to struggle through straight to the platform and join the long queue waiting patiently to board the train. Even on the platform, I couldn't see the end of the enormous Soviet-style train which stood there impassively in the early morning light.

We waited patiently as the queue, which easily numbered 1,500 people, shuffled slowly down the platform. As the ticket inspector intimated later, my ticket was different to Wu Shu's and stated that I was a 'foreigner'. If there were 1,500 people, there were 1,499 Chinese and one foreigner – yours truly – on the train that morning and we were going all the way to Xining city in Qinghai province, high on the Tibetan Plateau. It was the start of my 'honey trip', to use Professor Yu's memorable phrase after he wished me the best of luck for this journey. The Wu family had known for three days now that the foreigner had returned, and was heading towards them.

Wu Shu's mother apparently became very quiet and serious when she first heard the news that I was back. We would be at her door tomorrow evening at 6 p.m.

The night before, the director and political officer had hosted a lavish meal to celebrate my return. It even included senior members of the Beijing Parks Bureau, together with William, Mr Chen, Mr Huang and deputy director Li Wei Ming, among others, each with their smartly dressed wives. A latecomer to the dinner was Miss Zhang, head of micro-propagation, who Zhu Renyuan warned me to be gentle with. Elegant and poised, she smiled to everyone before the director rushed over to slide her chair in behind her as she sat down; he fussed over her throughout the meal, as was his habit.

Although late arriving, Miss Zhang had been an early supporter of 'our cause'; at one crucial point she took Wu Shu to one side and advised her to ignore silly gossip with the words: 'You only have to look into your foreigner's eyes, Wu Shu, they are so limpid.'

In contrast, Mr and Mrs Huang, who arrived punctually for the start of the dinner, were definite latecomers in their public support for us. Their recent, almost Damascene change of heart may have had something to do with the director's effusive and now very public championing of Wu Shu and me: 'Adrian, my director respects your return very much. He also appreciates the tasks you carried out for him in your England.' (I had met some members of the Parks Bureau in London and helped settle them in soon after I returned to England, and I had been working to establish a permanent link between the Garden and my college.)

At the end they all toasted us and wished us luck, tactfully not mentioning the area where luck would be paramount. I was touched when the political officer toasted me as 'old friend of the Garden'. Wu Shu had sat next to me publicly through all this for the very first time, a special moment for me after all the previous subterfuge. It released something deep inside and we thoroughly enjoyed the evening. I was chauffeured back to the hotel, dropping Wu Shu, very publicly, at her dormitory along the way.

Our seats – or rather bunks – on the train were carefully labelled as to which carriage and section within it we were to use. Spotlessly clean and comfortable, each carriage was provided with one stepped entrance and was monitored by a smartly uniformed female member of staff. Each wore a military beret on the side of the head with impeccably groomed hair beneath. They did not move, but instead stood to attention ramrod straight and gave the distinct impression that no nonsense would be tolerated. And no quarter given. We were not going to be treated as paying customers. No, we were lucky to be allowed on the train and that was that.

There were three classes of travel on the huge long-haul train. First class, if they called it that – which somehow I doubted – had four berths within a luxurious, closed compartment. It was lockable from inside and therefore theft could be prevented when the occupants were asleep, especially at night. Middle class, which was ours, consisted of six bunks, three on each side, with a small metal ladder to get to the upper bunks if you wished to sleep or merely lie down during the day. Ordinarily, all six occupants would share the bottom two beds to sit on during the long day. The lowest class consisted of a plain wooden seat with no sleeping facility. It was known simply as 'hard seat'. Everyone in the middle- and lower-class sections was aware of the risks of theft, and a system in which we all kept watch on each other's belongings was soon established. You were also expected to take a turn in filling the huge hot water flask that the six occupants shared.

Wu Shu settled us both in and started to go through an enormous bag that she had been very protective of from the first moment we got out of the Garden's car. It was the food bag. Before the other occupants got on, she went through everything, pulling out packet after packet of dried noodles, jars of pickles and sauces, all manner of breads, and at least a dozen hard-boiled eggs. When I asked if there was any meat, she plunged her arm back into the enormous bag and pulled out a sort of saveloy sausage that was the size of an elephant tusk.

I nodded my thanks. No problem in the protein department, I thought to myself, as she continued to sort everything out on the little table. The longest train ride I had ever taken until now was from London to Swansea, so I was clearly out of my depth here. Piped music started up from speakers set high in the ceiling. It was the usual Chinese military style that was sung by heavily made-up women on television, usually middle-aged, in full officer uniform and cap. There was nothing offensive about it, except that they persisted in playing it until it was the official time for lights out around 10.30 that night. By then, even I had begun to learn the words.

Wu Shu had already made two bowls of steaming noodles for our breakfast and was slicing rounds off the huge sausage as two other passengers joined us. For some reason there had been two unoccupied bunks, despite the train otherwise being full. The newcomers were two girls. One, quite young, and still a student, was going home to Xi'an city to spend time with her retired parents. The other girl was much older and was going for an interview to join the People's Liberation Army at Lanzhou, the last stop before Xining. She was a bit cagey about it, probably because it was a garrison town where the Chinese always believed the Russians, if they ever invaded, would advance through. Chinese engineers had even changed the gauge of the railway track so that it differed from the Russian one, making it difficult for them to transfer heavy military equipment into China. The Lanzhou valley was still a very sensitive military area for the Chinese, that much was clear.

The low early-morning winter sun slanted through our carriage as the massive train slowly pulled away from the West Station to begin its long journey west. The sun made everything sparkle and dance before our eyes. Wu Shu was serious, but I wanted to sing out loud. My spirits soared. For one thing I had Wu Shu to myself, which was a delicious prospect, although we were hardly alone on that crowded train. But all the patient waiting and all the preparations had worked and we were now on our way. Wu Shu's mother had apparently recovered after initially being stunned by the news of my return. Whether this had revised her view that I was 'a deceiver' was hard to tell, but she now made preparations for our arrival. We would stay with her in her apartment, but as it did not have a bath or shower, we would use the eldest son's apartment for that. He lived the other side of the city.

The family was most concerned about the bitter cold of the Tibetan winter and whether I was prepared for it. All other matters could wait. I had already tried on the thermal long johns, which made my legs itch like crazy. Thermal gloves, a thick hat and a scarf would be bought for me when we got to the city.

But now, 'alone' on the train, we allowed ourselves to relax and couldn't stop chatting, just as we had in the summer; we simply took up where we had left off. We talked and talked as the long train clattered along, crossing enormous stretches of dusty farm-land and occasional woodland. We were still talking as our fellow passengers dozed off under the hypnotic spell of the train's metallic rhythms. We watched as the train crossed the Yangtze River, which was as wide as a sea, and continued to pour out our innermost thoughts, hopes and wishes. Despite the similarities in our personalities, Wu Shu was still a product of a wholly alien system to mine. She asked me if I was good at sports and I said only 'OK', but added I was very good at 'throwing the cricket ball'. Wu Shu's face darkened abruptly when I mentioned this.

'Adrian, do you know I nearly failed senior school because of this activity.'

'What?' I said. 'But surely you didn't have to throw a *cricket* ball in China?'

'No, Adrian, it was a hand grenade.'

And it was true. Apparently every high school student was required to be able to throw a hand grenade a certain distance so that he or she could help defend China if the need ever arose. Wu Shu invariably came last; she just couldn't throw it the required distance. She didn't know how it happened – perhaps the sports teacher owed the Wu family *guan xi* – but one day she found she had passed. Simple as that.

I told her about a little thing that happened at my college after I returned from China. In a small community, it hadn't taken long for our story to become common knowledge. At coffee break one morning, one of the landscape students had overheard a question someone asked me about Wu Shu. He slowly lowered the tabloid newspaper he was reading, paused, and then said, 'What if you have a kid ... and it's born with one Chinese eye and one ... normal one?' Everyone shouted him down for being 'insensitive', but I couldn't help chuckling – it was the 'normal' bit that tickled me.

Later, more for the need of exercise than food, Wu Shu and I walked forward to the middle of the train to the sole dining car. Those Chinese who were awake nudged their friends as we passed through the carriages to get there. Some were even specially awoken in order to watch the big foreigner walk past them. I hated this, but had already reconciled myself to it before leaving England. It was part of living with the Chinese and it was also part of what made me so nervous on my return to China. Why anyone should ever aspire to be well known or a 'celebrity' was beyond me at those times.

The dining car, of course, was not in the romantic style of the *Orient Express*, but it still had that friendly Chinese charm of good home-style cooking and a beer served without ordering one. We sat there munching the hot food and talked and talked. This beautiful Chinese girl was so at ease with me – sometimes I had to pinch myself. I could talk to her about anything. It was easier to talk to her than anyone I had ever met in England. I told her about some of the other letters I had received from China.

'Oh, by the way, a couple of the design girls wrote to me in England. Miss Liu asked me to give her regards to Zhu Renyuan as she didn't know his address. But do you know what she also asked me to tell him? Not to eat too much butter or he would end up as big as me! Can you believe it, Wu Shu?'

'Yes. Because she is *right*, bad English man!'

'Oh thanks, darling,' I said, laughing.

'Adrian, I am not your English *darling*, I am *Chinese* girl ... Who else wrote to you?'

'Miss Han told me that she had started a part-time degree course at the Forestry University and she had to do more English lessons. Her American teacher asked them first to choose an English name. She saw my name – Adrian – apparently it means "brave". Her only comment was: "but I don't think Adrian is a very brave man ..."'

The steamed plain rice and pork with *pak choi* was all they had left in the dining car, but the salty soy sauce now soothed my belly instead of disrupting it. Plain Chinese home cooking. The meal for two cost less than £3, including the bottle of beer which Wu Shu, incidentally, would not let me finish.

Back in our compartment our two bunk mates were already asleep as the main lights, together with the piped classical Chinese songs, had already faded. Wu Shu, who lay on the middle bunk across from mine, was also soon asleep. I could make out her perfect little head with her arms above it, framing it, her tiny cat-like eyes now closed. She had been brave, I knew that. Strong – and then I remembered her lashing the driver that day in the Beijing park. If she believed in something she stuck with it and took the consequences, once she knew what was required of her. I respected it. She had made long train journeys home like this many times over the last eight or so years, but this time she was not alone.

I lay there in the darkness. The compartment was too hot for me to sleep. The increasingly cold winter climate did not penetrate the heavy train. Our bunk area was not sealed off like first class; it had only a thin curtain for privacy, and so I listened to the rhythm of the train and the slumbers of the hundred or so Chinese in the carriage. I hadn't been able to count the carriages, even when we were allowed out at one station for a five-minute stretching of our legs, because I never saw the end of the train up front. Or the engine. Drifting off at last, one thought entered my mind. Why did Madame Mao, all those years ago, ban Beethoven? It didn't make any sense.

I was suddenly awake, but when I heard the familiar rhythmic clatter of the train I allowed myself to relax. A soft Chinese ballad was playing from a speaker right above me. But that hadn't awakened me. What was it? I looked down to see Wu Shu and the two other girls tucking into steaming bowls of soup noodles. The eldest girl was adding more vinegar to her brew until she was satisfied with the amount of sourness produced. Yes, it was probably that distinctive nutty piquancy that jogged me awake.

All the passengers in the carriage were more muted than yesterday, I noted with some relief. The countryside was different too. Gone were the small peasant farms or smallholdings with their carefully tilled fields. Instead the scenery had become rugged and mountainous, with few signs of settlement. More grand. The low morning sun streamed through the windows once again, bleaching everything within the train into monochrome.

Wu Shu looked up at me and smiled discreetly. The other girls looked at each other and giggled. While I was still asleep they had asked Wu Shu what her relationship was with the big foreigner – her standard line of 'interpreter' was dismissed immediately.

'We can tell there is love between you. It's too obvious!' they said and looked at her intently.

Wu Shu gave in and told them the truth. And so it was with new eyes that they shyly greeted me as I came down the ladder that morning. Thankfully, they soon renewed their interest in their breakfast, and so I went for a wash and returned with a re-filled hot water flask that I nearly dropped as the train braked hard. The girls instinctively scooped up their bowls as the train screeched to a halt. I thought we must have hit something on the line, but I saw that everyone was putting on warm clothing and making their way out of the compartment.

'Come on, my *Mister* Webber, let's have some beautiful fresh air,' said Wu Shu smiling, and I dutifully filed out behind her.

The cold was unexpected and raw, and I fell down the small staircase that was put in front of the compartment door. I picked myself up and brushed myself down. The military-style attendant offered no help or reproof, but just stood to attention, aloof and expressionless. Wu Shu gave me one of her 'have you quite finished?' looks before laughing and shaking her head. It was now I understood the necessity for the long john thermals. My legs had already become paralyzed by the cold. The other passengers, including Wu Shu, had been wearing a pair of pyjamas under their ordinary clothes. You could spot the pyjamas when someone crossed their legs. Hadn't Margaret Thatcher been appalled when she visited China and noticed Deng Xioping was wearing a pair of pyjamas beneath his smart business suit during negotiations over Hong Kong in the 1980s? The man was only keeping warm it seemed.

With a sharp command from our attendant, we dutifully rejoined the train as quickly as possible. No dawdling now.

Wu Shu talked about her family, but particularly about her father, who she adored. He was always there for her; she was his youngest child and his only daughter. Wu Shu would send letters to him after she left home, telling him what she was doing and sometimes asking his advice. She had grown fonder of her mother relatively late in life. Her mother was the disciplinarian of the family; her father was more philosophical and relaxed.

Towards the end of her four-year degree at a university near the city of Xi'an, which we would later pass through, she was required to take an entrance examination to study for an MSc at the prestigious Shanghai Institute of Plant Physiology, Academia Sinica.

'It was the eve of Spring Festival,' she explained, 'and those who had applied for further study were asked to stay on after the end of term to prepare for the various entrance examinations that would be held in two weeks' time.'

'So you missed the beginning of your Spring Festival?'

She nodded. It must have been difficult, because Spring Festival was the most important festival in the whole Chinese year and it was particularly a time for families to be together.

'As soon as the examination was over, I fetched my suitcase from my dormitory and went to the train station.'

Later on, she explained, she had picked up the long haul train that we were now on to travel to Xining. No one drove a car at that time, so she hauled her suitcase through the snow towards her family home. Spring Festival was in full swing and fireworks began to drill their way into the sky as she walked through the gathering darkness. Families, muffled against the intense cold, called out to her lonely figure and wished her 'Happy New Year!'

'Adrian, do you know, the snow was so thick I could hardly move my legs. There was nobody to help me and I felt so alone until I passed the mosque, and knew then that it wasn't far. I was so happy in my heart when I turned the corner of our little lane and saw the house at the end of the street.'

She shook her head and tears welled up in her eyes.

'You see, as I got nearer I saw the antithetical poems on each side of the door in beautiful calligraphy, the best you know! But the colour, you see, the *colour*, was all wrong ...'

CHAPTER 17

刀子嘴，豆腐心

'Have a mouth as sharp as a dagger, but a heart as soft as tofu'

Many passengers got off at Xi'an, famous for its rediscovered armies of 'terracotta warriors'. But despite the recent influx of tourism, or perhaps because of it, the city was gaining a reputation for lawlessness. A rough sort of place, it certainly looked scruffy as we slowly chugged through it. Although it had been the train's second to last stop, there was still some sixteen hours left before we would arrive in Xining.

'What was wrong with the colour of the calligraphy, Wu Shu? What was its significance?'

She dried her eyes and continued: 'My father had been ill for a long time with cancer. It was his lungs; do you know he smoked all his life, those terrible cigarettes ... So when I saw the gate I knew he was dead. The paper of the decorations was *white*, you see, it should have been *red*. It was a time of celebration, you see.'

Frankly, I didn't understand it. Nothing made any sense.

'How long had your father been dead?' I asked tentatively.

'Twelve days,' she whispered softly.

'What! And they did not *tell* you? But that's *crazy* ...'

Then I realized.

'They *deliberately* didn't tell you, didn't they?' I asked. 'They kept it back. They didn't want you distracted from the entrance examination.'

Wu Shu nodded, tears welling in her eyes.

'Wu Shu ... that was very, very *hard*, you know.' It was all I could think of to say.

At the very end of his life, a lively young girl, who often visited another patient with her parents, had gone to see Wu Shu's father. Laughing, she had patted his arm and shouted, 'Wu Bai-Bai' ('Uncle Wu'). He raised his head one last time and smiled broadly. Wu Shu's mother was convinced that he thought it was his only daughter and he died shortly afterwards.

The family had decided to keep everything from Wu Shu. Friends of her father straight away offered to get word to her university and ask if everything could be delayed so she could see him for one last time, but they would hear nothing of it. The future came first. The youngest and brightest was to be given every chance to succeed and that was that. What I didn't quite appreciate was that despite their firm resolve, the family still missed and mourned him. The Ba Ba was such a huge central figure in the life of a family.

By now the train had largely emptied, and the staff seemed to have disappeared too. So we were free to roam the carriage and found some big soft seats with high backs to relax in with a few of the other passengers.

As we chatted, a middle-aged Chinese woman openly stared at me for what seemed like an eternity. Eventually Wu Shu got up and said something, tactfully, to the older woman. She was not in the least offended, but merely turned away to face the window; yet she managed to maintain her stare by looking at my reflection in the carriage window.

'Adrian, you must be the first Westerner she's ever seen!' Wu Shu laughed.

The train pulled into the dark station over three hours late. There were few lights, but Wu Shu saw her eldest brother and banged hard on the window glass as he paced the platform. He looked up, cigarette dangling from his mouth, and frowned. I saw the family resemblance immediately. He was the image of his dead father.

The middle brother stood behind him with a trolley; he took after his formidable mother, I thought. He was also puffing on a cigarette. They flung our luggage on to the trolley and, without a single word being spoken, we followed them out of the station and into the waiting car. It was pitch black and dark snow flurries whipped across the black car as we got in. There was little traffic along the wide streets of the sleeping city. After a few words with the middle brother about the train delay, there was a lapse back into silence. A couple of miles further on, the car slowed and turned into the large gated entrance of the university where Wu Shu's father had worked as a senior lecturer in mathematics.

A few toots on the horn eventually drove an old man, who guarded the gate at night, out into the snow. He peered into the car and recognized the brothers. The car nosed its way around a number of walls before coming to rest outside a tall apartment block. By the time we reached the third floor, via the dark unheated staircase, I felt dizzy. And the brothers had carried all the bags too. The brutal cold, together with the reduced oxygen level at the high altitude, unnerved me. It was pitiless. A thick thermal blanket stretched over the front door of the apartment. My head was still spinning as I was shoved into the heated corridor and then into a startlingly bright – from two long fluorescent lights suspended from the ceiling – warm sitting room.

My scarf was still over my face and around my head, but I was conscious of a lot of people in the room. Too many people, none of whom I recognized until a small woman, clearly in charge, bustled through the throng and stood four-square in front of me. She was wearing what looked like three or four jumpers with a tiny apron on top. I knew who this was. There was an enormous TV blaring out from behind them all. I recognized the actor on the screen immediately; it was Roger Moore in an episode from the sixties TV series, *The Saint*, speaking in perfect (but oddly) dubbed Mandarin. Bizarre, but at that moment anything seemed possible. I later learned that my 'Ayi' scoured the Chinese TV listings to check for programmes made in England. She had done this ever since the summer to learn about the English, hence the reason for Roger Moore on the screen.

'Ayi!' ('Aunty'), I shouted above the din. And then, more quietly, 'Ayi', as everyone suddenly stopped talking. Even Roger Moore had stopped talking and, I could have sworn, even raised one of his famous eyebrows straight at the camera before he and everyone in the room started talking Chinese again. This time it was even louder, and everyone was still talking at once. A couple of Chinese, each with a cigarette in his mouth, moved a little closer to inspect me, squinting through the smoke, until I backed away a step or two. I quickly looked around. *Where* was Wu Shu, I wondered? This was hardly the time to powder her nose, *surely*?

There was an impasse. No common language. But what to do? There was a bit of a commotion as a little girl silently pushed her way through the legs of some of the adults and stood up. Pretty in that familiar 'Wu' family way, which I recognized, she wore a denim romper suit over a heavy pink jumper. She couldn't have been more than seven. But now she took a few steps forward and stood directly in front of me, looked up, and without a hint of nervousness said, in English, 'Hello, you are *Uncle* Adie. Please welcome to you, if you please. And my name is Nan Nan, by the way!'

Complete silence from everyone in the room. And then ... applause! And they were still clapping as this sweet little girl shook my hand and then made a little bow to everyone gathered behind her. Wu Shu and her two eldest brothers burst into the room to see what the fuss was about, but they were too late, introductions had already been made. A feeling of relief swept the room. Again, as with my apology for the destruction of Yuan Ming Yuan in the summer, somehow in the Chinese, with the formalities over, everyone relaxed; they were now satisfied. Soon, most of the Chinese who were not close family began to leave; it was getting late. They had seen the big foreigner up-close with Wu Shu and something had happened which they perhaps could discuss later. Tomorrow, after all, was a working day.

'Oh, *there* you are!' I mimed to Wu Shu from across the other side of the room.

'I'm OK, *don't worry* ... And this is Nan Nan, by the way, *your* niece' – which I said with as much irony as possible.

Meanwhile, little Nan Nan had got my hand and she wasn't about to let go of it. I've already made a friend, I thought to myself. Not bad, not bad at all. Ayi appeared again in front of me and dropped a pair of heavy-duty slippers at my feet. I took my shoes off and went to put the slippers on, but she shook her head and waved me outside. I was taken into a small bedroom crowded with furniture. It was burning hot inside. She gestured for me to sit on the bed and, from behind her, someone brought a bowl, poured hot water from a flask into it, and then dropped in a small bar of soap. I took my socks off and plunged my feet into the scalding water and sat there. From behind the ruck of people at the door I at last heard the voice of Wu Shu.

'Adrian, you must wash your feet. It is very important for health, please understand. In winter, particularly here, the foot is the key to your body's well-being, you must understand this.'

Ayi, already bent down, was inspecting my feet.

'Please, Wu Shu, tell your mother she has very cold hands ...'

Back in the main sitting room some women in their thirties were preparing a low wide table for a meal while a number of children ran around. Wu Shu, meanwhile, pulled the gifts out of our luggage and gave her mother what I bought for her in London after obtaining the Chinese visa. She unwrapped the silver and a collection of expensive place mats that featured English countryside themes. They were all very carefully chosen by me in London's Bond Street, no less. Here in Tibet they were given a cursory look before being stored away in a cupboard in that now typical way of *not really accepting a gift*. One day I hoped I might get used to it.

The three brothers' gifts of Scottish whisky were received with more aplomb. The mysterious third brother, the youngest, was the image of Wu Shu. He was thin and handsome with a small moustache which lent him an old-fashioned raffish air. All the children clearly adored him and kept jumping up at him, demanding his attention, which he returned good-naturedly.

The whisky was carefully, scrupulously poured into small china cups. There weren't enough cups and so some was poured into china saucers. Wu Shu Bu, the eldest and now technically head of the family, made a quick toast before drinking the whisky. I wanted to say you are supposed to sip it, but gave up immediately. They had all drained their cups and saucers and waited patiently as they were re-filled. Wu Shu and her mother declined any drink and sipped hot water from thermal cups instead.

I offered a return *gan bei* or toast of *Wu jia ting, hao* which everyone pretended to understand, and raised their glasses and drank the whisky. 'Wu family, good' wasn't much, but it seemed to do the trick, or was it the whisky? Other people now got up to leave. The dinner was for close family only, which was understandable as there really wasn't room to eat comfortably with more people.

Wu Shu and her mother disappeared somewhere so I found myself alone with the three brothers, two wives, a girlfriend and a young boy, as well as my new friend, the adorable Nan Nan, who plonked herself down next to me as soon as we all sat down. Her little round face was framed by a pudding basin haircut while her very quiet cousin had a short crew-cut. They all looked at me without saying a word, and there was no more whisky. Embarrassing. But what to do? In the corner was my bag. I pulled it towards me and took out a pack of photographs of my family and friends. These were instantly seized from my hand and devoured, with the three brothers squinting at them through spirals of cigarette smoke.

Soon they were all laughing uproariously at the foreigner's strange life. Comments flowed between them, and the most innocuous things left them spellbound. Why, for example, did someone walk with a dog on a lead? It was stupid! Why was everyone dressed so formally? Unnecessary! And the red hair of one relative soon attracted attention and a queue formed for that particular photo.

Loud banging now came from the kitchen. I recognized the familiar sound of a couple of woks being worked hard and the roar from the gas burner; food was being expertly tossed and fried. Wu Shu Lu, the middle brother, was a very accomplished cook and quickly began to produce an enormous range of dishes, ferried into the room by the children. The Chinese at home did not worry about ensuring the dishes were served at the same time – each dish came out when it was cooked and eaten hot. I knew that Wu Shu Lu's mother had scolded him before we arrived because he had chosen to learn Russian, instead of English, while at university. 'What's the use of your *Russian* now?' she had demanded.

We all sat down on little stools around the low table. No newspaper covered my stool (as it did when I first came to China and fell over), so I achieved a perfect landing, just as a beautiful lacquered bowl of plain steamed rice was placed in front of me by the little boy who didn't seem to talk to anyone. I called *Xie xie* after him, but he simply ignored me and dutifully returned to the kitchen to get more food. Wu Shu and her mother returned and sat either side of me. Nan Nan was banished to the other side of the table to make way. Ayi didn't eat a thing, but sat there slowly going through the photos which everyone was still talking about.

Her little eyes, I noticed, missed nothing. Her wide mouth with its full lips, which Wu Shu obviously inherited, kept issuing statements or questions to Wu Shu. Each answer was considered very,

very carefully before she slowly, reluctantly, moved on to the next photo. I heard her ask Ba Ba (father), Ma Ma (mother, and oddly similar to English), Mei Mei (sister) Ge Ge (brother) Shu Shu (uncle) and of course Ayi (aunty) as she worked out who was who in my family. Once she finally reached the end she immediately went back to the beginning and started all over again. She went through the photos at least three times when I was present, but probably many more times when she was alone as she insisted on keeping them for the whole length of our stay.

Nan Nan, opposite me now, was working her way hungrily through a piece of chicken which had been cleaved through the bone. The Chinese knew where the sweetest meat lay and would never waste that flavour by filleting the meat from the bone before cooking it. Wu Shu told me of a conversation her mother had with the local butcher after she was widowed, which demonstrated this view: 'Miss Yu [a wife or widow always kept her maiden name], you are widowed now and so you will have to eat meat only. Bone, of course, is far too expensive ...'

The parts of an animal the Chinese covet are the parts where bone features predominantly. For example, with a chicken, the Chinese cook would ignore the breast meat, prized in the West, and want to pay the extra for a special meal using the wings, legs or backbone area. If a whole chicken was cooked nothing would be wasted; everything would be used and cuts would always be made through the bone to retain the flavour. In that way all the precious (and expensive) meat was used. The Chinese pride themselves on frugality – they waste nothing. I noticed before, when eating with the design office girls, that they could place a small joint of chicken in their mouths and strip the meat off it, before delicately placing the bone, now bare, beside their bowl. And all in the most ladylike fashion.

Although it was late the dishes kept coming; everyone was eating ravenously. The taciturn little boy, who was no older than four, still said nothing but just ate the food, which was more than his father was able to do while cooking. Eventually his father emerged, covered in sweat, and gave a little laugh as he looked down at the empty dishes. He must have expected this because he held a large bowl of soup noodles in his hand and placed it on the table in front of him. The youngest brother, Wu Shu Du, got up, went into the corridor, and returned with bottles of beer.

I looked up at the heavily curtained window and realized that nobody knew I was here. The Chinese immigration officials thought I would spend the whole month in the Beijing Botanical Garden's south hotel. I was now on the high Tibetan Plateau, alone with the Wu family. I knew I was to meet my test, but not yet. Not now at any rate; and I already had a friend – she was only seven but she could even speak English. Why hadn't Wu Shu mentioned this?

I looked across at the little girl. Despite it being so late she was as bright as a new pin.

'Nan Nan, you speak English very well,' I said to her slowly.

'Of course, Uncle Adie, I learn at school, why not?'

I explained that nobody had told me before I arrived, so it was a pleasant surprise.

'Wu Ayi [Wu Shu], she never sees me, she lives too far away. Doesn't know about my English. My teacher says I am very fast to learn, can you believe it?'

I could indeed believe it; she seemed to have an understanding far beyond her years. The 'Wu' effect perhaps.

We heaved ourselves up from the tiny stools and fell on to the couches and easy chairs. Nan Nan snuggled up to me like a little puppy and gripped my arm. I patted her head. She was so natural and sweet and I thanked her silently. It hadn't mattered a jot to her that I wasn't Chinese, and that was apparently that. What her mother and father thought, sitting across from us now, I could only guess.

Just as I began to relax everyone suddenly got up and prepared to leave. This involved putting on a lot of thick clothing, scarves and warm hats. Everyone checked everyone else to ensure they would be warm enough to face the cold. It was minus 10 degrees even during the hours of daylight. What the temperature was now, well after midnight, my whole body shuddered to think. My little *penyou* (friend), Nan Nan, made no such preparations as she lived with her grandmother during the school week. Both her parents worked long hours.

I quickly got up to say *wan an* (goodnight) and immediately regretted it. The whole room swam before my eyes and I sat back down straight away. The thin air punished all sudden moves; there simply was not enough oxygen to feed the body. Slowly this time, I got to my feet again but they had all gone. I heard their heavy boots tramping back down the staircase. Nothing had been said. They all knew why I was there, but somehow it would have been too impolite to make any statement of acknowledgement. Courteous, these Wus. They had shown great restraint and, with it, a certain respect. I was simply their guest. I knew that the dead Ba Ba, a product of a rich Chinese family, was respected by all for his impeccable manners and once again he dominated, even now, the family's partings.

CHAPTER 18

鸟鸣唱是因为有一首歌, 而不是因为有一个答案

'A bird does not sing because it has an answer, it sings because it has a song'

The blood on my pillow the next morning was only to be expected. It was the thin air combined with high altitude. I was assured later that it happened to everyone, particularly after the first night in that high place. Even local people who had visited a more low-lying area knew they would shed blood on their return.

Last night Wu Shu had stolen in for a quick kiss and warned me to expect blood before hurtling out of the room with the words: 'Please do not mind, Adrian, but I'm frightened of my mother.'

The following morning, I groggily pulled myself out of the warm comfortable bed, determined to get my first glimpse of the cold city. Everything was peaceful, and sunlight streamed through the window of the now quiet kitchen. It was spotlessly clean and ordered despite all the activity of the previous night. I looked out of a small window and saw nothing but other tall apartment blocks with high snow-covered mountains behind them. Then, looking down, I saw the playground of a local kindergarten full of Chinese toddlers running about, heavily padded and muffled against the cold. Strange, but why did the noise of children at playtime sound the same whatever language they spoke?

'Breakfast for my Mister Webber, an English gentleman, but unfortunately a rotten oak.'

I turned round to see Wu Shu holding a plate, with a radiant smile. She looked lovely.

'I can see you slept well, Miss Wu. Besides, I thought you told me that I was your tree?'

She laughed and said, 'But I am only qualifying my statement by explaining that you *are* my tree, Mister Webber, but it is a *rotten* English oak tree. My mother has prepared you this breakfast, by the way. She saw someone eating breakfast on English TV programme and has copied it.'

'So how does she know it was breakfast?'

'She told me the man who ate it had no manners. He was still wearing pyjamas, had not yet shaved, and yawned throughout the meal. His wife also scolded him – for getting up so late in the morning, she thought. Perhaps he did it often?'

'OK, OK, Miss Wu, you win! I can see your mother doesn't miss much, even with her tiny eyes. Now *please* let me eat, I'm starving, really!'

The omelette was delicious, although I would have preferred it without spring onions. A minor point. Bread turned out to be a cream-filled cake and there was also a large blob of soft cheese which Ayi had spotted a couple of days ago in a department store in the city. Perhaps that resembled scrambled egg? Wu Shu and her mother enjoyed a huge bowl of soup noodles while I, despite a fretful night, scrupulously refrained from yawning.

'Adrian, my mother says we must go into the city to buy you a warm hat. The one you have is too thin. And some thicker trousers too, maybe a jumper if they have one large enough. Your clothes may be good for English winter, but not here. It is too harsh.'

After we were all dressed ready for the big cold, Wu Shu's mother bent down and unselfconsciously lifted up one of my trouser legs before carefully patting it back down again.

'My mother wants to make sure you are wearing your tights, Adrian, it is very cold outside.'

The department store's main entrance was covered by two huge thick thermal canvases that you had to wrench apart enough to squeeze through. They were very heavy and greasy to the touch. No other customers were in evidence as we walked up the marble staircase to the first floor, which in the Chinese system was, confusingly, of course the *second* floor, the ground floor being the first. This perplexed me on first coming to China, especially having entered a lift to go down and out – there being no 'G' to press, only '1'.

Perhaps due to the lack of customers, when we enquired about a *mao zi* (hat) we found ourselves surrounded by at least five *xio jie* who all tried to help. Probably out of embarrassment, I started clowning around – throwing a hat into the air, then trying to catch it on my head.

My Ayi watched – at first with amazement, then with reluctant acceptance, followed by resignation. She went over to a table, buried her head in her arms, and sighed. Wu Shu, it had to be said, was far from amused although the *xio jie* laughed.

With a grey corduroy *mao zi* firmly stuck on my head, we walked on towards the city centre. We passed tiny shops and kiosks along the wide pavement, all heated by small charcoal burners; even in these everyone wore thick coats, heavy boots, and balaclavas or scarves to protect the face and head. Soon we reached the outskirts of the market area. Xining is famous for its outdoor market, or rather series of markets, spread like a web across the centre of the city, and reputedly the largest in the whole of China. It was possible to buy almost anything here and, provided you haggled, many a bargain could be yours. Wu Shu and her mother pretended to have nothing to do with me, the big foreigner, otherwise the price would go up rather than down. All foreigners were millionaires, after all.

Wu Shu saw an XXL warm jumper and bargained for it, but the trader wasn't to be fooled and kept holding out for the top price. Exasperated, she demanded an explanation for his stubbornness. He carefully explained that it was *she* who was being stubborn in not helping *him* get a good price from the foreigner.

'But we are one family!' she said, flabbergasted.

He thought about this for quite a few seconds before replying, 'But what about *China* ...?'

I started to get the giggles and walked away because he did have a point. But to my amazement, he ran after me and deducted 15 per cent off the asking price. Exhausted by the whole process, we paid him; there might not be another XXL jumper for miles and I was starting to feel very cold. But even after he'd been paid he continued with his complaints, to anyone who would listen.

I preferred the colourful food stalls selling live poultry and fish. There were myriad cages of scratching chickens and quarrelling fat ducks. In contrast, serene fresh water fish in bowls glided through their watery world. Ayi shooed me away before going up to one stallholder, haggled, and returned with a fish in a clear bag. Apparently it was for the pot that night.

We gave in to the seductive smell of hot noodles served in a fiery broth from an open-air stall. We sat outside, in the freezing air, gulping down the hot noodle broth; it soon warmed your belly and your face too if you bent over the wide bowl. I breathed in the salty tang and my eyes stung with the hot chillies and garlic floating on the surface, fried until they were nearly burnt. Soft, flat, unleavened bread was the only accompaniment.

The cold thin air meant we could barely climb up to Ayi's third-floor apartment with all the shopping. Wu Shu nodded to some old ladies who were exercising in the large sunny courtyard we passed through on the way to the apartment block. Her mother steadfastly ignored them, although they clearly all knew one another. For their part, the women all immediately stopped talking as we passed and stood and stared, open mouthed, at the three of us.

Apart from close friends and family, Wu Shu felt her mother was determined not to tell anyone about the foreigner and her daughter. If someone saw us and asked her later, she merely responded 'just a foreign comrade from work unit'. Whether anyone was actually convinced by this front was of course difficult to say. But they got no further and perhaps that was all that mattered to her.

I now had a routine. As soon as I got up and the kitchen wasn't being used, I would go in for a wash and shave. Apart from having no shower or bath, the apartment didn't have a bathroom either, so I used the tiny kitchen instead. As soon as I closed the door to strip my shirt off to shave, Ayi would fling the door open on some pretext or other, and come in. While I shaved she would be pretending to be at some chore, but was always looking up at me shaving. When I finished, it was time for her to bustle out again. She did this daily for the whole two weeks we stayed there.

Wu Shu, tactful as ever, said that she had noticed it too but explained that Chinese people believed that a house was not a proper home without a male living there. It was part of the *ying-yang* balance: too much *ying* (female) was wrong unless it was balanced by *yang* (male). I suppose this roughly translated into 'too many hens, not enough cocks ...'

I needed to write a number of Christmas cards and send them to England. Wu Shu Du, the youngest brother, watched me do this and commented that he found the giving of cards 'childish'; for all I knew he might be right, but we had to make our way to the city centre to post them. When we got there the place was heaving. There was much pushing and shoving. It took one and a half hours to send the cards. Why the post office was so busy was beyond me – it wasn't even a Chinese festival! However, there was a Christian church just around the corner and the Chinese seemed to like the *idea* of Christmas. But for them Christmas really was a Disney fairytale brought to life with a cheery Father Christmas dispensing gifts as if by magic. More importantly, perhaps, it provided another excuse, if they needed one, for that special meal out.

We eventually spilled out on to the equally busy street and made for Wu Shu Bu's favourite restaurant where the rest of the family were waiting. It apparently served the best Mongolian hotpot in town. With a cigarette in his mouth, he showed us over to a table where the rest of the family was already gathered. All his cigarettes were untipped, the equivalent of a roll-up. He also had another behind his ear in readiness, I noticed. The two little cousins were sitting together with Wu Shu Du, the youngest brother, and the one who most physically resembled Wu Shu. He always had a charming, easy smile, but from what I gathered he was the black sheep of the family and had given his parents their fair share of heartache over the years.

I knew that when he was perhaps eleven or twelve he went missing – he completely disappeared with a classmate. They left no note or message. It was over a month before word came through from a police department in Lanzhou that the boys were in a sort of lost children's collection unit, outside the city. Wu Shu and I had passed through it on the way – it was some six hours away from Xining. The boys had been apprehended on their way to enrol as Shaolin monks in the Shaolin Temple of kung fu fame, in He Nan province, right in the centre of China. Conditions in the collection unit at Lanzhou were foul and Wu Shu Du was later admitted to hospital in Xining in a coma. His temperature was off the scale and his parents received an official letter from the hospital that told them that he was close to death and 'to please make the necessary preparations'.

But he didn't die and he didn't become a Shaolin monk either. His family always believed that his brain had become overheated during the long period of fever and that this explained his subsequent bad behaviour. Now he sat there calmly, playing with the children seemingly without a care in the world. It was also quickly apparent that he was his mother's favourite, the Chinese prodigal son. For all her talk of her daughter, Wu Shu, which was really about her long absences, it was this youngest son who was at the centre of Wu Shu's mother's heart and he was the one she would forgive anything.

Ayi, it seemed, had a blind spot after all.

The owner brought over some chilled bottles of beer 'on the house' and made a great fuss of greeting the Wu family matriarch; Ayi, I noticed, made no effort to reply and simply ignored him. Her view was that all public restaurants were filthy places that she only visited, on sufferance, at family occasions such as this.

Soon tray upon tray of raw foods to be cooked in the gas-fired hotpot were brought over, carefully selected by the family cook, Wu Shu Lu. I loved his little laugh, a sort of chortle really, which broke out when he was amused by something. Both he and his wife were teachers and worked at the same high school in a remote town far from Xining. He taught physics, and she history. The subject of the Opium Wars was soon brought up by her, but I was an old hand at this now – I just pretended not to understand and switched the conversation to the 'return of Hong Kong' where I was on safer ground. We were to travel over to their school the following Friday, in Wu Shu Bu's car, and bring them back to Xining.

The stainless steel platters were piled with razor-thin slices of meat, particularly lamb, which the grasslands of the Tibetan Plateau were famous for. The huge Qinghai lake nearby was actually salt water, not fresh, a sort of lost high-altitude sea. It produced superb edible fish, unknown anywhere else in the world. Another whole dish was dedicated to the many organs and obscure parts of the cow – stomach lining, for example, all shiny and white (and, I discovered, utterly delicious). Everything was cooked in the large hotpot in the centre of the table. It was a matter of chance if you pulled out what you actually put in. Good food and good fun.

The next day we were due to visit the dead Ba Ba's memorial stone, high up in the mountains, in Wu Shu Bu's old banger of a car. The omens were not good as we left when a fierce wind kicked up and practically blew us down the street.

If anything, the wind was blowing harder the following day as

Wu Shu's eldest brother squinted through the smoke from the ever-present cigarette and the greasy windscreen as he tried to negotiate the best route up the mountain. The low cloud base didn't help, nor did the complete absence of road signs to indicate bends, uneven road, deep ravines left and right, the absence of crash barriers. Personally, I wanted to see a sign that said: 'Turn Back Now'.

Then, bang! We had a puncture. Wu Shu Bu quickly brought the swerving car to a halt and got out. Shaken, I knelt over the blown tyre and saw a hole in the middle of the front tyre the size of a small coin and around it the complete absence of tread. I pushed my finger into the hole to confirm what I suspected. The tyre was as thin as human skin. How on earth it had got this far was scarcely understandable, especially as we were halfway up a precipitous switchback mountain in icy weather. Wu Shu Bu chuckled as we changed the tyre for one in almost exactly the same condition, minus the hole of course.

'What does Adie think of my car?' he asked Wu Shu, who now stood nervously over us.

'Tell him it's probably the *worst* car I have ever been in during my *entire* life and I've been in some pretty rough ones over the years, mostly mine, believe me ...'

He was still choking on his laughter as we all climbed back in, completely frozen, just in time for his mother to give him an earful about the state of his car. What he needed, she told him, was an *Audi* car, they were sensible. Their tyres didn't burst. She had seen the adverts on TV. This only made Wu Shu Bu laugh all the more. I realized that I liked it when the Wu family laughed. Somehow, I thought, they were starting to, well, lighten up a bit. Nan Nan, who sat directly behind her father, started laughing too. Soon everyone was laughing, and so it was with a happy crew that at last we set off again on our perilous quest.

Ayi managed to light some candles, encased as they were in metal tubes on that high, blustery, mountain. She also burned handfuls of fake money for her dead husband. The Chinese believe that the departed can then spend the money in heaven. Nan Nan also lit a tiny candle for the beloved grandfather who cherished her as an infant. In the hospital, when hope for him was fading, a younger brother travelled all the way from Shanghai, forty-eight hours by train, to see him. He carried with him a live turtle in a clay pot. Turtle meat was considered good Chinese medicine for the very sick and he travelled with high hopes until he stood by his brother's bedside and realized it was far too late.

Safely back down the mountain, we spotted a mutton kebab stall and pulled over. As we got out of the car, the vendor immediately used his bellows to heat up the coals in the brazier. Wu Shu Bu reeled off a list of orders, before sitting down on the cold open bench. No one would join him, except me. Two large plates filled with long cold ribs of mutton were brought over, together with bowls of hot chilli sauce. I watched as Wu Shu's brother eagerly coated the ribs with the sauce before stripping the chewy meat from the long bone. I did the same. With his plate piled high with bare bones, he then called for the next course.

This eldest brother worked for the recently built huge hydroelectric dam powered by the mighty Yellow River, sister to the more well-known, but still local, Yangtze River. The dam provided for all the electricity needs of three provinces and their 80 million souls. He had negotiated a reduction in hours to pursue business interests with his formidable wife, helped by the new economic reforms in China.

Eight long skewers were placed squarely in front of us. Fascinated, I watched Wu Shu Bu put the skewer sideways to his mouth before pulling it all the way along the side of his mouth. As he did this he pulled the cubes of meat into his mouth with his teeth. He didn't even pause for breath before performing the same trick on the next one. Astonished, I nibbled a few cubes before I got the hang of it. Already, though, Wu Shu Bu was calling for another round which I was forced to decline.

The girls, meanwhile, stood around chatting; they clearly were not interested in any of the proceedings. Wu Shu, famous in her family for the dislike of any lamb product, had endured the scorn of her three older brothers during childhood – their joint response was to describe her as *Yaong Shi Dan*, meaning, roughly translated, 'Sheep's dung'. They were more charming now, I could tell! The brothers' nickname contrasted sharply to the one applied to her by her father as soon as she was born: *qian jin*, which translates literally as 'One Thousand Pieces of Gold'. Wu Shu's mother, for her part, often described her only daughter as ugly when she was growing up. This her father could not tolerate and it was a constant source of disagreement and friction between the couple. Another example of the 'knife mouth', I thought, with little evidence of the compensating 'tofu heart'. But, as they say, the past is a different country; they do things differently there …

'Xiao Shu! … *Xiao Shu!*' [Little Shu.]
Wu Shu Lu's loud shout for his sister not only led to me jumping out of my skin, but made me put down the knife I had just picked up.

Wu Shu stood in the kitchen doorway. 'Adrian, put that knife down this minute. What are you doing? *What* … trying to help! You are our *guest*. You cannot possibly help Xio Lu, now come out of the kitchen this second. You are embarrassing him. Please go into the sitting room – dinner will be served shortly.'

And yes, dinner was soon served, cooked solely by Wu Shu Lu once again. More confident now, I used my chopsticks to place some food into Wu Shu's bowl. This instantly drew a sharp word from her mother. 'Xiao Shu, your skill is better than his [with chopsticks] – you should serve *him*.'

And on another occasion, with chopsticks again, her mother watched Wu Shu carefully over dinner and kept nodding knowingly to herself.

'I always knew my Xiao Shu would live far from her home, do you know how I know?' she asked lightly … insinuatingly.

I just shook my head.

'Look, look how she holds her chopsticks – always at their very ends ...'

I looked down and, sure enough, Wu Shu *was* holding her chopsticks, not in the middle as most people did, but right at their very tips. Uncanny.

Chinese families, I began to notice, never seemed to kiss one another or show any affection in public; nor really in private, either. True, there was a lot of same-gender public hand-holding which, for my taste, seemed to be going too far the other way. But kissing *anyone*, no matter who they were, was definitely taboo. I was particularly struck by how the eldest brother treated his sweet little daughter, Nan Nan, when she went to bed. He was offhand to the point of callous with her: banging open her bedroom door and then just slinging an extra blanket on top of her, as she climbed into bed. Job done, he slammed the door behind him without any 'goodnights', let alone a story, and returned to his beer. No bedtime story or even a goodnight kiss. And yet the children seemed perfectly well adjusted, and gentle even. A paradox, really.

When I remarked about this to Wu Shu she merely smiled, 'He was just showing off to the foreigner! He adores Nan Nan, but in front of you he wanted to appear manly, so you would respect him. He was always showing off as a boy and Ba Ba chided him for it; yes, Ba Ba told him that he would rather be the head of a chicken than the tail of a peacock!'

It was then that I remembered a picture of him in Wu Shu's stout little photo album. He was in full PLA officer uniform, striking a heroic pose. I was impressed, until she told me he had simply borrowed the uniform from an army friend.

The following day Wu Shu and I walked together along the embankment of the frozen Huang Shui River, a tributary of the nearby Yellow River, while her mother had her afternoon nap. I bought us each a tin of the familiar almond milk I had enjoyed in the summer. The elderly vendor told Wu Shu that I was the first foreigner he had ever served. I nodded and smiled. We walked on; it was the first time we had been alone since our arrival.

'You know, Adrian, the news of your return to China and our visit here to my family will be common knowledge in the Botanical Garden by the time we return to Beijing, and many people will be surprised that it was to see me and not Miss Han.'

She said that Miss Han and I were seen together far more in public than she was with me. I put this down partly to the successful subterfuge that she had always insisted on; but if they had seen me more publicly with Miss Han, why had there been no gossip? But then Han Xu and I were working colleagues, after all.

Wu Shu stopped and looked up at me and we embraced tightly in the chill air. My feelings for this girl were so strong that I didn't know how to express them.

'One day after you left in September,' Wu Shu began, 'I was standing in the queue for lunch in the main building canteen you liked so much when I suddenly felt uncomfortable. I looked around to see Miss Han staring at me, obviously thinking something, and it was a long time before she realized I was looking back at her. She then looked down, embarrassed.'

I told her that Miss Han's fiancée, who she met at university, lived in a city far from Beijing. They were in a dilemma because he didn't like Beijing and she wasn't happy with the city he lived in. Until they worked out their future her weekends were free and she was kind enough to show me Beijing while Wu Shu continued with her weekend English lessons.

When Wu Shu and I returned, perhaps a little late, we saw Ayi in a thick black overcoat pacing up and down the street with a terrified expression on her face. She had been beside herself with worry after we failed to return on time. A brutal convicted murderer had escaped that morning from a high-security prison near the city and was still on the loose. The area was a favourite spot for prisons because of its remoteness and lack of transport links.

Wu Shu's mother refused to calm down even after we were all safely back inside her apartment. I wanted to mollify her. First, I handed her a sweet from a bowl on the table, but she turned her head to the wall. I offered her a thermal cup of hot water, but this too was rejected – so I offered her a piece of fruit from another bowl. This she shooed away, but I could see her heart wasn't really in it and so, finally, I picked up the TV remote control and gestured for her to put on her favourite programme to cheer herself up. She grabbed it from my hand, placed it on the table, and started giggling. To Wu Shu's complete astonishment, her mother giggled and giggled until tears ran down her face.

She then shook her head, got up, and disappeared into her bedroom to get a handkerchief. Wu Shu listened to her mother shaking with laughter next door with a look of complete disbelief on her face.

'Huh, they always crack in the end ...' I said, proud of myself.

The apartment's telephone was located in my bedroom for some reason. It jangled half-heartedly and I picked it up and said 'wei', the usual Chinese greeting when answering the phone. It was Wu Shu Bu and he seemed very upset, almost crying as I went to look for Wu Shu. After a few minutes on the phone, she quietly hung up and looked at me.

'He went out for a meal with old friends last night and they drank a great deal of Maotai – the usual nonsense drinking contests. This morning they all went to the swimming pool to sober up. His closest friend dived in spectacularly, laughing. After a while they realized he was not with them. In fact, after diving in he had gone straight to the bottom of the pool and laid there. When they got him out, he was unconscious.'

He lay in hospital for two days on a life support machine before he died, never regaining consciousness. Perhaps it was an omen, because a day or so later Wu Shu woke me up in the middle of the night and told me she dreamed that one of my relatives had just died. I didn't know what to do. Should I phone my family? I decided that it was probably just a bad dream and went back to sleep. On my return to England I found that a cousin who I was very close to had indeed died that very day. A heart attack. He was fifty years old.

That night, much to the chagrin of Ayi, Wu Shu and I ventured out into the city alone again, this time for an evening meal. Prospective son-in-laws were expected to spend the whole time with the family and eat with them. But I reasoned that our situation was different as we only had so much time to relax and talk quietly together. It would soon be Christmas and, strangely for a non-Christian country, the restaurants were now filling up.

'Chinese people are just using Christmas as an excuse to go out and eat,' I laughed.

Wu Shu said nothing, which I now knew meant that she might agree with me, but it would not be seemly to show it. After being turned away a number of times as the restaurants were full, we eventually found one that could take us, but it would have to be a private room. The room was vast. Oddly, we were given the whole private room treatment, including two *xio jie* to serve just us.

We were given the simple home cooking-style food we both preferred: two different pork dishes with vegetables and plain rice. But the bowls had been forgotten and so Wu Shu got up to ask for some. She overheard the two *xio jie* speculating on our relationship in a very earthy way. Standing unseen, she waited a few seconds before she interrupted them. They nearly screamed when they realized she was there, and both ran off together to fetch the rice bowls, returning with them, quite chastened. We couldn't stop laughing about it before returning to the hoary old subject of gossip. Wu Shu said that apart from the strange behaviour of Huang Yi Gong, when she washed her hair in her laboratory, there really hadn't been anything further to upset her. I was pleased by this because it nailed the lie Huang told me that there was much adverse gossip about our relationship and that it would reflect badly upon Wu Shu.

'Basically, Miss Wu, the problem with Huang is that he has always fancied you!' I said as lightly as I could.

At first Wu Shu shook her head modestly before saying, 'Strange, shortly after I joined my Botanical Garden, I visited central Beijing with Mr Huang and Mr Chen to get some materials for plant experiments. Mr Huang was our immediate boss. But after we collected them, Mr Huang instructed Mr Chen to return to the Garden with the supplies as he and I were required somewhere else in the city. Once we were alone he mumbled a little and then invited me out to dinner. He was my superior, so I didn't think anything of it at the time.'

She then told me that Huang Yi Gong spent a whole year in England at the Windsor Great Park, where my old classmate, Zhu Renyuan, was now spending his second year. He took an immediate and violent dislike to England and the English, spending all his free time locked in his room.

'So perhaps that's why my suddenly turning up in his Garden upset him so much? Another blasted *yin guo ren*!' I said.

'In fact, it was worse than that, Adrian. Ever since his time in England he has worn the green hat ... That is the rumour anyway,' she said quietly.

'Green hat? I don't understand.'

'It was rumoured that during his year abroad his wife took a lover, but he *forgave* her. If a man still allows his wife to live with him, we say he has decided to wear the green hat.'

Bouncing out of bed the following morning, for once I felt I was ready for anything. I walked down the corridor of the apartment, spooning the omelette I had just cooked into my grateful mouth. I could hear Wu Shu and her mother banging about in their bedroom and so, with a piece of freshly buttered toast in one hand, I threw open the door with the other. The strong sunlight streamed into the room so hard it momentarily blinded me, but in my carefree state I just laughed and bade them a very good morning. Today, the shortest day, was a Chinese lunar festival which by tradition meant the serving of the dreaded *jiao zi* dumplings. Ayi had been making different varieties for days now. They were to be served after the 'family meeting' tonight. I just hoped it wasn't a case of the last meal *after* the execution, rather than before it.

They both looked up from the inspection hatch and then went over to the small toilet and opened the door. The sewage pipe had become blocked overnight and every finger in the apartments below was apparently pointed at me.

'Adrian, they say that foreigner, you, must have tried to flush a scarf or handkerchief down the toilet last night, blocking the pipe.'

'But I didn't! Why would I do that? Have they actually found one or is it just an assumption?'

No one knew. But they blamed the foreigner, anyway. No such thing as coincidence was their thinking, I supposed, when tragedy struck. Anyway, we were off that morning to visit the local zoo. Wu Shu Bu would again drive us. The family meeting meanwhile was scheduled for 7 o'clock.

It was raining steadily when we arrived and the sprawling compound of the zoo was heavily dominated by drab concrete, but once inside the animals held your attention – especially one of the Tibetan vultures.

I looked at him and he looked at me. I shook my head slowly. There was no pity in those dark cold eyes, no love, no remorse, just death. He stood as high as an average man, his sharp horned beak matching the enormous talons on his bony feet, black and sharp. He continued to stare through me, then, with a high-pitched screech, lifted his huge wings, shook them up and down with great violence as if to intimidate, and screeched again. The wing span was impressive, but how the enormous heavy bird managed to take off and get into the air was beyond me.

The Tibetans had for centuries used the vultures to perform a so-called *sky burial*. As the ground for much of the year was too frozen to allow an earth burial, and meagre supplies of wood at this high altitude ruled out cremation, the deceased was cut up and fed to vultures at special sites or just left, in the traditional way, on the mountainside. Now it required a special licence, after a period when it was banned by the communist authorities.

While Wu Shu and her eldest brother waited for me, he passed the time criticizing his sister's dress sense. Her clothes, hairstyle and shoes, all of them he concluded, were 'ugly', especially the shoes. He apparently did this on all her routine annual visits. Once finished, he smoked a celebratory cigarette in satisfaction at a job well done. Wu Shu ignored him.

His wife joined us at the exit, having just come from the hairdressers and displaying a very high bouffant. She expected a compliment, but when she asked her husband's opinion, he laughed, 'It looks like you've got a Tibetan dog on your head,' he said gruffly.

She made a sort of Gallic shrug, told him that it had cost him a week's wages – and that *she* was very pleased with the result, thank you very much.

We drove on and out of the city eastwards. The market town of Da Tong lay some way off. There, both Wu Shu Lu and his wife worked as teachers at the large high school. We were to collect them so they could spend the weekend in Xining city and attend the all-important family meeting tonight to discuss the reason I was here. Soon the dusty plain gave way to cultivated farms, and woodland famous for its edible mushrooms. As we entered the town I noticed each house had an enormous bunch of bright red chillies strung from the eaves, slowly drying in the cold wind.

We entered the tall gate of the school and parked outside a series of low buildings which formed the teachers' residence. Wu Shu Lu was waiting outside to meet us, with his familiar broad grin. He embraced his elder brother before ushering us in to his tiny but cosy flat. It was warmed by a central wood-burning stove which his wife was stoking before placing new logs into it.

They were unfortunate not to have a traditional metal *kang* – a bed heated by a special wood-burning fire beneath it to keep warm at night.

The two teachers had to return to their duties for a further hour and so we had some time to ourselves. Wu Shu and I quickly decided to have a walk around the grounds, just to be alone together. It was an attractive campus, full of little gardens and frozen pools, but a little further on we were attracted by lively music being played very loud in the distance. A few minutes later we rounded a corner and were confronted by a huge courtyard where 300 or so teenage students were exercising to the commands of a stocky man in a tracksuit using a megaphone, high up on a balcony to one side.

He could not see us, but all the students could and they started to smile at us as they were put through their paces by the barked commands from the balcony. I took a few paces forward, looked at them, and then looked at the man on the balcony and nodded to myself. On his next command I stood on one leg, which must have looked incongruous in my corduroy hat and heavy coat. This drew a few smiles. On the next command I stuck one arm out and held it there, still perched on one leg, and waited for the next command. By this time there was a lot of giggling – the girls had their hands over their mouths to hide their laughs and stopped exercising completely when I started to topple over – so I beat a hasty retreat with a censorious Wu Shu, striding beside me, complaining about my 'naughty'.

On the drive back I bought a case of good Chinese beer, the one I knew the three brothers favoured – *Tsingtao* bottled beer. Quite expensive, but I needed all the help I could get to win them over. Wu Shu Lu had quickly heard about the big foreigner's antics at the exercise yard and confirmed the verdict of his sister: *naughty*. I hoped he wasn't going to hold it against me as tonight was the night. Wu Shu whispered to me the previous evening that her mother wanted the meeting much earlier and openly wondered why I hadn't called it almost from the first day. She had been champing at the bit these last ten days. It also vexed her that her eldest son, as head of the family, hadn't called it earlier too. My defence was that I thought we should get to know one another first, especially as none of them understood a word I said.

It was then decided to have the dumpling dinner *before* the family meeting instead of afterwards. A not untypical Chinese way of organizing things – decide or change everything at the very last minute. The immediate family was all there, eating without a care in the world. Trays of dumplings were brought out with their own special dips, but they seemed to share a common base of rich soy sauce. Wu Shu's mother, I noticed, bought soy sauce locally in clear plastic bags almost daily. Bottled soy sauce was completely unheard of.

The beer I brought to the feast was going down well, perhaps too well, because Ayi tutted every time I pulled a bottle out from behind me and topped up the men's glasses. She particularly scolded her eldest son, presumably wanting him at his forensic best to deal with the foreigner properly. As soon as the trays from Wu Shu Lu's kitchen started to slow, my hope-to-be mother-in-law was prompting her son, but Wu Shu Bu, who was clearly his own man, refused to be rushed, and continued to wolf down the remaining *jiao zi* like a true trencherman. For my part, I had given up after the first and just pretended to nibble the others in my lacquered bowl. The delay, though, was starting to fray my nerves and really I wanted to just get it all over with as well. Why we couldn't have had the meeting first, and the meal afterwards, was beyond me. Wu Shu said absolutely nothing to anyone and just sat there looking strained and not really eating either.

By this time the children were getting as fidgety as Ayi, so Wu Shu Bu sat up straight, pulled some soothing nicotine from a cigarette he had just lit, and cleared his throat. There was an awful silence, though, as he composed himself and Wu Shu prepared to translate – a stillness as though all the previous high spirits had been sucked out of the room and banished for ever out into the cold night air. But I was ready now. My speech was prepared and I was going to tell the Wu family what I thought. I knew this was not the time for sentiment; in a way, I needed to confront them.

'Adie,' Wu Shu Bu began, 'we realize that you have come a long distance from your England. And at no small cost to you. This we know and acknowledge.'

He was immediately interrupted by his mother who basically said 'stop all the introductory nonsense and *get on with it*'! But, to be fair, she already knew a great deal about me. Particularly due to the afternoons she would flash one of her tiny eyes at me to give me the once-over and then ask a searching question via Wu Shu. All the questions for the potential deceiver were based on the same, and by now, familiar theme: why do you like my Xiao Shu when you have so many pretty girls to choose from in your England? She had seen lots of pretty girls, apparently, on the English TV programmes she'd been scrutinizing since the summer. Her three sons obviously had different priorities: they were surprised to find anyone interested in their Mei Mei as she clearly could not even cook!

All this was pushed to one side as Wu Shu's mother now held centre stage. She bluntly asked, 'Why had I not talked to them formally before now, what was I holding back? Please answer this!' Her eldest son's attempt to put this to one side so he could continue with his speech was met with an icy dismissal. She then crossed her arms sullenly and waited.

I could feel the presence of the dead Ba Ba in them *all* now, not just his widow, who clearly still ached with grief; it was like a heavy slab of suffocating sadness that weighed them all down to the point where they distrusted the future. Nothing, in their eyes, would ever be right again it seemed.

So all eyes now turned to me, even the children's, which was heart-rending in itself. Wu Shu also looked nervous and bereft after her mother's harsh words; but that made me even more determined in what I wanted to say and I almost began to relax.

I told Wu Shu's mother I would have liked to have met her husband. 'My biggest regret,' I said, 'is not having met Ba Ba.' He was friendly towards the West and Wu Shu had told me that he had even taught himself English so that he could understand the BBC news and Voice of America.

'But Ba Ba's death is something I can do nothing about,' I continued. 'It was in the past and it occurred long before Wu Shu and I met. Perhaps we should not dwell on things we cannot change. When a close relative of mine was killed in a road accident at the age of seventeen the first words his father said to us all were: *Life goes on ...* This might seem hard, but I believe it is realistic and true. The clock cannot be turned back. We simply cannot change the past. All we can do is come to terms with it and, after a decent interval, accept it and move on.'

Each time Wu Shu quietly translated a sentence, there was silence. No one spoke, not even Ayi who now looked down at the floor, lost in thought.

'All I can do is help to make the future better! If, and only if, I am allowed to join this family I would do my very best to bring happiness to the Wu family. And I sincerely want this. Yes, I want to *marry* Wu Shu. And be a good husband, and father too, if we are so blessed. It was all I ever wanted ever since I met her. I love her. I know in my heart that I will *always* love her. And cherish her until the day I close my eyes, for ever. Ayi asks why I want Wu Shu and not a pretty girl in England? What can I say? I don't want to marry anyone but Wu Shu, no matter how *pretty* they are, or *where* they live!'

Silence.

'Words, as we know, are cheap, but please allow me, give me the chance, to be judged by my *actions*.'

This again was met by silence, but instinctively I felt it was a different kind of silence. The three brothers slowly looked at one another and then at their partners, and back at each other again.

Wu Shu's mother still looked down at the floor from her low stool and said nothing. All her fury and rage and frustration seemed spent now. A memory. She was clearly exhausted.

So it was left to her son to reassert his role. Again, he cleared his throat and began to speak, his voice now thick with emotion. The taboo subject had been put before them. It would be up to each to decide what he or she made of it.

'We have all seen Adie's character. He has not tried to hide it from us. We can understand it even though we understand not a single word he says. And so many words! Our view is "tacit". We feel affinity with you, Adie, that is all. Yes, you are a foreigner, we have many words to describe this, but it doesn't matter. What is in a person's heart is what is important. And nothing else.'

He used the word 'tacit' again. And then nothing. Silence. He had finished what he wanted to say. Wu Shu Lu tactfully slipped out of the room to the kitchen and began cooking again. Soon bowls of steaming noodles were being placed on the table and everyone, apart from Ayi, who shooed the food away, tucked into them. Noodles, one of China's best comfort foods, perhaps.

That night as I lay in bed I heard my bedroom door click open and quietly shut. Wu Shu, in her thick pyjamas and heavy dressing gown, sat silently on the side of my bed. I felt her gazing down at me.

'My mother asleep now,' she whispered. 'Do you know she cried herself to sleep ... like young girl ...'

I knew this wasn't the time to make any comment. Wu Shu quietly continued.

'When you first talked about Ba Ba's dying I was a little shocked and didn't know if I should translate your words, Adrian. It had a deep effect on me. You see I didn't want my family to be hurt by your words. That is why I was slow to translate and you looked at me; it was then that I saw in your eye spirit that you were trying to be kind to them – you wanted to lift the burden that has settled on them these past years.'

She lay her head on my chest.

'You undid this knot, I saw how they listened hard at your words. They had never thought this among themselves.'

I wrapped my arms around her and kissed her head.

'Perhaps even my tender foreigner had to be a little brave to win this Chinese girl.'

CHAPTER 19

雄辩只能给予劝告，但真理可以获取忠诚

'Eloquence achieves only persuasion, but truth brings loyalty'

The day started well as I had had a good sleep for once. Ayi heard me go into the kitchen and soon made an excuse to push open the door and busy herself behind me as I shaved. As soon as I finished, she disappeared again as was now her habit. By the time I re-emerged from my bedroom she was putting a mushroom omelette on the dining table – unusual because nowadays I made my own breakfast. She even made me coffee. That she had *never* done before.

The formal talk, it seemed to me, had confronted the past for the family, which was until now a source of guilt for them. If they embraced the future, it felt like a betrayal of the father's memory. This surely had to stop and now, perhaps, the process towards that had begun.

It was also Christmas Eve, and in this overwhelmingly non-Christian society I could still feel that tiny tingle, the childhood magic of Christmas, in my heart. Tomorrow was Christmas Day, and we had booked two sleeper train tickets back to Beijing. We would set off and arrive at Beijing's West Station early on the 27th, providing there were no delays.

While I ate I could hear Wu Shu call the Botanical Garden. She tried to get hold of Huang Yi Gong at first, but he was out. Instead, Sun Yi, my micro-propagation teacher from the summer, came to the phone very excitedly and asked Wu Shu where she was, and what on earth she was doing. The whole Garden was abuzz with the news of her trip to her homeland with the foreigner.

Eventually they found Mr Huang and he agreed to send a car to meet us at the West Station. Wu Shu was surprised by his apparent lack of curiosity. He asked no questions and made no comment.

Wu Shu Bu's car rattled even more that morning as we left the security of the city for the frozen wastes of the Tibetan Plateau, desolate, but achingly beautiful. The mountains on all sides were over 4,000 metres tall and completely snow-covered. The winding road was itself frozen and there was very little traffic around that morning. Groups of thin Tibetan prayer flags criss-crossed the route. Tibetans believe that by hanging flags in high places the Wind Horse will carry the blessings depicted in the flags to all beings. You could often hear them vibrating in the icy wind long before you saw them.

Our destination, Wu Shu informed me, was the town of Hu Zhu. It was here that the mysterious youngest brother, Wu Shu Du, now lived and worked. He would meet us there and show us the little printing company where he worked, producing beer bottle labels, from what I could gather.

After an hour or more of driving through stunning scenery beneath a deep blue sky, we entered the small town that appeared, at first sight, to be completely unpopulated and bereft of life. The main street was devoid of people or even a stray dog as we pulled up outside an undistinguished two-storey building. Wu Shu Du greeted us as we entered and then said absolutely nothing and lit a cigarette instead.

The manager of the printing works came out and invited us to sit down while tea was poured. A large, smartly dressed man, he had an easy charm and infectious laugh. He kept referring to Wu Shu's intelligence (he knew she had an MSc) – at one point rather cheekily asking the two brothers what it was like to have a younger sister more intelligent than they were! Everyone laughed, of course, but I reflected again on the nature of a Chinese joke: it pointed out an obvious truth which may or may not hurt the recipient, a form of 'better to say it than think it', perhaps?

We got up as Wu Shu Du wanted to show us his living quarters. I had to hide my shock as to how basic it was. It resembled a cowboy bunkhouse without the trimmings. Everything was so bare and utilitarian, made worse by the pervasive coldness. The walls could not have been painted for years. Its starkness was heartbreaking to witness – no homeliness, no comfort, no love. I was appalled.

A wizened old man appeared, who turned out to be Wu Shu Du's supervisor. He straight away fawned and fussed over us, which soon became embarrassing. Perhaps visitors to this remote unpopulated place were so rare they were more than a little flattered by being the subject of some attention, no matter how small or fleeting it might be? The whole area had the feel of the old Wild West about it. Its remoteness and loneliness made a visit, any visit, especially welcome, but particularly now in the depths of winter.

The little man bade us follow him. Wu Shu and her two brothers set off behind him; I followed more reluctantly, because we were going to a distillery nearby. It was the dreaded *jiu*, or straight alcohol, they made.

I could smell the *jiu* being distilled even though it was some distance away. The alcohol level was around an astonishing 59 per cent. Chinese men liked to drink it *with* a meal and soon started 'drinking games', even before the food had been eaten. Witnessing grown men retching outside restaurants in Xining was not a pretty sight, and at the same time seemed utterly pointless if you were eating a good dinner at the time. More than once I had been accosted by a drunk diner. They were usually good-natured and, because of the drink perhaps, had lost their usual shyness and just wanted to say hello, but you could never really tell. Tibetans usually carried knives anyway. Xining, remote as it was, could be a rough town.

The hot steam as we entered was a shock, and so was the intense heat. All the staff quickly gathered around us smiling, covered as they were by all their protective clothing; they left an old stooped man to guard the still itself. A very pretty young girl walked through the group of workers, holding a tiny tray in both hands, which she offered up to us, smiling broadly. On it were three large tumblers, each one more than half-full with a colourless liquid that had just come straight from the still. The two brothers clearly felt honoured, immediately shouted *gan bei* to me, and so with that and the expectant, not to say proud, faces of all the staff, I really didn't have a choice but to drink the fearsome stuff. And in one go too – as they had just done. It was slightly fragrant as I drank it, but it felt raw and burnt my throat. This made me do the time-honoured thing and I quickly bent over, coughing and retching, just as the two Wu brothers serenely accepted a re-fill. The staff all clapped for some reason and then returned to their duties. I staggered back out, with Wu Shu following discreetly. The jolting drive back was uncomfortable, but I felt uneasy too.

We eventually arrived back in Ayi's apartment car park where Wu Shu Bu, ever the one for the dramatic gesture, carved a beautiful arc in the snow with the car's wheels – 'my brother always was a show-off, Adrian, please do not mind' – intending then to silkily reverse into the vacant space in the car park. Unfortunately the car refused to reverse and eventually the engine just died. I got out into the snow; I'd had enough for one day and, despite the growing pain in my stomach, gripped the bonnet and pushed the wretched car back through the snow into its parking space with the last of my strength. I looked up as I heard loud tutting from the open third-floor kitchen window. Ayi was not impressed.

Ayi and Wu Shu Lu were still shaking their heads as we entered the welcoming warmth of the flat. It was our last evening in Xining and everyone had been invited for a big dinner. Ayi, together with a couple of old friends, had been helping Wu Shu Lu all day with the preparations and so it promised to be quite a feast. Personally, I was famished and needed some good home cooking, but it wasn't to be. What I also didn't know was that many of the dishes had been chosen with particular care. Apparently, from my very first evening eating with them, without saying anything they had scrupulously noted which sort of dishes I preferred; many of these had now been carefully prepared and would be served that evening. Ayi had whispered to her friends, conspiratorially: 'This is what *foreigners* like.'

The liquid time bomb was counting down its last few seconds within my stomach and, just as everyone sat down, in the buzz and excitement of the large family gathering, it went off. Bang! I got up fast, so fast I knocked my stool flying. Wu Shu Bu shouted *gan bei* to an empty stool and watched as I rushed headlong from the room, slamming the door behind me. I remembered there was a large plastic bowl for feet washing just behind the door in my bedroom, and my hand reached out and grabbed it as I slid through the doorway. I sat on the edge of my bed and waited like a condemned prisoner for the inevitable. I had already shooed Wu Shu out of the room with the lie that there wasn't a problem when seconds later up came a desperate unstoppable purge of my whole body. The sound of my retching obviously penetrated the wall shared with the dining room because I was suddenly aware of the bedroom being full of people each competing for a better look.

I managed to wave them away and say *chui fan fan*, 'eat, eat', and they reluctantly left, talking excitedly and speculating on what could possibly have happened to the foreigner? They didn't give a jot about the vomit of course. And neither did Wu Shu, who once we were alone kissed me full on the lips. Shocked, I turned away, full of embarrassment.

'Wu Shu! How can you possibly kiss me when I have just, well … you know?'

She didn't seem to understand the question and instead said flatly, 'I belong to you, why do you ask such a *silly* question? You are my tree but I am also responsible for you in my China, please understand this.'

Someone discreetly took my used bowl and put a fresh one in my hands. Meanwhile, Wu Shu's sugar was instantly replaced, to my mind at least, with vinegar; although to her, as I was to understand much later on, there was simply no difference, just honesty.

'Adrian, do you know that my eldest sister-in-law can drink *four* cups of this alcohol without any problem at all,' she whispered to me.

Only a tender foreigner expected charm, I reflected, vexed somewhat. The meal over, everyone was now trying to get another look at the ('what *is* the matter with him?') foreigner. The first and worst attack over, I now tried to entertain them with mimed imitations of a wounded animal taking its last breath before going under, in high dudgeon. They all laughed at the foreigner's one-man Christmas pantomime, which eventually just morphed into part of the evening's entertainment. My little friend Nan Nan crawled through the throng to climb on to the bed and was soon jumping up and down on it – which only encouraged the other small children to join in and do the same.

Wu Shu Lu, in the meantime, had slipped out of the apartment and bought me a woolly Father Christmas to cheer me up, which he laughingly tucked under my pillow – but the kids soon pulled it out and started playing with it. They didn't even know who Father Christmas *was*.

Wu Shu Lu, usually undemonstrative, came back in, told people to be quiet, and made a little speech to everyone in my bedroom and those out in the hall before slapping me good-heartedly on the back, which immediately had me fishing for the plastic bowl again. Ayi then took charge and abruptly waved everyone out of the room; the 'entertainment' was over. When the last person had left and the door quietly closed I flopped back down on the bed, exhausted. I felt terrible and the prospect of a thirty-six-hour train journey to Beijing didn't help.

Wu Shu Lu again returned and even tucked me in, chortling all the while. The Father Christmas was placed under my left arm and the light was turned out. Ayi kept coming in to check on me throughout the night apparently, like I was a little sick schoolboy. I was now in the second stage of alcohol 'poisoning', a sort of toxic listlessness that refused to go away for the next two or three days.

Someone was whispering in my ear. I opened an eye, it was Wu Shu. She was fully dressed and ready to go; Wu Shu Bu stood behind her, talking slowly to me before looking at his watch.

'My brother is talking as head of the family; please understand this, Adrian, they came to a final decision about you last night, after you went to sleep.'

It must be Christmas Day already, I realized. But what was Wu Shu talking about? What decision? I had forgotten everything for the moment.

'All the family discussed you last night and do you know they have said "Yes"; they approve of my choice and will sign the government form, and they will do everything they can to help us. Adrian, you look so strange, do you understand what I am saying? My family, Wu Shu Bu, has said "Yes" to us ... Adrian, *please* wake up ...'

CHAPTER 20

如你食用两袋面包，出售一袋去买百合花

'If you have two loaves of bread, sell one and buy a lily'

The train's familiar metallic rhythm strayed in and out of my consciousness as Wu Shu looked out of the cloudy window and then back at me, with an indulgent smile.

'How is my tender little foreigner? My *Mister* Webber?' she asked in mock concern.

I tried to sit up, but my belly ached too much and so I rolled on to one side in the bunk bed to face her. Then I remembered; when I had been only half awake that morning, Wu Shu and her brother had been standing over my bed, telling me things I couldn't understand.

'Your family said "Yes", didn't they?'

She nodded and smiled, 'They said they have a tacit' – that *tacit* again – 'understanding of your character and they think they can trust you although you are rotten English oak tree really ...'

And what clinched their assessment of me? Apparently it was nothing at all to do with my speech, my big appeal to the family. Instead it was my behaviour the previous night, when I was ill, that impressed them. The middle brother, Wu Shu Lu, had made the little speech in my bedroom, I now remembered, while I lay there, with the children bouncing up and down on the bed.

'Adrian, Wu Shu Lu told everyone that, despite all the discomfort, that your first thought was not to interrupt the dinner party, and after you apologized you even tried to entertain everyone when they could see you were grey with sickness. Chinese people appreciate that sort of thing, do you know? And that is what Wu Shu Lu said to everyone when he stood by your bedside. This they can understand and respect. Even my tender foreigner did not wallow in self-pity. Perhaps you have even become a *little* Chinese?'

'Wu Shu, please stop all this – it hurts when I laugh, you know.'

'Do you know what you said, in reply?'

I shook my head.

'You thanked them for their hospitality and said that you would always look after me and that you loved me very, very much.'

'I remember your mother running around like a two-year-old afterwards,' I said, 'which at the time I put down to that blasted alcohol. But seriously, she seemed so happy – or was it perhaps relief?' I asked.

'Relief mostly. She was able to stop *worrying*, for the first time since the summer. It was a very long time for her. She is widowed after all, Adrian, you must remember this.' Also, apparently, her opinion of me had been downgraded from 'deceiver'.

It now stood, officially, as 'mischievous'.

Funny, but after all the pretty speeches it had come down to a glass of high-octane Chinese alcohol at high altitude on an empty stomach to convince the Wus about me. The distillery had even given me a case of the stuff: 'To take back to your England, foreigner, because you have come from so far away, to be here.'

As soon as we got back to the car I had donated the whole case to the Wu brothers.

It was barely 5 a.m. when the train's hypnotic rhythm was interrupted by loud metallic shrieks and vibrations as it changed tracks to enter the Beijing railway system. As I peeped through the sea-green window curtain, I saw the outskirts of Beijing's west side, twinkling in the cold darkness.

I looked around, but everyone was still fast asleep. Miss Wu was still buried beneath her warm blankets with only the crown of her head visible. Still feeling drained, my spirits perked up straight away at the thought of the long journey's end. All the overhead lights suddenly flickered on like a starburst. And if that wasn't enough to wake you, the speakers then exploded into life with some strident Marshall music, which in turn was interrupted by a public announcement ordering everyone to pack their things carefully and make ready to get off the train smartly. No dawdling allowed, I thought to myself.

Wu Shu looked up from her bunk with those beautiful little eyes and, as ever, resembled a cat slowly unfurling itself as she forced herself awake.

A few minutes later we were down the slippery steps and on to the grey concrete platform where we seemed to sleepwalk, along with everyone else, in the cold, white Beijing dawn. The car from the Garden arranged by Mr Huang was waiting patiently for us out front.

We had less than one week before I would have to return to England.

It was New Year's Eve and we went to see *Mission Impossible* starring Tom Cruise. Wu Shu thought the scenes set in London were alienating and made her generally uncomfortable. I tried to reassure her that it was merely a theatrical device in which to inject a sense of menace and was totally unlike the real London I knew. I reminded her how most Chinese people thought that London still suffered from terrible fogs – the old pea-soupers that had been eradicated before I was born. Wu Shu, though, was not convinced.

As we walked along the street I looked up at a tall narrow hotel which seemed to have a revolving restaurant on top of its twenty or so floors. There was a large neon sign advertising a special New Year's dinner, 'Western style'. I puffed up my chest and invited Wu Shu to dinner, which she agreed to, laughing at me for some reason. I just hoped there was a table left, but I need not have worried. It turned out that the Chinese didn't much care about the calendar New Year; they were waiting for the lunar-dictated, Chinese New Year due in only a few weeks' time, and so we found a table easily. We took the lift up to the twenty-fourth floor where a gaggle of *xio jie* were waiting to greet their guests.

In their black glitzy dresses, they clutched enormous menus and wine lists, and one showed us to a table by the window. The view of central Beijing at night was breathtaking. The whole atmosphere was pleasingly romantic; there were no fluorescent lights to be seen anywhere, neither were there chopsticks on the lush linen tablecloth, only heavy cutlery. A large avocado seafood starter was carefully placed in front of each of us but – to my eternal shame – I couldn't understand why Wu Shu was making such a fuss over what cutlery to use. First, she picked up a knife, then a fork, before putting them both down again and settling on the soup spoon. What was the matter with the girl?

'Adrian, please do not mind, but I don't know how to use these metal things except this horrible spoon!' she whispered across the table.

Oh, how could I be so *stupid*, I thought?

'I'm so sorry, Wu Shu. Why would you know these things? Let me show you and, if it doesn't help, I'll ask for chopsticks of course.'

Wu Shu nodded, picked up a piece of smoked salmon on the edge of her knife, and pushed it into her lovely mouth with her other hand.

'That's the spirit, well done! Took me *years* to master chop-sticks, I can tell you!' I whispered encouragingly.

But Wu Shu always had the ability to surprise. Next, she picked up a jumbo prawn, which she was clearly more at home with. After twisting off its head, I thought she would place it on the side of the plate in her usual ladylike way, but she was having none of that. She pushed the juicy tail to one side of her plate and brought the head end to her mouth and proceeded to suck the brains out of the prawn. Wiping her mouth delicately with the linen napkin, she appeared satisfied before having a go at the salmon again.

'Please, Adrian, why are you looking at me like that, my knife action is good, isn't it, much improved, yes?' she asked quietly.

'It's *excellent*, darling, fantastic, the best! But actually, I was sort of wondering why you were eating prawn brains. You can tell *me*, surely?'

'To improve my brain power of course. Why else do you think I would do this, *silly* foreigner?' she replied, and smiled at me in that straightforward, guileless way of hers.

But then I remembered her director picking off the protuberant eyeballs of the prawns one lunchtime, and he always wore glasses, too.

I ordered another glass of chilled white wine which turned out to be a very expensive way of drinking it. Should have ordered a bottle because there was a lot to celebrate, after all, as the Wu family had given their verbal consent and promised to sign the government form when the time came. We were to visit the British Embassy the day after next to ask what the protocol was for getting married in China. And the day after that I would fly back to England.

Later, I held Wu Shu in my arms, feeling so happy. I was even stoical about returning to England and the long absence until Easter, but Wu Shu sensed my mood and looked me straight in the eye.

'Adrian, I want us to marry. All I can bring to our marriage is my physical integrity. It is all a young girl has to bring. Can you understand?'

She didn't have to say any more, I felt guilty enough. It was now that I realized that I was only beginning to appreciate her depth of understanding. In the summer my misunderstanding was driven by her fear of what she knew would happen; her fear of the gossip that would surely follow the public outing of her relationship with the foreigner. She saw it clearly and was rightfully afraid. Intelligent and, in that truly Chinese way, unsentimental, she knew what would happen and immediately took steps to meet it. This, combined with her instinctive chasteness and ladylike attitude to everything, meant that misunderstandings were, perhaps, inevitable.

Early the following morning Wu Shu rapped on the hotel room door and dragged me out of the warm room to a little noodle bar around the corner which served delicious Chinese dumplings in a hot broth. To my surprise, I actually enjoyed this odd sort of breakfast. We strolled through the snow back to the hotel where Wu Shu had a good look around my room as I had decorated it with some flowers. She was impressed, commenting, 'I will have rich [artistic] life with you, even if we are poor. You can create rich atmosphere with very little, that is easy to see. Is that right, my *Mister* Webber?'

A typical, slightly coquettish Wu Shu comment; what she gave in one hand she instantly discounted with the other. I found that we were becoming so easy and relaxed with one another. As one Western man I read about, who had married a Japanese girl, said: 'The main difference between Suki and me is that she is a *woman* ...'. I was beginning to understand the full meaning of that candid comment.

Wu Shu also said she only ever felt completely true and whole with me. Something she never felt even with members of her family, with the possible exception of her beloved Ba Ba.

'Adrian, I told you before, sometimes I can feel your blood flow through my vein. And, do you know, I am a polite girl except with you when I can be so rude and naughty. Why *is* this, my Mr Webber?'

I smiled and said I didn't know, but perhaps it was catching. I remembered a day when we were eating in the canteen and the tall deputy director of the Botanical Garden, Li Wei Ming, had careered over to us and, without any greeting, said, 'Webber, you are a very very lucky man to have a lovely girl like Wu Shu. Yes! A very very very very *very* lucky man, indeed!'

I didn't even know he spoke English ...

'You see, Wu Shu is a very very very very ...'

I raised my hands to say I understood. He bent down and put his face next to mine, clearly wanting a response.

'Yes,' I whispered, 'Wu Shu is, as you *rightly* say, a *very* lovely girl and I am a *very* ... lucky man and I would like to thank you for pointing this out.'

I reasoned it was the sort of reply that might appeal to a drunk, even if he wasn't drunk after all.

'Good answer, yeah ... good,' he spluttered in my ear and lurched off, puffing on a cigarette.

It was New Year's Day and a holiday, so I had arranged to give the design office girls lunch in Xiang Shan's best – although not most expensive – restaurant. My treat was for all they did for me the previous summer. Wu Shu was in her laboratory catching up on her work. It was snowing hard as I walked through empty streets before crossing the road to the Garden's main building which housed the design office. I was worried that the terrible conditions would prevent Miss Han and Miss Shi from getting in from their homes in Beijing city but, sure enough, as I walked in they were there, looking cold but happy.

Miss Han had a haunted look on her face, a look that, despite all her smiles, never really left her face throughout the entire lunch. My other 'older sister', Shi Jin Yu, looked completely lost under a huge woollen floppy hat which I teased her about; she couldn't have cared less, I was pleased to note! Later on she returned from the Ladies and dashed the back of my neck playfully with the water still on her hands. And, yes, I had to laugh because the wet hands did seem to suit her ... *this* Chinese girl at least....

In view of the cold, the girls decided on Mongolian hotpot as the only sensible choice, but with a cold beer. The lunch turned out to be great fun. The girls always saw the funny side of everything; they laughed and giggled and teased me relentlessly about everything, except to ask *why* I was back in China. But they were enjoying life much as before and went to the cinema as often as possible, particularly if a Western film was being shown. Still the same girls, thank goodness.

At the end of the long meal I presented each of them with a gift from England which I had earlier lodged with the bar staff. I sensed that they would have liked to have had Wu Shu there too, but she almost certainly would not have agreed to come. First, she knew none of them well and, second, thought it would intrude on the easy rapport I enjoyed with them.

We pulled our coats on and prepared to leave. The snowflakes were lighter and the wind had dropped as we trudged through the snow, and I followed them as they immediately ducked into the post office in their supremely confident but ladylike way. They wanted to look at the stamps. There had been a recent new release and Miss Shi and Miss Han were both keen collectors. They ordered the new trays to be brought out and put on the counter for their perusal. The post office assistant patiently stood there as they took a long time making their choices – a very long time indeed. Each sheet was expertly scrutinized before judgement was passed.

I admired their careful study. It was a privilege to watch that scene being played out. In a way it belonged to their private world. Their *Chinese* world. And, standing there, I knew I could never, ever forget it.

After we shook hands and waved our goodbyes, I watched them go with a lump in my throat. They turned and shouted, 'We'll see you again, won't we? A special occasion, perhaps…'. I just nodded and waved. I couldn't speak, so I reluctantly turned on my heel and trudged back through the deep snow.

And so it was under a cold and fitful sun that I climbed the familiar steps and entered the research building where I was surprised to see the little caretaker's office empty. I peered into the office through the tiny double windows. Bare walls, an empty bed, just the mattress and a few bits of furniture was all I could see. Where was he? What had happened to him? I turned to see

William standing at the bottom of the stairs. He wouldn't meet my gaze and started to climb the stairs to his living quarters, but I strode over fast to head him off.

'Where's the little caretaker?' I asked sharply.

William quickly turned to see if anyone else was around before whispering, 'He has been sacked, Adrian.'

'What!' I said incredulously. '*Why* exactly? What did he do?'

William gestured nervously for me to calm down. 'Mr Huang thought that he was on the verge of a great sickness and so would be a liability to the Botanical Garden and ...'

'What! So you slung him out on his ear, with nowhere to go, just when he needed everyone's help?'

I stood there, furious with Huang Yi Gong. I knew that he had caused mischief for Wu Shu and me, but that was nothing, just the hurly-burly. But *this*? I could see in William's eyes that he didn't want to defend what had happened, so at last I patted his shoulder good-naturedly and strode up the stairs ahead of him to Wu Shu's office. She had left a note on the door to meet her at her dormitory.

But on the way back out I met a heavily muffled Mr Huang coming in. I stopped in front of him, took one long look into the caretaker's empty office, and immediately cut him dead. Now I knew it was none of my business, but frankly he was lucky to get away with that.

The cold gate of the British Embassy in the heart of Beijing's embassy district was at last thrown open by a smartly uniformed Chinese guard who clearly didn't relish being out on the frozen pavement to deal with another long queue on that cold bitter morning. The queue was for Chinese nationals who needed a visa to visit the UK, but as we were making a general enquiry we were shown straight in by the unsmiling guard. Minutes later a tall thin official, in a double breasted suit, came out and showed us into a semi-private area and, with a beaming smile, bade us sit down.

I was forced to admit that after the noise and chaos that went with Chinese life, the official's easy charm and calmness came as an overwhelming relief. He was not going to get upset, become vague, or suddenly obtuse. And he clearly knew his job, too. He didn't waste any time and spelled it all out slowly, so I had time to copy it all down:

1 I was required to have a legal affidavit stating that I wasn't already married, and so I was therefore free to marry.

2 The affidavit needed to be officially translated into Chinese Mandarin, within China.

3 My British passport needed to be translated into Chinese Mandarin, again within China.

4 All the above would first need to be officially stamped by a Public Notary within England.

5 All the above would then have to be taken to the Foreign Office in London for official sanction.

6 Once sanctioned by the Foreign Office, the documents had to be taken to the Chinese Embassy in London for official sanction. This would take two weeks, and then I must return to the Embassy to collect them.

7 I would then have to return to China and make contact with the Marriage Bureau in Beijing where we had to apply to marry.

8 We would then both have a full physical medical in a Beijing hospital. It would include blood tests and chest X-rays.

9 When the above was completed, a number of official photographs of us together would be required for various documents, not least our marriage passports that each of us would be issued, if all went well. Wu Shu's mother would be required to sign a special form to allow her daughter to marry a foreigner.

If all the above was achieved and there was no other unforeseen hiccup, they could then marry us. Once we were married in China, Wu Shu would be free to apply for leave to remain in the UK. This in turn would require her to obtain a Chinese passport sanctioned by her work unit. The application to remain in the UK would require a search into Wu Shu's background and payment of £300 in local currency, cash only. If the application was refused for any reason, they would still keep the money.

And that was that. It had to be said that the somewhat intimidating list was conveyed to us by the official with much charm and no little humanity. We were grateful to him. He gave us a rueful smile as he watched us take it all in. We were going to have to co-ordinate all this at a distance of 5,000 miles by post and phone – the world wide web and email were still in their infancy.

We thanked him again and walked back through the security gates. I felt very different to the way I felt when we walked in that cold morning. Our first task was to find somewhere warm to talk, and hopefully get some breakfast; we had been up since before six that morning to get here in time. I would then be able to explain to Wu Shu in detail what all this meant for us – as much as I *understood* anyway. I was numb with all the detail and officialdom.

All the relief at getting the Wu family's support for us died in that moment. Another huge obstacle, which was really a series of obstacles, had been placed squarely in front of us.

'Adrian,' Wu Shu began, 'that officer he is very kind, but his long list is horrible. What is *Public Notary?*'

'I have absolutely no idea, Wu Shu. But I'll tell you this: it all sounds very difficult to me, and very, very expensive.'

That evening was my last in China and the director had arranged a farewell dinner for me with many old friends present: William, who now liked to be known as 'Billy', Mr Chen, Vice-Director Ming, and their wives, and Miss Liu and Miss Zhang, with their husbands. Unfortunately many friends who lived off site could not come because of the bad snow conditions, but it was still quite an occasion.

I could see that we had been quietly accepted. Those who had gossiped before had now gone quiet. The foreigner had not only returned as he said he would, but he had also visited the Wu family. This, combined with the director's and political officer's very vocal and public support before we even left for Tibet, had sent a clear signal around the Garden.

At the end of the evening, with everyone exhausted from their turns at the karaoke machine, I made a little speech and told everyone that we were trying to build a permanent bridge between the Garden and my college to allow regular student exchanges. As I sat down I passed the microphone to the director, who got up straight away and feigned deep worry and anguish. He gripped the table for support very theatrically before saying: 'More Englishmen! Only on one condition – they are engaged to be married at least – we don't want you coming over here *pinching all our best women!*'

This drew a thunderous burst of applause and a group *gan bei* to the director, followed by cheering. He turned, slapped me on the back, and picked up Wu Shu's left hand, holding only her ring finger. This drew more cheers. I smiled and nodded, embarrassed.

The following morning he accompanied his driver to my hotel. I thought he was just coming to say goodbye when he entered, wearing a handsome dark-blue overcoat and matching French beret, grinning from ear to ear. But standing next to my bed, he casually dropped 2,000 yuan in 20-yuan notes on to it. Wu Shu silently picked up the money and took it out to pay my hotel bill.

We dropped him off at the main building on the way to the airport and he stood at the top of the steps to wave us goodbye. I told him not to work too hard as we shook hands. And then, simply, *penyuo* (friend).

Once in the terminal I shook hands with Wu Shu, and then

holding both her hands tightly said, 'At least we are now seen to be "holding hands" – publicly, I mean – how does it feel to be engaged?'

'Go to your England quickly, Adrian,' she replied. 'Here in China has a young girl waiting for you.'

CHAPTER 21

看似容易，却身负千斤

'It takes little effort to watch a man carry a heavy load'

What worried me, apart from the usual apprehension before returning to China, was the medical check. All the documentation was simple by comparison – it just needed patience and a readiness to pay; the surest sign that everything was in order was an immediate request for payment.

Zhu Renyuan hadn't helped when we met up in London before I left: 'Adrian, they will check all your body, every single possible thing. If you have a problem – China will find it!'

Wu Shu had had her medical check the previous week and, needless to say, passed with flying colours. It had been followed by a compulsory teaching video on appropriate sexual relations, family planning and the all-important one-child policy of China (and the heavy financial penalties for exceeding it).

Once through customs, I saw Wu Shu waiting patiently. I had too much luggage – one huge case alone contained the gifts I had bought. Chinese weddings stipulated that the bridegroom gave presents to all the family. In return they would buy his wedding suit, usually tailor-made.

'Adrian, you are so verbose in your luggage, it's *horrible*.'

'And the flight was perfectly *fine*, darling, no need to worry …' I called after her.

She immediately turned on her heel, 'I am *not* your English *darling*, Mister Webber. I am Chinese girl!' She smiled dreamily and we both laughed. The hypnotic spell of another long absence broken, I wanted to hug her.

The director could not meet us; he was busy with plans for a new show-piece conservatory for the centre of the Garden. He was due to fly to Europe soon to look at established conservatories there.

'Adrian, the driver has instructions to take you to the Wofosi Hotel – you had your send-off there last summer, remember?'

The hotel was a nice gesture as the accommodation there was very comfortable and close to Wu Shu's dormitory. Within an hour we were inside and alone at last.

'Miss Wu, you are a *tiny* bit bigger, I'm sure.'

'Adrian, do you know I eat more each day after I left your England. I cannot prevent myself. I don't eat candy, but I eat much more noodle until I nearly burst I swear!' she replied, smiling.

'Well, I think it suits you. My parents send their love by the way. And they really appreciated the gift and card you sent them when you returned here.'

Wu Shu had flown to England in the summer with Professor Yu who, despite his age, saw as much as he could and thoroughly enjoyed himself. He stayed as a special guest of my college where he was shown many famous local gardens. The last few days he spent as my parents' guest with Wu Shu and me; they were charmed by both.

We entered the large airy lobby of the huge hospital and were directed at once to the 'blood testing unit' on the next floor. The cheerful nurse, dressed from head to toe in white, made a big show of stripping all the sterile packaging off the brand-new needle and syringe before she found a vein. The syringe filled, she smiled again before popping it into a plastic bag with all my details, handing it to Wu Shu, and directing us to a reception area where an enormous queue of Chinese men snaked out of the large waiting area and into the corridor.

Without a blink, Wu Shu strode past them straight up to the reception counter where she jumped in behind the man being served. A ripple of protest went through the queue; there was tutting and moaning, a few hard stares and then ... nothing. Wu Shu came away carefully pocketing the receipt, looking at me with her brightest smile, 'X-ray of bad man's chest this way,' she said, pointing down the corridor.

A few other checks – my height and weight – and it was over. We walked down the long drive while I muttered my relief to Wu Shu.

'*Yin guo ren ... yin guo ren!*' We turned to see a middle-aged nurse running towards us. As she drew near she stopped, breathless, and quickly said something to Wu Shu.

'Adrian ... they haven't checked your teeth.'

The Marriage Bureau had a low spacious building all to itself. Inside, an air of rarefied calm prevailed, and everyone spoke in low whispers. 'Adrian, please give me the photographs ... no, just three, they only need three.' I passed her the A4-sized photos.

The Marriage Bureau official calmly accepted the photos, together with all the documentation, now officially translated, and our medical check results.

The following day, shortly after nine in the morning, we returned and they married us. Two kindly officials quietly presented each of us with a bright-red marriage 'passport' with the Chinese national symbol embossed on the front; each included our official wedding photograph. No witnesses were required.

Wu Shu reached into her bag and offered the traditional gift of chocolate, which they at first politely refused and then reluctantly accepted. We were free to leave.

Warm autumn sunshine welcomed us as we emerged from the building, a little giddy, as Mr and Mrs Webber. I looked at Wu Shu for the first time as my wife. We were alone in that deserted street. No family, no well-wishers, no one. Wu Shu looked so beautiful I wanted to take her in my arms, but I sensed that even outside the place where we had just been married it would have embarrassed her. Instead she looked up at me, smiled, and in her teasing way said, 'Chinese girl very hungry, so why doesn't her husband feed her? And when my husband has given me breakfast ... I must ring my mother.'

The train pulled out of Beijing's West Station on time and the journey time had even been cut by a whole three hours – it was now thirty-three hours to Xining. The enormous train was far from full, and so we had lots of space to relax during the day. There was only one other passenger in our sleeping compartment and he spent most of the time reading; although at one point we were joined by members of China's national wrestling team. They came to say 'hello' to the foreigner. They were very gentle and good-natured although they completely filled our cabin. I gave them each an under-arm deodorant stick, a novelty in China at that time. They went off happy after offering their congratulations and bowing deeply to Wu Shu.

'Well, I hope your brothers are going to be as friendly, Mrs Webber, or should I say Miss Wu? Funny, but somehow you will *always* be Miss Wu to me,' I said.

As soon as Wu Shu had telephoned her mother we had celebrated our civil ceremony by visiting a traditional bridal shop in an old quarter of Beijing. Surrounded by large colour photographs of Chinese brides in Western white dresses, we selected a beautiful traditional full-length Chinese dress, with the customary split-leg opening. Wu Shu tried it on. She looked both lovely and natural; the rich wine colour set off by sparkling sequins and tasteful styling made a stunning combination. I paid for it immediately. Encased in a luxurious gold bag, it now lay in a rack above Wu Shu's head.

'My mother said on the telephone that my family will take you to a special tailor in Xining and pay for your wedding suit. They want to take you there the morning after we arrive because it will take a few days to be made.'

'Was she happy?' I asked.

'Yes, I think so, but she knows there is plenty more to do and she is always practical. She still thinks you're mischievous, by the way – a mischievous son-in-law, it's her fate, she says.'

'Come on, Wu Shu, I can see she said something else too ... I know you too well!'

Wu Shu laughed. 'My mother also wants to make a speech at the family wedding ... don't look so worried, Adrian, no one would let her. She wanted to say how the foreigner was so lucky to find a *chaste* Chinese girl. He is neither old nor young, but who arranged his good fate? Was it his God ... or was it Buddha?'

The train pulled in to Xining the following evening, right on time. There were hardly any other passengers as we got off and I could see a tight huddle of Wu family members down the long platform. Almost immediately one member detached herself and ran headlong towards us. Nan Nan left the ground a good few feet away and slammed into my chest with the words, 'Uncle Adie, Uncle Adie, Nan Nan *miss* you!' I held her in my arms as the rest of the family came up a little more shyly with trolleys for our luggage. They smiled quietly as they accompanied us down the long platform to Wu Shu Bu's new vehicle – a pick-up truck.

'Adrian, my family say they want to visit the temple to pray,' Wu Shu said smilingly.

'What for? Oh, our marriage of course.'

'No, they want to thank Buddha for loss of your heavy weight and donating some to me – they think I'm a *tiny* bit chubby.'

We were to have a meal out in one of the new seafood restaurants that had recently sprung up in a fashionable part of the city. Even before we got there I could see that the family was still slowly taking it all in. After months of waiting, everything had happened very fast, and we were now there.

My three brothers-in-law sat opposite me across the huge table, smoking and nonchalantly perusing the thick menus, while their wives inspected Wu Shu's rings. After much scrutiny, careful weighing and general discussion, they pronounced themselves satisfied with the foreigner's choice.

'Wu Shu, I'm soon to be part of this family and they still refer to me as *the foreigner*, what's the matter with them?' I asked plaintively.

'Adrian, you *are* part of this family, or soon will be, but you are not a *Chinese*, that's all. Really your question is like drawing feet on a snake,' she replied firmly.

'What on earth does that mean?' I asked.

'Unnecessary, Mister Webber ...'

The suit, made of pure wool, fitted like a glove. The tailor continued to fuss over his creation while Wu Shu and her mother looked on. They clucked and nodded their appreciation; it did have a rather fetching style. Ayi bent down and tugged here and tugged there, but found no flaw. A matching hat was lowered on to my head to complete the ensemble.

'Adrian, you look *almost* handsome! Really you should thank this poor tailor from the bottom of your heart,' Wu Shu said finally.

Wu Shu Lu appeared in the shop and came over to do his share of the suit tugging. He whistled when he saw the silk lining; the tailor smiled and told him it was 'export' quality. Wu Shu Lu chortled in reply, lit a cigarette and, with everyone satisfied, slipped off to pay the bill.

We walked back through the city's famous markets, stopping to purchase different items for the family wedding. Wu Shu Lu and I watched as his mother and sister bargained for various scrolls of antithetical poetry couplets and beautiful ancient wedding scenes, elegant lanterns, many 'double happiness' marriage signs, money envelopes for the children, and dragon and phoenix candles. But everything they bargained for had one thing in common: they were all bright red. The symbol of marriage and happiness.

A head-dress flower, a large red veil really, to be worn by Wu

Shu before the marriage itself was purchased in a tiny shop down a backstreet that specialized in them. It was beautiful and elegant and brought a lump to my throat as it was carefully draped over Wu Shu's head by two smiling *xio jie*. I tried to pay, but Ayi merely ushered me out of the shop. And Wu Shu Lu did the same after we entered another store, which was so dark you could barely see, and bought a 2-metre roll containing 1,000 firecrackers. Devoid of all light and heat, they wanted nothing in the store that could ignite the huge boxes of gunpowder stored there.

And then there was the car. Wu Shu Bu had spotted an open-topped car in the classic English sports tradition; he had been admiring it for the best part of an hour before we arrived. It was cherry red, obviously aimed at the wedding market, and came with its own driver too. Wu Shu Bu frowned at the price, haggled, and was at last satisfied as his mother peered cautiously inside – she'd been told it *wasn't* an *Audi* – and shook her head doubtfully. Wu Shu was also far from convinced.

'Adrian, this is too Western romantic style for our wedding car. I am modest Chinese girl. Only Xiao Bu could find such a brag-gadocio thing.'

I lay alone in bed that night thinking. It had been a very long road, but I was nearly there; perhaps that explained the near panic I sometimes felt. Wu Shu had just left after a quick cuddle – she would sleep in her mother's bed until the night of the family wedding celebration. If anything, she seemed more nervous than me. I knew that the two huge red candles we bought today would be placed by our marital bed. Once lit, they would be allowed to burn through the night, symbolizing the couple's life burning together in harmony; not until morning could they be extin-guished.

I would leave here tomorrow and travel to the other side of the city to stay in Wu Shu Bu's apartment for the eve of the wedding. It was to be my symbolic family home from which I would set off to collect Wu Shu, my bride, in the little Chinese sports car.

The following morning I had never seen Ayi so nervous, but she insisted on making my breakfast all the same. A large bowl containing an incredible four-egg omelette was banged down in front of me packed with fried spring onions, 'otherwise no taste', along with a smaller bowl containing coffee. Three generations of Wu women sat across from me now, slowly chewing their noodle breakfast: Ayi, Wu Shu and little Nan Nan – who wasn't going to be left out of anything.

'Adrian, do you know my mother just mentioned that she and Ba Ba also married in Beijing so many years ago – she never thought her only daughter would also marry ...'

'A *foreigner*!' I said sharply enough to startle Wu Shu Bu into looking up from his newspaper.

'No, to a rotten English oak tree! An effrontery man! A *bad* ... man.'

'Whom you are to marry shortly, Miss Wu ...'

We both laughed.

Wu Shu Bu had come over early because we were to go to the hotel where the wedding feast was to be held to check all the arrangements; the dishes had been ordered days ago. We also wanted to lodge with them the various alcohols to be served, and in what order, on the day. We would stop at an ancient department store on the way; it had recently opened a modern drinks store in the basement including, it was rumoured, 'foreign concoctions'. My other motive for being involved was to steer the emphasis away from the *jiu* alcohol and all its ghastly variations. It was my wedding day after all.

The big store was indeed ancient. Nan Nan gripped my arm tightly as the three of us entered the basement. Wu Shu Bu was immediately fascinated by the heavy ceramic bottles of Maotai and the like, while I was drawn to some hefty bottles of champagne which had been given pride of place in the centre of the store.

The champagne turned out to be sparkling wine produced in China, in co-operation with French vineyards. Something had clearly been lost in translation because as I peered closer I noticed the labels said '*Spanking* Wine'. I could afford two magnums of the rosé; the colour would match the red marriage tradition. I managed to steer my soon to be brother-in-law away from the Maotai, which had a graphic picture of a foreigner on his knees clutching his throat.

We cracked open a few bottles of Chinese beer over dinner that night; Wu Shu Bu and I clinked glasses and *gan bei'd* each other many times that evening and long into the night.

Tomorrow Wu Shu and I would be properly married.

CHAPTER 22

远水救不了近火

'You cannot fight a fire with water from far away'

I could hear someone giggling and eating at the same time, so I rubbed my eyes and sat up slowly in the couch-bed. Nan Nan had positioned her tiny stool next to my couch-bed and was watching me sleep as she ate her breakfast. She chuckled to herself before spooning another dollop of sticky rice into her mouth.

'Uncle Adie, Ma tried to make you some coffee, but it all went wrong ... Ba Ba is doing it now, can you smell it?'

After all those beers last night, I was going to need it. My head ached and my throat felt parched as I looked at my watch; the driver with the sports car would be here in a little over an hour – just time for a quick shower. Wu Shu Bu, already smoking and wearing his smart coat, brought over a huge bowl of coffee. And before I knew it, there was a loud tooting outside and Nan Nan was jumping up and down at the window shouting, 'It's here! It's here!' in Chinese and English.

The car had been polished so hard it positively glowed. At the end of the long bonnet there were two tall puppets in Western marriage dress: the bridegroom sporting full black tie and top hat while holding the hand of his bride, who wore a pure white wedding dress and matching veil. The red carnation in his buttonhole matched mine. The three of us got in and, with Nan Nan squashed in the middle, we set off.

A mellow autumnal sun gently bathed the dusty streets as we motored along at a leisurely pace. The car was attracting many stares, from both sides of the street; people were pointing at us and shaking their heads. A few waved, rather doubtfully. A traffic policeman held up a whole lane of vehicles to let us cross into the university campus; all the students then charged out of their dormitories to look down from their high balconies. The Wu family and friends were standing around in groups, quietly enjoying the sunshine.

I looked up at the third-floor apartment windows. The bridegroom would normally be expected to go up to Ayi's apartment and to post red packets of money through the door until the bride's family on the other side of the door was satisfied with the amount. Then the door would finally be opened, perhaps to reveal a bridegroom slumped across the doorway in a sort of numb, penniless stupor. Wu Shu Bu, as head of the family, had ruled this out. 'Adie, you have paid enough just to be here,' he told me firmly.

And then everything became hushed. I turned to see Wu Shu Bu holding his sister in his arms. My bride was wearing a dusky mauve Western-style suit (later on she would wear her Chinese wedding dress), but was almost unrecognizable beneath the beautiful red veil. She looked lovely, chaste (as her mother had said) and dignified. Something stirred within me that wouldn't calm itself. Perhaps it was pure love, love for one's bride, to whom at that moment I wanted to give everything – everything in this world.

I bowed deeply to her brother, stepped forward, and took Wu Shu in my arms. I was about to tell her through the veil how much I loved her when an enormous explosion ripped through the air, echoing off the courtyard walls, instantly followed by another and then another. Wu Shu Lu had let off the firecrackers to ward off evil spirits from his sister's marriage; everyone was shouting and clapping in between the explosions as I sat my bride in the car and quickly got in the other side.

I coughed again before saying hoarsely, 'Wu Shu, I had no idea that Chinese firecrackers were so *loud*.'

We looked at each other and laughed. And we were still laughing as the driver carefully drove over the three bridges necessary for a happy marriage. At the hotel, where a crowd quickly gathered around us, I recognized Wu Shu Du escorting his mother through the throng to greet us. She grabbed our hands tightly as we tried to get out, but there were far too many people surrounding the car so we just slumped back in.

'Adrian, Chinese people are very curious!' I heard Wu Shu say from behind the veil.

They were soon rocking the car, laughing good-naturedly. Eventually a detachment of *xio jie* came out from the hotel; they marched two abreast to collect us and the crowd obediently parted to let them through. They bowed as one, and invited us to join them. Wu Shu and I held hands tightly as we were escorted through the crowd into the hotel's huge lobby. Inside everything was calm and we were quietly ushered up a wide marble stair-case to the banqueting suite. The rest of the wedding party eventually picked their way through the crowd still milling outside and silently followed us into the hotel.

I wanted desperately to hug Wu Shu, but there was no chance of that as the room quickly filled. In that moment I suddenly felt alone. Here I was surrounded by well-wishers, but I was the only Westerner there. England, at that moment, seemed very far away.

But I was quickly swept up by proceedings and carried along. I looked at Wu Shu and then around at the gathering; everyone was very relaxed, many were smoking. Even Ayi seemed carefree – she was laughing, frivolous and, I swear, *joking* with familiar female friends. Perhaps it was the ultimate relief? She had become recon-ciled to her fate. At the same time I noticed that she had become more caring towards me and even complained whenever I left. She said it was too quiet; just a loss of *yang*, perhaps?

An endless stream of dishes was laid out on the huge circular table; one particular dish caught my eye as everyone kept adding it to their soup. Stacks of little cubes, crimson red in colour – which turned out to be chilled pig's blood.

It all looked fine to me, although people were soon asking why dessert and soup were being served first and not at the end? Wu Shu Bu tried to laugh it off, but the questions kept coming. On my prompting, Wu Shu stood up and apologized for the strange order. 'It is the way they do it in England,' she explained, while I smiled broadly.

Time for a toast, I thought, and gestured for the 'champagne' to be brought in; again perhaps it wasn't in the right order, but I knew that as soon as Wu Shu and I drank the wine from the same cup in front of everyone we were *married*. The '*Spanking* Wine' was carefully opened with a huge *pop!* – now it was the turn of the Chinese to be startled.

Two sisters-in-law delicately drew the elegant red veil away to reveal Wu Shu's face, as beautiful and radiant as I had ever seen it. She wore no make-up, and blushed as I tried to speak but could not find the words. My eyes stung as I stared at her. A silent message, perhaps, after everything we had been through.

Both our glasses were filled, so I offered her one and picked the other up, wrapping her arm through mine, Western style, to drink the wine, but we also raised each glass to the height of our eyebrows. This drew a huge round of applause. It symbolized the *raising the tray to the eyebrows*, which signified mutual respect between husband and wife.

Then everyone stood up. Wu Shu Bu made a speech as head of the family, before leading the salute to our marriage and happy life together. After everyone sat down, I looked across at my mother-in-law, but she remained firmly seated. There was going to be no speech from her, that much was clear.

Western wine wasn't to everyone's taste, and soon the men were calling for other refreshments. Huge glasses of beer were soon carried in on trays, together with bottles of Maotai, surrounded by small shot glasses. Now where had Wu Shu Bu got that from, I wondered? But I was soon back on my feet for the wedding kiss, which no one had told me about. Wu Shu looked into my eyes steadily as I leant forward and kissed her lips delicately. More applause and shouting followed; we then toured the room as a couple, inviting everyone to eat more, drink more. The men, in high spirits, *gan bei'd* me while their wives quickly gripped Wu Shu's hand, carefully admiring the rings the foreigner had brought 'from his England'.

'Wu Shu, what did your brother say in his speech?' I asked later. 'It went down very well, didn't it?'

'Yes, Xiao Bu first used old Chinese saying: "Fate can bring people together from a thousand miles away ... those destined to be married to each other, although a long way apart, are drawn together by a single thread." Then my brother make joke, he said in all the years he knew me I had only one shortcoming, "My Mei Mei cannot cook, as Adie will soon realize to his discomfort!" Everyone laughed at that of course, and then more seriously he went on to say ... "His Mei Mei, he knew, would be a virtuous wife." Embarrassed me really.'

'There was a lot of hammering on the table after he said that, wasn't there?' I said.

Wu Shu nodded, and said at the end he used an ancient description of a good Chinese wife:

> ' ... as delectable as a peach or plum,
>   and as cold and frost as ice ...'

With those words buzzing around my mind, I cautiously approached our marital bed later that night. The room seemed dark at first, illuminated as it was by two huge red candles, but then as my eyes adjusted to the low light I saw the bed covers had been pulled back. I moved closer and was startled – red fruits and nuts had been strewn across the bed sheet. I quickly turned to Wu Shu.

'Adrian, these are for fertility. Can you understand? It is for our happy life.'

I calmed down and nodded, before taking her in my arms at last. She lay her head on my chest, which I always loved. Wu Shu wiped a tear and so I gripped her tightly. 'It's been a long road, old girl, hasn't it?' I whispered softly. She nodded and pressed her little head into my chest. 'Young girl needs her tree,' she said and gripped my shoulders tightly.

'But you've been very brave, Wu Shu, God only knows ...' I whispered to her gently.

We lay together in the soft candlelight giggling. 'Wu Shu, what is your mother *doing*?' I asked. This made her giggle even more.

'My mother is ... well ...'

'Being your *mother*,' I said ironically.

We looked at each other and then at the wall. On the other side my mother-in-law was noisily sluicing and scrubbing every bucket and bowl she possessed and it seemed all her neighbours' too. She kept carrying them in and out, slopping past our bedroom door in her wet sandals.

'Wu Shu, I think she is trying to defend your honour and your chastity!'

Wu Shu smiled sweetly, 'Adrian, she can't keep it up all night, can she?'

'Well ... I wouldn't bet on it,' I replied.

Wu Shu told me her inner circle of friends and work colleagues took our news calmly and were quick to offer their congratulations. Those who had least to do with her were the most shocked and censorious; this extended to the academic South Garden, too. People could talk of nothing else.

The gossip didn't affect me; I only had a few days before my return to England and much of that time was spent dealing with paperwork and visits to the British Embassy. Wu Shu would have to bear it alone, yet again.

There were many tears at Xining's station as everyone saw us off. My mother-in-law was beside herself; no one could calm her. She was heartbroken. Her only daughter, newly married, was to leave her and then fly away to a foreign land and be lost *for ever*! She would die a lonely old woman ... and ... and ...

'Ma!' Wu Shu said. 'Please listen. Adrian wants me to return to see you before I go, whatever happens. He has said this many times now, please believe his words. I shall come back to see you ... I *promise* ...'

People started to pat her shoulder, uttering soothing words, but she shrugged them off.

'Adie also wants you to come to England, have a look, stay as long as you're ... *allowed*,' Wu Shu told her pleadingly. But she just stood there, pained and surly, tears welling up in her eyes.

I bent down to face her. 'Ma!' I said, and looked her straight in the face.

Her little eyes flicked up for a brief second ... then at last she reached out and gripped my hands tightly; after a while she sniffed, and dabbed her eyes with a tiny handkerchief. Everyone relaxed and started to say their goodbyes. Wu Shu embraced her mother while I shook hands with my three Chinese brothers-in-law.

'Ge Ge' (brother), they said shyly and grinned. We had no words in common but we were easy with one another, affectionate even ... in a manly, no-nonsense way of course. I found out later they wanted to get Wu Shu and me a room for a few nights in a Xining hotel – a short honeymoon – but their mother had vetoed the idea.

She said it was 'unsafe'.

Director Zhang stood and looked at us. For the first time since I'd known him that look was not accompanied by a smile. Instead he slowly walked towards us, shaking his head with his arms out wide, and gripped Wu Shu and me tightly. Our 'Red Mama' had just returned from a European trip and looked tired, 'I just didn't believe it would happen. Really, I didn't!' He looked at each of us in turn and said, 'Now China is *truly* open ... by the Buddha. Many congratulations! Happy marriage also.'

He laughed loudly and, still holding us tightly, called for his driver to take him home; he'd wanted to see us first as soon as he heard the news on the way back from the airport.

'China is really open now!' he shouted back as he got into the car.

With the director and his senior staff all abroad, we needed help with our living arrangements when we first returned. It came in the form of Professor Yu's formidable daughter. Middle-aged and happily married, she viewed herself, first and foremost, as her famous father's daughter. She organized a car for us at the station and then arranged for another bed to be put into Wu Shu's office. This required a lot of furniture moving and many staff were pressed into service. The bed, once assembled, was carefully placed, with some ceremony, next to Wu Shu's tiny office bed; and it was probably this symbolic act that caused the gossip around the Garden.

Unperturbed, Wu Shu decided to make the rounds to offer the traditional marital gift of 'candy' to staff. And so after purchasing boxes and boxes of chocolate sweets, we set off. Despite all the heated gossip, the sight of us together drew no adverse comment. In fact, everyone was all smiles and thanked us profusely for the gift.

A day or so later, equally unexpectedly, we ourselves were the recipients of a number of gifts. Many of the staff had apparently contributed to the purchase of some exquisite silk-covered Chinese photograph albums for our marriage day and future happy life. And it had all been organized by none other than Huang Yi Gong, who led the delegation. Wu Shu made a quick recovery, but my mouth was wide open in disbelief long after they left us. It seemed a good omen, but I was still uneasy.

I enjoyed living in Wu Shu's office those last few precious days; it had its own routine, a sort of working honeymoon. Wu Shu had to get up before 8 o'clock each morning to work in her laboratory. Those days were sun-filled and happy, blunted only by our impending separation – and for how long we had no way of knowing. The Embassy had said the visa would take six weeks at least.

And then the day finally came. I think we were as prepared as we were ever going to be. We even joked about it. Perhaps we had done it enough times now and knew the routine? For a start, we pulled away from each other. It had to be done. Each began to treat the other as if they were wholly to blame for the predicament: 'if only ... if only ...'

As one poet said: 'When I know you are leaving, I miss you before you've gone.' And I suppose it was a form of mourning, a long dull ache that might diminish, but would never properly fade; the actual parting was in many ways irrelevant.

Professor Yu's daughter wanted to accompany us to the airport and I decided to invite my old classmate Zhu Renyuan as well. He had recently returned to China from England after two years away, but my reason for inviting him was not sentimental.

And so it was four of us who climbed into the director's car to set off for the airport. Wu Shu and I clenched hands while our companions steadfastly looked out at the passing scenery; we said nothing to each other, it had all been said.

But still it wasn't enough. I felt itchy, impatient, frustrated by it all. People in England before I left listened in disbelief when I said that I couldn't bring Wu Shu back with me. The reaction was always the same: 'What! Once you're married you can't bring her back here? What a lot of nonsense. You're *married* for goodness' sake!'

It was at moments like these that I felt proud to be British. The innate common sense, and the suspicion of officialdom, was a comfort to me as we got out and arranged the luggage on the trolley. Once inside the terminal, I took Zhu Renyuan to one side.

'Now Mister Zhu Renyuan,' I began, 'You started all this and now you are going to help me *finish it*,' I said sharply. 'I am now leaving China and Wu Shu, my wife, is going to be left here on her own, understand?'

He nodded slowly, wary now.

'And she is going to need some special help. She has friends, but it isn't enough – what she needs is someone to *look out for her*. I don't mean some silly check each evening. What she needs is someone who can spot trouble *and head it off*. Someone intelligent, who knows his way around. *You*, in other words. Yes, *you*, my tough ... young ... friend.'

Zhu practically snapped to attention. 'Of course, Adrian! Of course ... my *duty*!'

'Good, now take this piece of paper. Ring that number if there is any trouble, day or night, you understand? Leave a number I can call you back on. *OK?*'

He took the paper thoughtfully and immediately went for a cigarette. I walked back over to the girls, smiling. Professor Yu's daughter shook my hand and then tactfully joined Zhu Renyuan.

'Hello again, Mrs Webber,' I said to Wu Shu. 'How are you?'

'The same as I always am on these occasions ... airport is like monster in my eyes, always hurt me. Why? Difference is, I am your wife. Adrian, we marry, we should look after one another, cherish and enrich other's life *for ever* ...'

'Hey, my little tiger ... I understand, and it's my fault, I'm very sorry ... you are my wife and I should look after you always.'

Wu Shu leant her head on my arm and gripped my hand tightly as I tried to soothe her. But she wasn't going to fall for that and immediately perked up and became practical.

'Adrian, I'll keep you informed of all official things here. You have done your half, it's finished now. Your naughty girl is now your wife, she must do her duty too, yes? And keep her free time busy.'

She was looking down and I knew she was crying, but there was nothing I could do.

'I love you, bad girl, I'm sorry it all makes you sad. It makes me sad too, but it is you I worry about. Now take care of yourself, old girl, we shall be together soon ...'

Wu Shu kept her head bowed and whispered, 'My China

cultivates this girl so many years, but she hasn't given her to you yet, my kind husband.'

Slowly she let go of my hand and stood there as I pushed the trolley through the security gate into check-in. If I looked back, would she still be there? I turned round and she waved before slowly re-joining her friends.

My whole body ached as I boarded the plane. Different emotions flowed through me: sadness, loss, frustration, anger and bitterness. Frustration and helplessness were the worst. I felt caged, hemmed in, beaten ...

Economy class was empty, which suited my mood as I stowed my hand luggage and slumped down in an aisle seat. I looked up to see an elderly steward peering down at me above his half-moon glasses.

'And what brought you to China, Sir, if I may be so bold ...?'

I managed a smile before replying, 'To get married.'

He looked around. 'Haven't we *forgotten* something, Sir?'

'Yes, I have forgotten something,' I said quietly.

Slam! A glass tumbler with ice was banged down in front of me, quickly followed by two malt whisky miniatures. 'Courtesy of British Airways, Sir, I take it congratulations are in order?' he whispered.

'Yes ... but it's ... a long story ...'

'I bet it is ... I bet it is,' he muttered and walked away to greet another passenger.

What do you say to a man who marries a beautiful girl, then flies 5,000 miles away from her with no guarantee that she will ever be allowed to join him? The answer is you adopt the British stiff upper lip – you make a few sympathetic noises and then change the subject. And I can't say I blamed those who did so.

But Wu Shu was more philosophical. In one letter she wrote:

Please don't worry about me. I'm very happy, hope you're the same. Care for yourself, my 'tree' ... Sometimes I cannot believe myself. Change my mind to have baby. Any other man cannot change me, only you, bad man! Before I swear that who wants to marry me he must agree, wish me, don't let me born baby. It's a very important condition for me to marry, but now everything's changed up to down. Crazy!

And in another letter she talked about the staff reaction:

Adrian, do you know, so many people, often kindly, ask the same question: 'Why you marry with this foreigner?' Chinese people are very curious about this phenomenon!

My answer is always the same: 'Happy when I stay with him!' Some people understand, but others just show bafflement in their eyes, perhaps they can never understand in their whole life really?

Also you tease me that I am not suited to marry a Chinese. Perhaps a Chinese man isn't suitable to me. They have burden of heavy Chinese history, they're too realistic, so realistic that make them lose interest in life. I respect them but maybe difficult to love them.

Wu Shu's first obstacle was to get the formal consent of the Garden to release her temporarily from her five-year employment contract to travel to England and, at the same time, formally allow her to apply for a private, non-work-related passport. Only the Garden's political officer was authorized to do this. She planned to see him in his office the following week. Later on she told me what happened.

'You will visit England for three months ... in the New Year, Wu Shu?' he asked, puffing slowly on his cigarette.

'Yes,' she replied.

He looked at her evenly, laid his cigarette carefully in the ashtray, and picked up the form. He studied it for a few minutes before carefully laying it on his desk, rubbing it flat.

'You understand that you must return to the Garden after

three months, it is a contractual obligation. You may of course continue to visit England providing you complete the remaining two years of work you owe the Parks Bureau and the Botanical Garden of course.'

Wu Shu nodded and smiled. He appeared far from convinced, but after a few more questions she watched nervously as his pen hovered over the signature box. He exhaled noisily, quickly signed, and tossed the form across the desk. He leant back heavily in his chair and remained seated as Wu Shu slowly got up, folding the form as she did so. She closed the door quietly behind her. Now she could apply for a private passport from the Chinese government, although it would still take some weeks even if the application was successful.

And so we waited. And waited. And waited as the calendar New Year came and went and the Chinese lunar New Year loomed. It was now February. On the telephone we wished each other a 'Happy Three Months Wedding Anniversary' just as Wu Shu received her Chinese private passport; but from the embassy ... nothing. A complete blank. One day, out of sheer desperation, I rang them from England and was told: 'Soon, very soon ...'

And then ... nothing. Days went by, but still no word came. We waited. And waited.

I slowly awoke. The phone was jangling by my bed.

'Adrian, I must tell you what just happened, were you asleep?'

'No,' I yawned, 'What on earth's the matter, Mrs Webber?' It was 2 a.m. Wu Shu had just left the British Embassy with her entry visa for the UK. She then related the whole story. I replaced the handset and slumped back in relief. It had taken over three months. Wu Shu would return to her mother's home as promised for a couple of weeks to say 'goodbye' to her family; then she would surrender her identity card to the local security bureau on her return to Beijing.

*

Air China's flight to Heathrow was right on time. The arrivals lounge was packed, mostly with Chinese families waiting for a family member, presumably. My parents, the only Westerners apart from myself, sat, outnumbered, in the middle of them. Then everyone suddenly erupted into activity as the first trolleys exited the hall. After a while things became quieter as the flight's stragglers made their way out. We looked back down the empty hall passageway. Where was Wu Shu? We looked up at the electronic screen – it showed the flight's status as closed.

'Look, there she is!' my father shouted. We turned and watched, a little awed, as a very composed and dignified Wu Shu walked out completely on her own (she had been detained for a routine TB check). And while my mother tried to tame the huge unruly bouquet of flowers we had brought, my father reached out and grasped the trolley, leaving me, giddy with emotion, to pick up my wife. Time slowed and sounds became muted as I whirled and whirled her around me – my tiny angel smiling shyly back seemed stationary against the blurred light dancing behind her.

And soon we were laughing ... laughing until our jaws ached ... until our arms ached ... until people stared ... until tears ran down our faces ... it didn't matter ...

We'd made it.

结 束

EPILOGUE

头尾相接

*'The beginning and the end reach out their
hands to each other'*

Wu Shu didn't return to the Botanical Garden to finish her contract – in fact, she wasn't to see China again for more than six years. She had lost weight dramatically while waiting to come to England (she floated in the bath), but soon fell pregnant after her arrival. In China, Professor Yu, rather impishly, broke the news to Director Zhang during a formal meeting within the Garden. He responded, 'Clearly Western medicine is not as strong as China's ...'

The view from Tibet was less phlegmatic. Wu Shu's mother practically exploded with rage: 'How could Adie do this to my poor Xiao Shu! She only just arrive and now look ... her mother so far away ... how can she possibly *cope*?'

But Wu Shu did cope; in fact, like many young women new to childbearing, she seemed to positively blossom. Only once were we concerned when a blood test showed a risk of abnormality and an invasive procedure was called for. As Wu Shu recovered in a ward upstairs, I mentioned to the Sister that it was possibly an *age* thing (Wu Shu was in her late twenties). But she misheard me and replied, 'Oh yes, all our *Asian* ladies are so tiny they always distort the blood test!' And so it proved.

Back in China other pregnancies were being celebrated and they didn't stop over the next few years. They all had one thing in common – every single baby was male. Each of the design office girls gave birth to a boy, with Miss Liu leading the way, quickly followed by Miss Han, who left the Garden to join her fiancé and married soon after. Miss Shi eventually followed, having now married the childhood sweetheart she met at primary school.

The old research building staff were not to be left out. Mr Chen and William became proud fathers, and Miss Sun Yi, now married to a doctor, also gave birth to a boy. Her boss, Miss Zhang, cut her troubled ties with China and emigrated to Canada with her husband. My old classmate, the estimable Zhu Renyuan, responsible for this story, married, amid great secrecy, a local Beijing girl who soon gave birth to a sturdy son.

One night a thousand miles away in Tibet my mysterious brother-in-law Wu Shu Du had to quickly arrange transport to the hospital where his wife bore him a son. A few months later in the middle of the night in England, his sister dug me in the ribs to whisper that her waters had broken. Only a few hours later I was handed a little bundle – a girl – and a quick check satisfied me that her eyes were both beautiful ... if not 'normal'.

We returned to China when our daughter, Sophia, was five to introduce her to all the Wu family, first in Shanghai, where Wu Shu's paternal family lived, in time for the 'Sweeping of the Tomb' festival where families traditionally cleaned family tombs and burned money for the dead. Sophia rested a small posy of flowers against her grandfather's tomb and bowed her head as firecrackers exploded around her.

We flew on from Shanghai, landing heavily at Xining's tiny airport late in the evening where the whole family were waiting to get their first glimpse of the new young member.

The eldest brother, Wu Shu Bu, appeared to be in a sort of trance as he stared at his niece who looked up at him, grinning; his younger brothers, shuffling and smoking, shyly snatched glances at Sophia. Her grandmother, the Wu family matriarch, patted her head and knelt down to look at her properly – but she was soon nudged out the way by Nan Nan, who wanted a proper look at her foreign cousin. She bent down and hugged her tightly; despite the age difference, they became immediate friends. Her father, meanwhile, had to be guided back to his pick-up truck, having still not got over the shock, his hands shaking as he tried to light a cigarette.

They all said the same thing, 'Wu Shu, how did you manage to give birth to a completely *Western* baby ...?'

Meanwhile, in the Botanical Garden, Director Zhang, our 'Red Mama', continued to develop the Garden with the huge new conservatory, as well as adding new visitor-friendly facilities. We were told that he always kept a framed photo of Sophia on his desk right up until he finally retired in the spring of 2008. He then became a consultant for the Garden, sitting on many committees and planning its future development. Retirement also gave him more time, he said, to spend with his family and his many friends. We never forgot all he did to help us. Or Professor Yu, now widowed and in his nineties, who still maintains his thirst for knowledge and life while continuing to write horticultural books from his tiny, book-lined study.

And what about Wu Shu, who adapted readily to English life while maintaining a thorough Chineseness in her attitude to her new experiences? She gave up her scientific career, preferring administrative work – English style – where her gentle smile and patient manner beguiles all before her, perhaps to the point where people forget that she is from such a different society – until they look down at her shopping list written in Chinese pictographs. 'Wu Shu, can you *read* this?' they ask incredulously.

A pay bonus to Wu Shu is 'a rich harvest'. An enthusiastic colleague is 'a leaping frog'. A person wishing to appear rich 'wants to show chubby face'. And yes, if something is unnecessary it is 'to draw feet on a snake'.

Wu Shu will always look at things differently, perhaps less sentimentally, less charmingly – which in its way seems to have its own charm. As someone once said: 'You can take the girl out of China, but you can't take China out of the girl.'